Float Planes &
Flying
PLANES &
BOATS

Float
PLANES &
Flying
BOATS

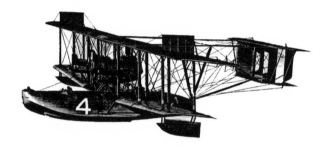

The U.S. Coast Guard and Early Naval Aviation

CAPT Robert B. Workman Jr.
USCG (Ret.)

Naval Institute Press
Annapolis, Maryland

Naval Institute Press

291 Wood Road

Annapolis, MD 21402

First Naval Institute Press paperback edition published in 2017.

ISBN: 978-1-68247-184-5 (paperback)

The Library of Congress has cataloged the hardcover edition as follows:

Workman, Robert B.

Float planes & flying boats : the U.S. Coast Guard and early naval aviation / Capt. Robert B. Workman Jr.

p. cm.

Includes bibliographical references and index.

ISBN 978-1-61251-107-8 (hbk. : alk. paper) 1. United States. Coast Guard—Aviation—History—20th century. 2. Seaplanes—United States—History—20th century. 3. United States. Navy—Aviation—History—20th century. I. Title.

VG53.W66 2012

359.9'4097309041—dc23

2012014683

♾ Print editions meet the requirements of ANSI/NISO z39.48-1992 (Permanence of Paper).

Printed in the United States of America.

25 24 23 22 21 20 19 18 17 9 8 7 6 5 4 3 2 1

First printing

This book is dedicated to my wife Gail, without
whose enduring love, support, and patience
I might have abandoned this project long before it
came to completion,

and to . . .

Elmer Fowler Stone, U.S. Coast Guard, member
of a team of early Navy, Marine, and Coast Guard
aviators without whose loyalty, expertise, and
perseverance we would not have recently celebrated
one hundred years of naval aviation.

CDR E. F. Stone, USCG official portrait, Washington, D.C.

DEDICATION

CDR Elmer F. "Archie" Stone, USCG
Naval Aviator #38
Coast Guard Aviator #1
1887–1936

A fierce winter storm was raging off the mid-Atlantic coast on April 4, 1933. LCDR Elmer F. Stone, USCG, was flying his twin-engine RD-4 amphibian in the morning twilight headlong into it. He flew low above the wave tops, just below the clouds, in marginal and obscured visibility, to maintain visual contact with the ocean.

He had just learned that the Navy's new rigid airship USS *Akron* had crashed shortly after midnight and been destroyed off Barnegat Inlet, New Jersey. The German tanker *Phoebus* had recovered only three survivors out of seventy-six souls on board. Heavy seas and a strong winter storm had prevented further rescues and hampered other searchers. On board *Akron* was RADM William A. Moffett, USN, and other friends from the time Stone tested seaplanes for the Navy, was pilot of NC-4 during the First Transatlantic Flight, and from when Stone led development of shipboard aircraft catapults and aircraft carrier arresting gear.

When Stone arrived on scene, he found no other survivors from the crash. He did, however, manage to locate two bodies. One was that of *Akron*'s commanding officer. An offshore landing in heavy seas and low visibility was a dangerous operation. But he had done it before during the First Transatlantic Flight, other rescues, and law-enforcement missions. Flying at an airspeed 10 percent above the flying boat's power-on stall speed, with full flaps down, Stone looked for the back side of an ocean swell, one without cross swells, where he could land. Stone chopped back on the throttles and raised the flaps, putting the amphibian into a full stall, falling to the ocean's surface in order to land at the slowest ground speed.

As if his aircraft were a stone skipping on water, he aggressively moved the flight controls to counter violent forces from the rough seas and to maintain level wings and a slight nose-up aircraft attitude until the RD-4 came to a complete stop. He then maneuvered the flying boat on the water so his crewman could recover the two bodies. He lined up thirty degrees right of the takeoff heading, letting the torque from full power pull the aircraft around to the correct heading as he skipped across the wave tops until flying speed was reached.

The bumpy instrument flight to Naval Air Station Anacostia was full of sad feelings. After Stone's landing, a *Washington Times* reporter asked him why he had taken such a grave risk for the rescue attempt. His response:

"It was the least I could do."

CONTENTS

FOREWORD

VADM Gerald L. Hoewing, USN (Ret.)

The twentieth century saw a leap in technology that eclipsed any period in the history of man. Certainly, one of the greatest advances of that time was man's conquest of the air. For the U.S. Navy the challenge of marrying air and sea power captured the imaginations of a small number of men, their efforts eventually to take naval aviation in the mere thirty years from the hairy shipboard takeoffs and landings by Eugene Ely to the fast carrier task forces that dominated the Japanese, won the war in the Pacific, and are today powerful symbols of American might worldwide.

Certainly naval aviation's pioneers could not have envisioned what our navy would look like by the end of the last century but struggled with the problems at hand, gradually conquering the small challenges and, in a step-by-step process, producing advances that collectively yielded the most unique and versatile arm of our nation's defense.

U.S. naval aviation encompasses Navy, Marine, and Coast Guard air arms. The doctrine, training, and equipment are common, and there is an ease with which they may join in a common task. Among naval aviators there is a common bond, and nowhere was this more evident than among the pioneers. Then the science of flight was largely unexplored, and funds were limited by budget constraints, pedestrian skeptics, and a stingy Congress. Experimentation was dangerous, and progress was measured in baby steps. Nonetheless, men like Mustin, Whiting, Towers, and others persevered. Among the early believers was the Coast Guard's first naval aviator, Elmer F. Stone, a man destined to leave his mark as a test pilot, engineer, and visionary.

Bob Workman's painstakingly researched history traces the efforts of Stone and others as they faced one challenge at a time. The title itself tells us of the major steps in the naval aviation's evolution, from flimsy float planes hoisted aboard ship that would bring them in range of the enemy, to seaplanes designed to cover large areas of ocean in order to protect shipping lanes—and to eventually conquer the Atlantic—to ADM Joseph Mason Reeves's work in developing the modern aircraft carrier and defining its role in the fleet. More important, it highlights the role that CDR Elmer Stone and other U.S. Coast Guard officers played in those years and then later in the development of the helicopter and its tailoring to the very important role of search and rescue in peace and war.

To those with only a passing knowledge of naval aviation's rich history, I commend this work. Not only is it a detailed story of trial and error, failure, and eventual success, but it gives witness to the common bond among those of us who wear the Wings of Gold. We may be Navy, Marine, or Coast Guard airmen, but when the chips are down, the bond among us makes us one.

VADM Gerald L. Hoewing, USN (Ret.)
PRESIDENT & CEO
NAVAL AVIATION MUSEUM FOUNDATION

MajGen Joseph T. Anderson, USMC (Ret.)

Captain Workman apparently deliberately shaped his manuscript pointing to the joint-ness of the three sea services during the initial growth years of naval aviation. There is history written about what the Navy did and not much, if anything, about joint collaboration. This is a painstakingly researched work that demonstrates that perhaps our naval service would not have been ready for World War I if it were not for the three sea services pulling together. The very fact that all wear identical Wings of Gold deeply symbolizes our common roots, values, and traditions. We had always trained together, operated together, and, most importantly, held a deep respect for the likeness of our missions as much as their variance. There are more bonds than differences, and Captain Workman points them out with precision. He emphasizes Navy, Marine Corps, and Coast Guard joint collaboration in aviation mission areas and cross training. These mission areas include, but are not limited to, narcotics interdiction, counterterrorism, security, and search and rescue. He pointed out to me with pride that even he had pulled a few Marines from the drink after they had to bail out. The most interesting was seven hundred miles offshore in the Pacific. He wrote about this in an article in volume 29, Spring 2008, *Foundation* magazine from the National Naval Aviation Museum, in Pensacola. In fact, two current joint Coast Guard–Marine operations are security for Navy ship fueling stations in the Mediterranean and Middle East ports, and security for Iraq's offshore oil rigs and the port of Basra. For the fueling stations, the Marines are responsible from dockside inland, and the Coast Guard is responsible for dockside–offshore and around the ship. There is also a joint school at Camp Lejeune for both services to train for security missions. Captain Workman also reports that the Coast

Guard has joined the U.S. Navy SEAL program to carry out its port security mission and that Coast Guard aircrews are now trained for rapid insertion of port security teams.

For me, the bottom line is that all of our services are moving toward seamless interoperability and truly joint forces for effective warfare. Much of this has been driven by exterior and political influences. Regardless, truly joint operations are required for today's challenges. Captain Workman has amply demonstrated that this imperative was recognized, embraced, and executed very early on by the U.S. Navy, Marine Corps, and Coast Guard. Captain Workman: Congratulations on your scholarly work and your very personal contributions to naval warfare and our nation's defense.

MajGen Joseph T. Anderson, USMC (Ret.)
DEPUTY DIRECTOR
SMITHSONIAN NATIONAL AIR AND SPACE MUSEUM

VADM Vivien S. Crea, USCG

It gives me enormous pleasure to see this extensive effort to research, collect, and document the birth of naval aviation and the pivotal role played by Coast Guard aviators and engineers. From the black-uniformed crew of the U.S. Life Saving Station at Kitty Hawk who served as the "ground crew" for Orville and Wilbur Wright to the heroic efforts of Elmer Stone, Coast Guard Aviator number 1 and pilot/crewmember for the NC-4 on the first successful Atlantic crossing, Coast Guardsmen have played a key part in the foundation of naval aviation.

The history and successes of the U.S. Navy, Marine Corps, and Coast Guard have been intertwined since our nation was formed over two hundred years ago, and never more effectively than now. We operate jointly every day, leveraging each other's strengths, authorities, and capacities, surging to support our mutual responsibilities of defense, maritime and homeland security, and protection of life and property. Strategically, we are linked more closely than ever, as articulated in the concept of a National Fleet that spans the spectrum of maritime missions, presence, and capabilities, and the Cooperative Strategy for 21st Century Seapower, jointly developed and signed by the Chief of Naval Operations, the Commandant of the Marine Corps, and the Commandant of the Coast Guard.

It is difficult to imagine success in our current mission sets without the capabilities that naval aviation assets bring to bear—from ship-based and maritime patrol aircraft to rescue helicopters, to vertical insertion capabilities, and airborne use of force that has proven pivotal in curbing the success of drug smugglers.

As the Coast Guard's Ancient Albatross, I have always been immensely proud to have graduated from naval flight training and to wear my Wings of Gold. This book provides even more clarity on our services' joint heritage in the birth of naval aviation.

VADM Vivien S. Crea, USCG
ANCIENT ALBATROSS #21
(LONGEST-SERVING COAST GUARD AVIATOR ON ACTIVE DUTY)

PREFACE

This book was born of the frustration of looking for an answer and not finding it or of finding, after a long search, an answer so elementary as to be inadequate. I was highly curious about my Coast Guard aviation heritage but was, except for a few platitudes, unable to find any information about it. There are many books and motion pictures about naval aviation. Few, if any, books and motion pictures are written or made today covering events and people living from the beginning of the twentieth century up to the volatile times of World War I and aviation's rapid advancement to 1938. There is a resulting curiosity about that period and its people and events. This is especially true for aviation enthusiasts. It is surprising how many naval aviators, be they career active-duty members, short-timers, or retirees, know very little about the three sea services' early aviation and their collaboration to grow naval aviation during and shortly after the world war. There are no firsthand experiences shared, since there are no longer survivors of that period available, and few comprehensive books exist.

I wanted a single, easy to understand, comprehensive volume to learn from, one that would reveal the heritage of U.S. naval aviators: Navy, Marine Corps, and Coast Guard. I wanted a book that celebrated the centennial of naval aviation in the year 2011. I wanted a book containing the unified history of all three sea-service naval aviators, their interrelationship and mutual support. As I gathered material for the book, I discovered massive amounts of rarely reported information and seldom-seen photographs tucked away in rarely used archives.

Float Planes & Flying Boats: The U.S. Coast Guard and Early Naval Aviation is completely documented, with 426 endnotes, and it features 271 interesting vintage aviation photographic images, as well as a nautical chart of historical note embedded within its text. This balance of photographs and endnote documentation provides additional visual historical context that will come alive for the reader. I think you will find, as I did, once you learn something of the history of early naval aviation, that enormous creativity was involved in the birth, development, and advancement of Navy, Marine Corps, and Coast Guard air forces and their aircrews' capabilities.

What began with frustration has ended with much pleasure. I hope that your venture into the world of early naval aviation will be every bit as enjoyable as mine continues to be.

ACKNOWLEDGMENTS

I gratefully acknowledge my indebtedness to CAPT Mont J. Smith, USCG (Ret.), for his valuable editorial assistance. Mont was president of the Coast Guard Aviation Association until 2012 and is Coast Guard Aviator number 1520. Mont is currently director of safety for the U.S. Air Transport Association.

I am also thankful for the encouragement to research and record early naval aviation history that I received from the U.S. Coast Guard Historian, Dr. Robert Browning, and by three Coast Guard naval aviators, VADM John Currier and retired vice admirals Donald C. Thompson and Howard Thorsen.

I must thank the research assistants at National Archives in Washington, D.C., for their professionalism and for two and a half years of patiently pulling massive amounts of requested documentation and photographs. I thank the volunteer librarians in the Research Library at the National Naval Aviation Museum in Pensacola, Florida, for archived information and photographs. I also appreciate the editorial assistance provided by Col Denis J. Kiely, USMC (Ret.), editor of the Naval Aviation *Foundation* magazine and of the Marine Corps Aviation Association *Journal*.

INTRODUCTION

Sea Change

It is 1914, and LT John H. Towers, USN, has reported to the Chief of Naval Operations (CNO) for duty in the Office of Operations. Lieutenant Towers has been watching an escalating war raging on the continent of Europe, and he can foresee his country being dragged into the war. The country is not prepared for war! There are few trained people or combat-ready ships. Most available resources are leftovers from the Civil and Spanish-American Wars, and there are no combat aircraft like the ones fighting in Europe. To top it off, the Wright brothers and Glenn Curtiss are in Europe developing and selling aircraft to Europe's military! Why are they not here helping their own country prepare for war? Where is the congressional support? Fast forward—it is now three years later, and the United States has joined the war, in April 1917. Now a lieutenant commander, John Towers is still very concerned that the country's military aviation forces are unprepared for war. The total status of U.S. Army aviation forces is thirty-five Army pilots, fifty-five noncombat aircraft, and three airfields.[1] The total status of U.S. Navy aviation forces is forty-eight Navy and Marine Corps pilots, nine of which are academy-trained in engineering, mathematics, and physics; fifty-four noncombat aircraft; one airship; three balloons; and Naval Air Station Pensacola.[2] U.S. Coast Guard aviation forces comprise eighteen pilots, eight of whom are academy-trained in engineering, mathematics, and physics; an aviation engineer line officer, trained by Glenn Curtiss; and a new office at headquarters for an "Inspector of Aviation."[3]

Twelve Navy and eight Coast Guard aviators with engineering training will ultimately manage and participate in the development and growth of naval aviation to 2,107 new aircraft, fifteen dirigibles, and 215 balloons; 6,716 Navy officers and 30,693 Navy enlisted men, as well as 282 Marine Corps officers and 2,180 enlisted men.[4] At last the Wright brothers and Glenn Curtiss have returned home to contract the design and manufacture of combat aircraft.

The Navy, Coast Guard, and Marine Corps pulled hard and pulled together to bring U.S. naval war-fighting capability to at least a modest level as the country entered World

War I. All naval services aircraft at the time belonged to the Navy. The Marine Corps and Coast Guard did not have any aircraft in their inventories. All three of the sea services flew Navy aircraft on Navy missions. The conduct of antisubmarine warfare (ASW), to protect convoys transporting critical war matériel to Europe, was the Navy's priority during World War I.[5] Navy, Marine Corps, and Coast Guard pilots all flew Navy aerial ASW patrols and missions in Navy aircraft, from Navy commands, during the war.

At war's end in 1919, a number of senior officers in both the Army and Navy, steeped in traditional surface-warfare tactics, shunned aviation and the use of airpower as a major asset in the order of battle. The field was a career buster. In 1919, BG Billy Mitchell, USA, was deputy chief of the Army Air Service. He attacked both the Navy and War Departments as shortsighted in the use of airpower. He made his point with dramatic bombing tests, sinking several German battleships ceded to the allies at the end of hostilities. He later accused senior leaders in the Navy and Army of incompetence and "almost treasonable administration of the national defense." He was found guilty of insubordination by a court-martial and resigned his commission in the Army.

Even after World War I, U.S. airpower was considered weak. A December 14, 1925, *New York Times* headline in bold print stated:

> # AVIATION SITUATION DECLARED ALARMING IN REPORT TO HOUSE; Special Committee Says We Do Not Realize Importance of Air Power. FOR DEFENSE DEPARTMENT Annual Expenditure of $10,000,000 by Each Service for Next Five Years Advised. OUR RANK NOT ABOVE THIRD Congress Is Urged to Determine Respective Fields of Operation of Services. AVIATION SITUATION DECLARED ALARMING
>
> Special to The New York Times.
> December 14, 1925, Monday
> Page 1, 2167 words
>
> **WASHINGTON, Dec. 13.** -- "An alarming situation still exists in the Army and Navy Air Services," states the report which will be submitted to the House tomorrow by its special committee appointed last March to investigate aircraft conditions. [END OF FIRST PARAGRAPH]

Modern naval historians have written about early naval aviation development largely with little regard for the pooling of talent by all branches of the naval services and the friendly collaboration between them. They have ignored the stories of the extreme shortage of engineering-trained officer-aviators in the U.S. Navy and Marine Corps as our country entered World War I and of the contributions of Coast Guard engineering-trained officer-aviators to fill the gap in the buildup for war. This book reveals the extraordinary role of aviators from the three sea services and focuses on their effort to establish naval aviation as an important, indeed indispensable, capability for protecting the United States in times of war and peace.

CHAPTER ONE

Emergence of Naval Aviation

*F*loat Planes & Flying Boats: The U.S. Coast Guard and Early Naval Aviation* is the *first* written history that describes the Coast Guard's contribution to early naval aviation and early Coast Guard aviation development. The Navy and Coast Guard were so entwined in this endeavor that history is distorted when only one service's story is told. During the early years, both services were developing flying boats and seaplanes; prior to, and eighteen years after, the world war, both services had almost equal numbers of engineering-trained officer-aviators. Following the world war, the two services began to diverge. Coast Guard aviation continued to develop and depend upon seaplanes for its mission sets; however, after launch of the first three aircraft carriers, Coast Guard contributions to advancement of naval aviation diminished as Navy aviation developed carrier task forces and antisubmarine warfare aircraft for its own missions.

Published history has ignored the shortage of engineering-trained officer-aviators in the U.S. Navy as the country entered World War I and the matching contribution of U.S. Coast Guard engineering-trained officer-aviators in the buildup to the war. It was an era of float planes, flying boats, of the birth of aircraft carriers, and of the first transatlantic flight. It was a time of constant change and excitement, as each new day brought many remarkable ideas and events that mankind had not even imagined before. It was a time of keen competition between inventors to be the first to attach one's name to an invention, discovery, or process. It was a time when a significant part of the population was moving from the farm to the city in response to new thinking and better technology.

The emerging "second industrial age" changed the nature of commerce and naval warfare. Climbing a ship's rigging to scout the strength of an enemy force or deployment was replaced with observers in kite balloons towed by ships. Use of kite balloons was at its height in 1911. As World War I approached, scout and patrol aircraft would replace kite balloons.

One of the most significant changes was the arrival of the airplane and its impact on the safety of maritime commerce and on naval operations during and following World War I. Prior to the airplane, the careers of both Navy and Coast Guard officers were built solely on experience in shipboard operations and with strategies and tactics involving the maneuver of fleet components. The airplane changed the order of battle and required a coordinated ship-and-aircraft operation.

The military academies adapted to new technology with increased instruction in engineering and science disciplines, and the services were short of academy- and university-trained engineers. Prior to 1900, Naval and Coast Guard Academy graduates had been trained to perform as officers on sailing ships. Officers on board modern naval ships had to be familiar with engineering plants and how they operated. Airplane development only heightened the need for engineers.

Characteristic of an isolationist nation, American political leaders ignored the need to update the nation's armed forces and to provide funding for necessary personnel and equipment. Farmers with only basic educations, if any, constituted the majority of the country's population.

The U.S. Navy prepared for World War I with major battle fleet upgrades and a major expansion program. Line-officer orders to aviation training at Naval Air Station (NAS) Pensacola were suspended for the duration of the war, and only warrant officers and enlisted personnel received orders to Pensacola. Prior to the war, naval aviators who were graduates of the Naval Academy (Ellyson, Rogers, Towers, Mustin, Bellinger, Richardson, Byrd, Mitscher, Read, Griffin, Westervelt, and Chevalier) along with an interested line officer (Hunsaker) and Constructor Taylor led the effort to develop and expand the Navy's air force. Eight Coast Guard Academy officers (Stone, Donohue, Sugden, Wishar, Von Paulsen, Parker, Coffin, and Eaton) completed aviation training at NAS Pensacola prior to the war and contributed significantly to the development and capability of the Navy air force.

The need to upgrade and expand Navy resources was recognized early by President Theodore Roosevelt. The Japanese navy had grown to dominate the Pacific and threatened possessions newly acquired in the Spanish-American War, the Philippines, and Guam. Also, between 1906 and the world war a naval-expansion race between Great Britain and Germany caused rising tension between them. Between 1904 and 1907, eleven new U.S. Atlantic Fleet battleships were built, requiring additional experienced and trained personnel. Roosevelt then ordered the Atlantic Battle Fleet, with its new battleships, to sail around the world—as the Great White Fleet—from December 16, 1907, to February 12, 1909. Additionally, Roosevelt wanted to test the fleet's ability: "I want all failures, blunders and shortcomings to be made apparent in time of peace and not in time of war." This grand cruise demonstrated the president's deep conviction that only a strong navy could project a nation's power and diplomacy abroad. He also believed that a successful Great White Fleet would help obtain funding for four additional battleships.

The Great White Fleet's success was not unmixed. In 1906, Great Britain launched HMS *Dreadnought,* whose awesome size and firepower rendered the Great White Fleet's battleships obsolete. According to the Naval History and Heritage Command, the two oldest battleships in the fleet, *Kearsarge* and *Kentucky,* were already "Obsolescent and unfit for battle. Due to mechanical troubles, two others, *Maine* and *Alabama* had to be detached at San Francisco." *California* also experienced major mechanical troubles. In addition, the voyage revealed ship-design problems. Heavy weather revealed a need for larger size and displacement; the ships' habitability and ventilation were inadequate; casement shutters did not prevent the entry of seawater during rough seas; rapid-fire guns placed close to the waterline could not be used, due to spray and water driving into gun ports, distracting their crews; ship superstructure and mast design was not practicable for battle; and torpedo-defense guns and fire-control equipment needed upgrading. As Great Britain and Germany engaged in the world war, Britain had twenty-nine dreadnoughts and Germany had seventeen. Additionally, Britain had nine dreadnought battle cruisers, and Germany had seven. U.S. Army, Navy, Marine Corps, and Coast Guard aviation resources were meager at best.

It is not surprising that the early days of naval aviation were marked by concern, excitement, and extraordinary collaboration between Navy, Marine Corps, and Coast Guard officer-aviators with engineering skills. Early aviators in the three services helped each other to develop aircraft and to convince skeptical "Gun Club" shipboard officers of the relevance of aircraft in service operations. The Navy loaned aircraft to the Coast Guard, Coast Guard aviators were trained at NAS Pensacola, and over five hundred World War I Navy pilots were trained under a Coast Guard commanding officer at NAS Key West. Coast Guard aviators were assigned to Navy aviation engineering projects, operational commands, and training centers.

Events leading up to the world war inspired a few visionary men from each of the armed services and civil aviation. There were stars among them, such as Navy officers Washington Irving Chambers, Theodore G. Ellyson, John Rogers, David W. Taylor, John H. Towers, Holden C. Richardson, Jerome C. Hunsaker, George C. Westervelt, Godfrey deC. Chevalier, Richard E. Byrd, Marc A. Mitscher, Albert C. Read, and Virgil C. Griffin; Coast Guard officers Elmer F. Stone, Stanley V. Parker, Norman B. Hall, Eugene A. Coffin, Charles E. Sugden, and Phillip B. Eaton; and Army officers Eddie Rickenbacker and William "Billy" Mitchell. Within the Coast Guard, Stone stood out foremost. Indeed, Stone was also considered exceptional by the Navy. These men's vision and forward thinking transcended the norm and changed the world forever. They all knew each other, and most were close friends. They were committed to the improvement of aircraft and to the greater good rather than their own personal interests. Indeed, fourteen of these men are included in the National Naval Aviation Museum Hall of Honor:

PATRICK NEISON LYNCH BELLINGER

1885 – 1962

VICE ADMIRAL, UNITED STATES NAVY
NAVAL AVIATOR NUMBER 8

GRADUATED FROM THE UNITED STATES NAVAL
ACADEMY IN THE CLASS OF 1907. ARRIVED
PENSACOLA ABOARD THE USS ORION WITH THE
FIRST AVIATION GROUP JANUARY 1914. PILOT OF
FIRST UNITED STATES AIRCRAFT TO BE HIT BY
HOSTILE GUNFIRE - OCCUPATION OF VERACRUZ,
MEXICO, 6 MAY 1914. PILOT-IN-COMMAND OF NC-1
ON ATTEMPTED TRANS-ATLANTIC FLIGHT. HELD
MANY SIGNIFICANT COMMANDS INCLUDING USS
LANGLEY, USS RANGER, PATROL WINGS PACIFIC,
COMMANDER, AIR FORCE, ATLANTIC FLEET.
DEVELOPED MANY INNOVATIVE PROCEDURES AND
SET SEVERAL ALTITUDE AND DISTANCE RECORDS.
CONTINUOUSLY STRIVED TO ADVANCE THE
STATE OF THE ART.

VADM Patrick N. L. Bellinger, USN

RICHARD EVELYN BYRD, JR.

1888 – 1957

REAR ADMIRAL, UNITED STATES NAVY
NAVAL AVIATOR NUMBER 608

GRADUATED FROM THE UNITED STATES NAVAL
ACADEMY IN THE CLASS OF 1912. MADE THE
FIRST FLIGHT OVER NORTH POLE ON 9 MAY
1926 AND THE FIRST FLIGHT OVER SOUTH POLE
ON 29 NOVEMBER 1929. ORGANIZED AND LED
EXPEDITIONS TO ANTARCTICA IN 1928 -'30,
1933 - '35, 1939 - 41, AND 1955 - '56 WHICH
CONDUCTED EXTENSIVE EXPLORATION OF THE
VAST POLAR REGIONS, ACCUMULATED VALUABLE
WEATHER DATA AND ADDED FURTHER TO
KNOWLEDGE OF COLD WEATHER OPERATING
CONDITIONS.

RADM Richard E. Byrd Jr., USN

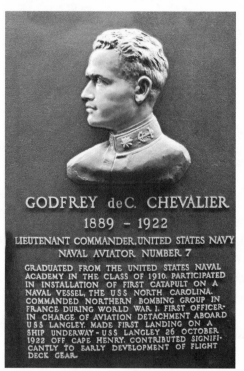

GODFREY deC. CHEVALIER

1889 – 1922

LIEUTENANT COMMANDER, UNITED STATES NAVY
NAVAL AVIATOR NUMBER 7

GRADUATED FROM THE UNITED STATES NAVAL
ACADEMY IN THE CLASS OF 1910. PARTICIPATED
IN INSTALLATION OF FIRST CATAPULT ON A
NAVAL VESSEL, THE USS NORTH CAROLINA.
COMMANDED NORTHERN BOMBING GROUP IN
FRANCE DURING WORLD WAR I. FIRST OFFICER-
IN-CHARGE OF AVIATION DETACHMENT ABOARD
USS LANGLEY. MADE FIRST LANDING ON A
SHIP UNDERWAY - USS LANGLEY 26 OCTOBER
1922 OFF CAPE HENRY. CONTRIBUTED SIGNIFI-
CANTLY TO EARLY DEVELOPMENT OF FLIGHT
DECK GEAR.

LCDR Godfrey deC. Chevalier, USN

GLENN HAMMOND CURTISS

1878 – 1930

INVENTOR
EARLY CIVILIAN AVIATOR

TRAINED THE NAVY'S FIRST NAVAL AVIATOR.
DEVELOPED THE FOLLOWING: FIRST AIRCRAFT
TO TAKE-OFF FROM A NAVAL SHIP; FIRST AIR-
CRAFT TO LAND AND TAKE-OFF FROM A NAVAL
SHIP; FIRST FLYING BOAT; FIRST AMPHIBIOUS
AIRCRAFT; NAVY'S FIRST AIRCRAFT; THE "JENNY"
OF WWI FAME; AND THE NC-4, THE FIRST AIR-
CRAFT TO FLY ACROSS THE ATLANTIC OCEAN.
DEVELOPED MANY IMPROVED AIRCRAFT THROUGH
THE 1920'S.

Mr. Glenn H. Curtiss, Civilian

THEODORE GORDON ELLYSON
1885 – 1928
COMMANDER, UNITED STATES NAVY
NAVAL AVIATOR NUMBER 1
GRADUATED FROM THE UNITED STATES NAVAL
ACADEMY IN THE CLASS OF 1905. FIRST NAVAL
OFFICER ORDERED TO AVIATION DUTY. FLEW
FIRST NAVAL AIRCRAFT ON DAY OF RECEIPT.
MADE FIRST NIGHT FLIGHT BY A NAVAL AVIATOR
TWO NIGHTS LATER. PARTICIPATED IN DEVELOP-
MENT OF SHIPBOARD LAUNCHING DEVICES
INCLUDING SUCCESSFUL TAKE-OFFS FROM AN
INCLINED WIRE AND FROM A BARGE-MOUNTED
CATAPULT. ESTABLISHED AVIATION CAMPS AT
ANNAPOLIS AND SAN DIEGO. ESTABLISHED
SEVERAL ENDURANCE, ALTITUDE AND SPEED
RECORDS. SERVED WITH DISTINCTION IN
ENGLAND DURING WWI IN SUBMARINE CHASER
OPERATIONS. SERVED WITH FLEET AND BUREAU
OF AERONAUTICS PRIOR TO FITTING-OUT OF
USS LEXINGTON.

CDR Theodore G. Ellyson, USN

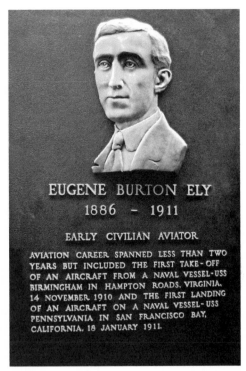

EUGENE BURTON ELY
1886 – 1911
EARLY CIVILIAN AVIATOR
AVIATION CAREER SPANNED LESS THAN TWO
YEARS BUT INCLUDED THE FIRST TAKE-OFF
OF AN AIRCRAFT FROM A NAVAL VESSEL-USS
BIRMINGHAM IN HAMPTON ROADS, VIRGINIA,
14 NOVEMBER 1910 AND THE FIRST LANDING
OF AN AIRCRAFT ON A NAVAL VESSEL-USS
PENNSYLVANIA IN SAN FRANCISCO BAY,
CALIFORNIA, 18 JANUARY 1911.

Mr. Eugene Ely, Civilian

WILLIAM ADGER MOFFETT
1869 – 1933
REAR ADMIRAL, UNITED STATES NAVY
NAVAL AVIATION OBSERVER NUMBER 1
GRADUATED FROM THE UNITED STATES NAVAL
ACADEMY IN CLASS OF 1890. DISTINGUISHED
SERVICE AS COMMANDING OFFICER OF USS
CHESTER DURING BATTLE OF VERA CRUZ IN
1914. COMMANDANT OF NAVAL TRAINING
STATION, GREAT LAKES, DURING WORLD WAR I.
SERVED AS THE FIRST CHIEF OF THE BUREAU OF
AERONAUTICS 1921 TO 1933. LEADER IN THE
FIGHT TO RETAIN AVIATION IN THE NAVY.
STRONG ADVOCATE OF THE AIRCRAFT CARRIER.

RADM William A. Moffett, USN

ALBERT CUSHING READ
1887 – 1967
REAR ADMIRAL, UNITED STATES NAVY
NAVAL AVIATOR NUMBER 24
GRADUATED FOURTH IN THE UNITED STATES
NAVAL ACADEMY CLASS OF 1907. SERVED AS
PILOT-IN-COMMAND OF THE NC-4 AIRCRAFT
DURING HER HISTORIC TRANS-ATLANTIC FLIGHT
IN 1919 WHICH WAS THE FIRST FLIGHT ACROSS
THE ATLANTIC OCEAN FOR ANY AIRCRAFT.
COMMANDED NUMEROUS NAVAL AIR STATIONS,
SQUADRONS AND SHIPS. COMMANDING OFFICER
OF USS SARATOGA. CHIEF OF NAVAL AIR
TECHNICAL TRAINING, HIGHLY INSTRUMENTAL
IN IMPROVING AND EXPANDING NAVAL AVIATION
THROUGH THE END OF WORLD WAR II.

RADM Albert C. Read, USN

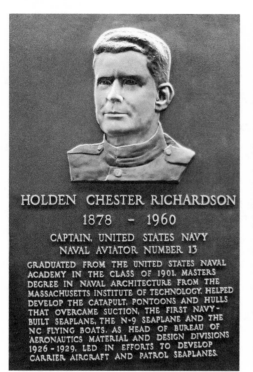

HOLDEN CHESTER RICHARDSON
1878 – 1960

CAPTAIN, UNITED STATES NAVY
NAVAL AVIATOR NUMBER 13

GRADUATED FROM THE UNITED STATES NAVAL
ACADEMY IN THE CLASS OF 1901. MASTERS
DEGREE IN NAVAL ARCHITECTURE FROM THE
MASSACHUSETTS INSTITUTE OF TECHNOLOGY. HELPED
DEVELOP THE CATAPULT, PONTOONS AND HULLS
THAT OVERCAME SUCTION, THE FIRST NAVY-
BUILT SEAPLANE, THE N-9 SEAPLANE AND THE
NC FLYING BOATS. AS HEAD OF BUREAU OF
AERONAUTICS MATERIAL AND DESIGN DIVISIONS
1926-1929, LED IN EFFORTS TO DEVELOP
CARRIER AIRCRAFT AND PATROL SEAPLANES.

CAPT Holden C. Richardson, USN

JOHN HENRY TOWERS
1885 – 1955

ADMIRAL, UNITED STATES NAVY
NAVAL AVIATOR NUMBER 3

GRADUATED FROM THE UNITED STATES NAVAL
ACADEMY IN THE CLASS OF 1906. ASSISTANT
DIRECTOR OF NAVAL AVIATION DURING WORLD
WAR I. COMMANDER OF TRANS-ATLANTIC
FLIGHT OF NC AIRCRAFT IN 1919. CHIEF OF
BUREAU OF AERONAUTICS AT BEGINNING OF
WORLD WAR II, THEN COMMANDER AIR FORCE
U.S. PACIFIC FLEET FOLLOWED BY DUTY AS
DEPUTY COMMANDER-IN-CHIEF, U.S. PACIFIC
FLEET AND FINISHED WAR AS COMMANDER TASK
FORCE 38. LATER SERVED AS COMMANDER-IN-
CHIEF PACIFIC FLEET. PRIMARY SPOKESMAN FOR
NAVAL AVIATION AFTER REAR ADMIRAL MOFFETT'S
DEATH IN 1933. HIGHLY INSTRUMENTAL IN
ACQUIRING MAJOR ROLE FOR AIRCRAFT CARRIER.

ADM John H. Towers, USN

MARC ANDREW MITSCHER
1887 – 1947

ADMIRAL, UNITED STATES NAVY
NAVAL AVIATOR NUMBER 33

GRADUATED FROM THE UNITED STATES NAVAL
ACADEMY IN THE CLASS OF 1910. COMMANDED
USS HORNET DURING LAUNCH OF DOOLITTLE
RAID AND BATTLE OF MIDWAY. AS TASK FORCE
COMMANDER DURING LAST TWO YEARS OF
WORLD WAR II, MASTERFULLY PLANNED AND
EXECUTED AN EXTENSIVE SERIES OF DEVASTATING
AND DECISIVE AERIAL VICTORIES OVER MAJOR
TASK FORCES OF THE ENEMY. HIGHLY
INSTRUMENTAL IN PROVIDING THE LEADERSHIP
NECESSARY TO PUSH THE ENEMY TO HIS
HOME SHORES. A RECOGNIZED AND DEMON-
STRATED EXPERT IN THE TACTICAL EMPLOYMENT
OF NAVAL AIR POWER.

ADM Marc A. Mitscher, USN

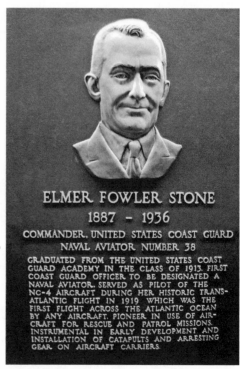

ELMER FOWLER STONE
1887 – 1936

COMMANDER, UNITED STATES COAST GUARD
NAVAL AVIATOR NUMBER 38

GRADUATED FROM THE UNITED STATES COAST
GUARD ACADEMY IN THE CLASS OF 1913. FIRST
COAST GUARD OFFICER TO BE DESIGNATED A
NAVAL AVIATOR. SERVED AS PILOT OF THE
NC-4 AIRCRAFT DURING HER HISTORIC TRANS-
ATLANTIC FLIGHT IN 1919 WHICH WAS THE
FIRST FLIGHT ACROSS THE ATLANTIC OCEAN
BY ANY AIRCRAFT. PIONEER IN USE OF AIR-
CRAFT FOR RESCUE AND PATROL MISSIONS.
INSTRUMENTAL IN EARLY DEVELOPMENT AND
INSTALLATION OF CATAPULTS AND ARRESTING
GEAR ON AIRCRAFT CARRIERS.

CDR Elmer F. Stone, USCG

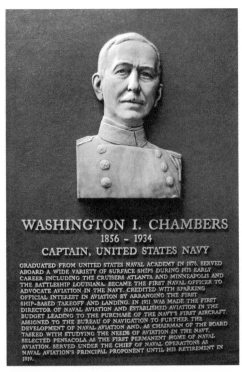

WASHINGTON I. CHAMBERS
1856 – 1934
CAPTAIN, UNITED STATES NAVY

GRADUATED FROM UNITED STATES NAVAL ACADEMY IN 1876. SERVED ABOARD A WIDE VARIETY OF SURFACE SHIPS DURING HIS EARLY CAREER INCLUDING THE CRUISERS ATLANTA AND MINNEAPOLIS AND THE BATTLESHIP LOUISIANA. BECAME THE FIRST NAVAL OFFICER TO ADVOCATE AVIATION IN THE NAVY. CREDITED WITH SPARKING OFFICIAL INTEREST IN AVIATION BY ARRANGING THE FIRST SHIP-BASED TAKEOFF AND LANDING. IN 1911 WAS MADE THE FIRST DIRECTOR OF NAVAL AVIATION AND ESTABLISHED AVIATION IN THE BUDGET LEADING TO THE PURCHASE OF THE NAVY'S FIRST AIRCRAFT. ASSIGNED TO THE BUREAU OF NAVIGATION TO FURTHER THE DEVELOPMENT OF NAVAL AVIATION AND, AS CHAIRMAN OF THE BOARD TASKED WITH STUDYING THE NEEDS OF AVIATION IN THE NAVY, SELECTED PENSACOLA AS THE FIRST PERMANENT HOME OF NAVAL AVIATION. SERVED UNDER THE CHIEF OF NAVAL OPERATIONS AS NAVAL AVIATION'S PRINCIPAL PROPONENT UNTIL HIS RETIREMENT IN 1919.

CAPT Washington I. Chambers, USN

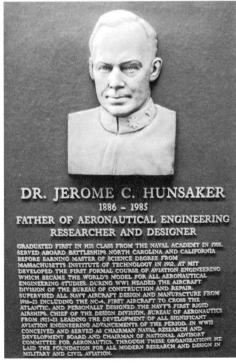

DR. JEROME C. HUNSAKER
1886 – 1985
FATHER OF AERONAUTICAL ENGINEERING
RESEARCHER AND DESIGNER

GRADUATED FIRST IN HIS CLASS FROM THE NAVAL ACADEMY IN 1908. SERVED ABOARD BATTLESHIPS NORTH CAROLINA AND CALIFORNIA BEFORE EARNING MASTER OF SCIENCE DEGREE FROM MASSACHUSETTS INSTITUTE OF TECHNOLOGY IN 1912. AT MIT DEVELOPED THE FIRST FORMAL COURSE OF AVIATION ENGINEERING WHICH BECAME THE WORLD'S MODEL FOR ALL AERONAUTICAL ENGINEERING STUDIES. DURING WWI HEADED THE AIRCRAFT DIVISION OF THE BUREAU OF CONSTRUCTION AND REPAIR. SUPERVISED ALL NAVY AIRCRAFT DESIGN AND MANUFACTURE FROM 1916-23 INCLUDING THE NC-4, FIRST AIRCRAFT TO CROSS THE ATLANTIC, AND PERSONALLY DESIGNED THE NAVY'S FIRST RIGID AIRSHIPS. CHIEF OF THE DESIGN DIVISION, BUREAU OF AERONAUTICS FROM 1921-23 LEADING THE DEVELOPMENT OF ALL SIGNIFICANT AVIATION ENGINEERING ADVANCEMENTS OF THE PERIOD. IN WWII CONCEIVED AND SERVED AS CHAIRMAN NAVAL RESEARCH AND DEVELOPMENT BOARD AND CHAIRMAN OF NATIONAL ADVISORY COMMITTEE FOR AERONAUTICS. THROUGH THESE ORGANIZATIONS HE LAID THE FOUNDATION FOR ALL MODERN RESEARCH AND DESIGN IN MILITARY AND CIVIL AVIATION.

Dr. Jerome C. Hunsaker, Civilian

CHAPTER TWO

Naval Aviation Conception and Birth

1898–1912

*D*uring the early years, the Secretary of the Navy was responsible for deciding the number and *type of ships and other major naval resources that would be carried in the Navy's inventory. Congress would decide the funding. Therefore, the Naval Aide for Matériel to the secretary exercised significant influence. The decision-making process for adding aircraft to the battle fleet would be no different than adding a new type of ship.*

Conception

The Navy's interest in aircraft as scout planes for the battle fleet began as early as 1898, with Assistant Secretary of the Navy Theodore Roosevelt and Professor Samuel P. Langley's flying machine. Later, Navy observers LT George C. Sweet, USN, and Navy Constructor William McEntee were assigned to report on Wilbur and Orville Wright's aviation demonstrations in 1908 and 1909. Their report led to a proposal for procurement of two "heavier than air flying machines." The Navy Department rejected the request, because aircraft had not advanced enough to make it practicable. On September 1, 1909, CDR Frederick L. Chapin, USN, naval attaché in Paris, France, reported observations from the Rheims Aviation Meet and expressed his opinion that aircraft would be useful in naval war fighting. On November 3, 1909, Lieutenant Sweet became the first Navy officer to fly, when he was carried aloft as a passenger in an Army Wright aircraft piloted by LT Frank P. Lahm, USA, at College Park, Maryland.

This early interest led to the assignment of CAPT Washington Irving Chambers, USN, assistant to the Aide for Matériel, in the office of the Secretary of the Navy, on September 26, 1910, as custodian for all aviation correspondence and information. Also in 1910, Navy constructor CAPT William McEntee, USN, was ordered to attend the first large air meet in the United States at Belmont Park, New York. He witnessed demonstration flights and the technique of aerial bombing by civilian pilots in rain, fog, and twenty-mile-per-hour winds. After hearing Captain McEntee's report, Captain Chambers was convinced that aircraft would become an important part of naval war fighting. To sway critics, he requested the Wright brothers and Glenn Curtiss provide demonstrations of landplanes flying off and onto ships. The Wright brothers used a catapult for their first flight, but they thought it too dangerous and impractical. They declined to participate, and the early relationship between the Navy and Glenn Curtiss began.[1]

Indeed, an early Coast Guard relationship with Glenn Curtiss also began in 1914, with initial training and lease of flying boats to develop the service's search, patrol, aerial law-enforcement capabilities, and ultimate introduction into naval aviation.

To facilitate the demonstrations, the Norfolk Navy Yard built a crude, sloping wooden platform on the bow of the light cruiser *Birmingham* (CL-2), and on November 14, 1910, Mr. Eugene Ely, a pilot employed by Glenn Curtiss, made the first shipboard aircraft takeoff. Ely flew off the drooping bow, dipping low to the water's surface, and "with his heart in his throat" recovered and landed on Willoughby Spit, near the site of future NAS Hampton Roads and Naval Operating Base, Norfolk.[2] Following up on the successful *Birmingham* takeoff, Glenn Curtiss sent a written offer to the secretary to train one naval officer for flight duty so as to assist "in developing the adaptability of the aeroplane to military purposes."

Following that first shipboard takeoff, Mare Island Navy Yard built a sloped 119-by-31-foot wooden platform over the armored cruiser USS *Pennsylvania's* aft turret. Thirty arresting lines, with fifty-pound sandbags on each end, were laid out three feet apart.

Curtiss 40-HP Pusher on first shipboard takeoff, USS *Birmingham* (CL-2)

Curtiss 50 HP Pusher first shipboard landing, USS *Pennsylvania* (ACR–4)

First shipboard landing, USS *Pennsylvania* (ACR–4)

The lines rested between sandbag pairs one foot off the deck. The axles between the landing-gear wheels were fitted with three pairs of arresting hooks to snag the lines. As a result of the perilous takeoff, Curtiss replaced Ely's original Curtiss Pusher aircraft engine with an improved, fifty-horsepower engine, and on January 18, 1911, Ely made the first shipboard landing.[3]

Curtiss Pusher Amphibian close up

Curtiss continued modifying his biplane by removing the tandem triple floats and replacing them with a single main float with a sled profile. Two successful flights proved that the sled profile float had superior performance. It became the standard for hydroplanes in the Navy until World War I.

Recognizing the need for communication between land, ship, and aeroplane, Acting Navy Secretary Beekman Winthrop directed the Navy's Point Loma Wireless Station to cooperate with CAPT Harry S. Harkness, U.S. Aeronautical Reserve, in wireless communications with aeroplanes.

The Navy theorized that the only practical approach for an aircraft to support the battle fleet was for it to land and take off alongside a ship, on the water. When not flying, it would be hoisted on board for storage. LT Theodore G. Ellyson, USN, was assigned to assist Curtiss on Coronado Island, at San Diego, California, in developing an aircraft to meet this requirement. On December 23, 1910, Lieutenant Ellyson received orders to Curtiss's Aviation Camp at North Island, San Diego, and a week later, hanging on to the main float, he would become the first passenger and pilot-in-training on a flying "hydroplane." A significant push for naval aviation came on February 17, 1911, when Curtiss successfully demonstrated for the Navy in San Diego Bay his "hydro-floatplane," the first practical floatplane to be developed. Curtiss landed his sixty-horsepower hydro-floatplane alongside the anchored USS *Pennsylvania*. The hydro–floatplane was hoisted on board and then lowered for a getaway (takeoff) and landing in shallow water off the beach. This demonstration met the Secretary of the Navy's first formal requirement to qualify the aeroplane for naval operational use: "The flying machine must be capable of landing on water alongside a warship and be fitted for hoisting aboard." It could provide aerial observation and gunfire spotting for the fleet.[4]

Curtiss hydro-floatplane hoisted on board, then lowered to water for getaway and landing by beach

Curtiss modified his hydroplane into an amphibian with both landing gear and float. He named it Hydro-Terra-Aeroplane, or TRIAD for short. His first TRIAD flight departed from the water at Spanish Bight on Coronado on February 26, 1911, and flew offshore and along the beach to a landing on the beach near the Hotel Del Coronado.[5]

Glenn Curtiss in water along beach with hydro-floatplane at North Island, 1911

A–1 in flight over Coronado, California, near Curtiss Airfield, 1912; Del Coronado Hotel in background

May 8, 1911—naval aviation's birthday

After the first flight by the Wright brothers at Kitty Hawk on December 17, 1903, the race was on between the early aviation pioneers to produce aircraft of military and commercial value. In particular, Glen Curtiss and the Wright brothers were locked in competition to sell aircraft to governments for military applications.

Airfields and engineering test facilities required large tracts of land with no real estate or manufacturing development within a broad boundary zone around them. San Diego's North Island, owned by the Coronado Beach Company, was just such a large tract of prime land, near other military facilities and a major port city.

By 1910, the Army Signal Corps, the Navy, and Marines were competing to use North Island land, already leased for three years by Glenn Curtiss for airfields.

Aviation advancements were finally recognized by Congress when naval aviation's first appropriated development funds ($25,000) were received by the Bureau of Navigation on March 4, 1910. Recognizing Curtiss's head start, the Wright Company needed to catch up, and it made a written offer to train one Navy pilot unconditionally, contingent upon purchase of one Wright flier for five thousand dollars. The first naval aviator, Lieutenant Ellyson, completed flight training at the Curtiss Aviation Group, North Island, in 1911.[6] The second naval aviator, LT John Rogers, USN, reported on March 17, 1911, for flight training at the Wright Company in Dayton, Ohio; on June 27, 1911, the third naval aviator, LT John H. Towers, USN, reported for aviation instruction at the Curtiss School in Hammondsport, New York.[7] Because NAS Pensacola was not operational until 1914, some argue that the "Cradle of Naval Aviation" was North Island, and not Pensacola. Indeed, one could argue that the cradle of Army Air Corps (Air Force) aviation too was North Island.

Curtiss instructing Lieutenant Ellyson at San Diego Aero Club Meet, January 29, 1911

Original Curtiss Flight Class, January 1911. Surrounding Curtiss, left to right: Army lieutenants G. E. Kelly, John Walker; Navy lieutenant T. G. Ellyson; Army captain Paul W. Beck

Following these shipboard and floatplane demonstrations, Captain Chambers requisitioned the Navy's first three aircraft on May 8, 1911: TRIADs A-1 and A-2 from Curtiss and a B-1 from the Wright brothers.[8] The three aircraft were to be assigned to each of three pilots, two trained by Curtiss and one by the Wright brothers. May 8, 1911, would become the official birthday of naval aviation.

First Navy Aeroplane

The Navy's first aeroplane, TRIAD A-1, was powered by a sixty-horsepower engine turning two chain-driven, metal-tipped tractor propellers. It was required to have dual tandem pilot controls, to be able to land and take off from both land and water, fly at least forty-five miles per hour, and carry one passenger seated at a second set of pilot controls. A-2 was powered by a single pusher propeller on a sixty-horsepower engine. The Navy's first aircraft trial (acceptance test flight) was made by Curtiss in A-1 on July 1, 1911. The same day, Curtiss flew A-1, with Ellyson under instruction, and Lieutenant Ellyson soloed in A-1 in the final flight of the day. During a daring flight in A-1 on July 3, Lieutenant Ellyson departed Lake Keuka, near Hammondsport, New York, on the first Navy night flight, and after two attempts following his arrival, landed on the lake without artificial lighting. New aircraft and pilots needed a structured environment to develop operational capability.[9]

Naval aviation had learned to walk and now, in 1911, was trying to run. Many firsts were experienced in rapid-fire sequence. On July 6, 1911, Captain Chambers was assigned to temporary additional duty at the Naval Academy, in Annapolis, Maryland, to establish an aviation experimental station on Greenbury Point, the first Navy flying camp. On July 10 at the Curtiss facility in Hammondsport, Curtiss flew A-1 to demonstrate a getaway from land, followed by landing in the water after raising the landing gear. Aircraft trials were undertaken for the recently completed A-2 on July 13, with two flights, one by Curtiss and one by Ellyson.[10]

On August 23, the new aviators were ordered, with their aeroplanes, to "Greenbury Point Flying Camp, in connection with the test of gasoline motors and other experimental work in the development of aviation, including instruction at the aviation school."

The secretary's approval criteria for the development of naval aviation stated, "Land and takeoff alongside a ship on the water. When not flying, it would be hoisted on board for storage." However, launching *from* and recovery of aircraft *on board* ships remained at the heart of every Navy officer's desires.

At Hammondsport on September 7, 1911, Lieutenant Ellyson launched a hydroplane hanging from an inclined wire ending at the water's edge. Navigation capability for overwater flights out of sight of land was improved when on September 20 a boat compass was ordered from the Naval Observatory for experimentation with the TRIADs.

Aircraft maintenance support for naval aviation became a reality when on October 10 Lieutenant Richardson became the Navy's first aviation engineering and maintenance

Navy's first aircraft, A-1, Lieutenant (junior grade) Ellyson, and passenger, Captain Chambers

officer, reporting to the aviation division of the Bureau of Construction and Repair at the Washington Navy Yard. Also, on October 16, the first test of hydroplane floats was made at the model basin in the Washington Navy Yard. The next day, Captain Chambers theorized that engines propelled by diesel oil, or kerosene, would be used for aircraft: "In my opinion, this [jet] turbine is the surest way of all, and the aeroplane manufacturer who gets it first is going to do wonders."

The roll of naval aviators continued to expand. On November 8, ENS Victor D. Herbster, USN, reported to Greenbury Point for flight instruction to become naval aviator number four. On October 25 and November 26, naval aviators seven and eight, respectively, ENS

Curtiss and Chambers on A-2

Godfrey deC. Chevalier and LTJG Patrick N. L. Bellinger reported to Greenbury Point for pilot training.

Since all Navy aircraft were required to operate from water, a float system to modify the Wright B-1 landplane to a hydroplane was ordered from the Burgess Company, in Marblehead, Massachusetts, and from Glenn Curtiss on November 14, 1911. Following B-1 modification, ENS Charles H. Maddox experimented at Greenbury Point on December 20, 1911, with wireless transmissions, using a long-line antenna trailing from A-1, flown by Lieutenant Towers.

LT Holden C. Richardson, USN

The capability to launch and recover aircraft from ships continued to receive priority. On December 26, 1911, the Bureau of Ordnance notified Captain Chambers that it was interested in developing a launch catapult for aeroplanes using a design similar to compressed-air torpedo launchers. Launching torpedoes from heavy cruisers and battleships was no longer practical for naval warfare, and unused air compressors took up much important space on board the ships. To facilitate this effort, research, development, and testing had to be conducted near the battle fleet. At year's end, December 29, 1911, the TRIADs and pilots were transferred from Greenbury Point to Curtiss's facility at Coronado.[11]

Wright B-1 after pontoon installation

1912

Until the end of World War I, Marine Corps air operations basically supported Navy aviation development efforts and antisubmarine air operations. For example, during World War I aerial surveillance and bombing patrols against German U-boats, U.S. Marine pilots would fly day search patrols, Navy and Coast Guard pilots at night.

Combined Marine air/ground support operations and other now-traditional Marine Corps operations were developed following the war.

The year 1912 was one of continuing operational performance innovations: Marine Corps entry into naval aviation; engineering strength-of-materials and aircraft-engine tests; wireless communications; catapults; and ordnance innovations for aircraft.[12] A March 9, 1912, letter from Assistant Naval Constructor Lieutenant Richardson to Captain Chambers expressed interest in aluminum and steel alloy aeroplane construction: "From all I can gather, there is little doubt that much greater confidence would be felt if pontoons were constructed with metal skin. . . . It would be unwise to make any requisition for such a construction until a practical standard design has been developed."[13]

On board Armored Cruiser Number 5, USS *West Virginia* (later renamed *Huntington*), on March 11, Chief Machinist Mate F. E. Nelson, USN, recommended in a letter to the Secretary of the Navy that models be used for experimentation in the development of a helicopter design. The Navy policy reply was to authorize expenditure of not more than fifty dollars for experiments and to keep watch while others developed the helicopter.

U.S. Marine Corps Aviation Is Born

On May 22, 1stLt Alfred A. Cunningham, USMC, reported to the Burgess Company for flight instruction. He would become naval aviator number five and the first Marine Corps aviator.

The first aircraft strength-of-materials engineering tests for the Navy were conducted at Greenbury Point on July 20, when Curtiss's Monel rigging wire was tested against Wright's steel rigging wire. The Monel wire resisted corrosion and was 50 percent stronger.

At Greenbury Point on July 26, Ensign Maddox, on board B-1, piloted by LT John Rogers, USN, sent wireless messages to Torpedo Boat 19, *Stringham,* at a distance of one and a half nautical miles. On July 31, Lieutenant Ellyson attempted a catapult launch in A-1 from Greenbury Point. A crosswind caught A-1 and caused it to crash, but Ellyson was not injured.

On September 18, Marine Corps aviator number two, LT Bernard L. Smith, reported to Greenbury Point for pilot instruction.

Ordnance-delivery capability was added to naval aircraft when tests were conducted on October 3, at the Indian Head, Maryland, Proving Ground for a recoilless rifle designed by CDR Cleland Davis, USN. The design provided for a cartridge large enough to damage a submarine, yet with recoil small enough not to damage the airframe carrying the weapon. On October 8, Greenbury Point successfully tested a fifty-horsepower Gyro radial engine in a laboratory setting.

A–1 on first catapult attempt at Greenbury Point

Lieutenant Towers began tests on October 26 to evaluate an aircraft crew's ability to identify submerged submarines. His report of December 18, upon completion of tests, concluded the best search altitude for submarines was eight hundred feet and that submarines could be detected a few feet below the surface of the muddy waters of Chesapeake Bay. Urgency would lead to deployment of the entire Navy aviation element, on March 3, 1913, to Fisherman's Point at Guantánamo, Cuba, for battle fleet operations and tests. Flying boats would become highly successful in detecting submarines and mines at depths of thirty to forty feet and in scouting for the fleet.

Davis recoilless ASW gun

LT Theodore G. Ellyson, USN, was successfully catapulted in C-1 at the Washington Navy Yard on November 12, and from this point, naval aircraft development would be almost exclusively centered around the flying boat until the end of World War I.[14]

FLYING BOAT LEAVING CATAPULT 16630 - NOVEMBER 1912.

C-1 catapulted at Washington Navy Yard

After successful shipboard landing and takeoff demonstrations, the Navy envisioned four aircraft carriers with a sustained top speed of thirty-five knots. The high speed was necessary to accelerate aircraft to forty to forty-five knots for takeoff and permit landing at approximately forty-five knots, using only brakes to stop.

Congress saw things differently, deciding that a ship that could make thirty-five knots would be too expensive.[15] Slower aircraft carriers would be the rule. This led to the need for a variety of alternative aircraft "platforms" and devices—seaplanes, amphibious aircraft, catapults for battleships and cruisers, and aircraft-carrier arresting gear. Over time, aircraft and ordnance would become much heavier than the very early models, necessitating both catapults and arresting gear for aircraft carriers. Congress's frugality ultimately hastened development of catapults and arresting gear.[16]

When Captain Chambers's tour of duty ended, CAPT Mark L. Bristol, USN, relieved him as assistant to the aide for matériel for the Secretary of the Navy. Captain Bristol's assignment was to "Take the Air Service to sea!" The Navy's efforts added development of the shipboard catapult to launch aircraft.[17]

In 1912, the Navy accepted delivery of its first flying boat, the Curtiss C-1. Lieutenant Ellyson conducted the aircraft trial for C-1 at the Curtiss plant in Hammondsport on November 30. Early flying-boat hulls left much to be desired, requiring extensive engineering development. The C-1's power was limited to only sixty horsepower, and early flat-bottomed hulls were difficult to lift off the water during getaways. Unless there were stiff wind and choppy sea conditions, hydrodynamic suction on the hull resisted lift forces, thwarting flight. To solve the problem, the Navy began experimenting with deep V-shaped hulls at the hydro model basin in the Washington Navy Yard and in San Diego.[18]

Other important firsts occurred in 1912. LT B. L. Smith, USMC, took off in the first amphibious aircraft, landed ashore, and returned for a water landing. In mid-December, Lieutenant Ellyson in C-1 was successfully launched from a pneumatic catapult mounted on a barge at the Washington Navy Yard. LT Alfred A. Cunningham, USMC, attempted the first pneumatic catapult shot from the deck of a warship under way. He crashed, because of the unreliability of the air pressure firing the catapult.[19] Improvements were made, and soon the flying boat became operational on board warships under way at sea.

Float Planes vs. Flying Boats

A float plane had a single main float for buoyancy on the aircraft's centerline under the fuselage. Two small floats were located under each lower wing tip to prevent capsizing. The float plane–type configuration was also used on both gliders and powered machines. In fact, the Wright brothers experimented with a lashed canvas canoe beneath the center section of their lower wing in 1909.[20]

Following the invention of the float plane, the flying boat was developed. The term "flying boat" was coined to differentiate it from a float plane. A flying boat was an aircraft designed with a boat-shaped hull, or fuselage. It had a small float under each lower wing tip to prevent capsizing. It was, therefore, a combination airplane and boat. To facilitate these developments a wind tunnel and hydrodynamic model basin were built at the Washington, D.C., Navy Yard.[21] Funding for research and design was funneled to developing more efficient flying-boat hulls, wing-tip floats, airfoils, and airframe structures.

The Navy theorized that the flying-boat design was more seaworthy and reliable for operations than the float plane, due to its larger mass and its shape. It offered structural and aerodynamic advantages over a float plane, with its larger fuselage providing flotation, instead of a shorter and thinner float.[22] The flying-boat hull had less aerodynamic drag than a large main-float appendage suspended under the aircraft.

All these events led the Secretary of the Navy in 1912 to appoint Captain Chambers to chair a board to develop a plan for "organization of a Naval Aeronautic Service." The board recommended an air training command at Pensacola, Florida; an aviation office under the Secretary of the Navy to coordinate the technical bureaus; a training ship for aviation operations at sea; and an aircraft assigned to each major combat ship. The recommendations were implemented, and the fiscal year budget for 1917 established a 150-officer and 350–enlisted man Naval Flying Corps and a Naval Reserve flying force.[23]

Wind-tunnel model of first aircraft designed and manufactured using wind-tunnel tests

In the meantime, events overseas foretold of hostilities that would imminently erupt into a large European war. War-fighting capability, particularly antisubmarine warfare against German U-boats, became an important part of the developing naval aviation mission.

CHAPTER THREE

Development and Growth

1913–1919

Since the early days of U.S. history, long before steamships, Atlantic coastal trade and trade with Caribbean and South American countries had been an important part of the economy in the eastern United States. Smuggling was also a common coastal event. Most coastal trade was carried by large, wooden-hulled schooners of three, four, or more masts. They were built in New England and Nova Scotia shipyards with sturdy designs and were sailed by experienced Down East sailors who had been born to the sea. As the eastern United States and Caribbean nations developed, trade continued to expand along the North American coast. And, in spite of the advent of steamships in 1871, wooden-hulled lumber schooner trade still existed in a small way until the end of World War II.[1]

Schooners were at the mercy of storm systems, wind, sea, and current. In 1916, the radio had yet to be developed for reliable maritime communication, so weather, navigational hazards, and hurricane-warning broadcasts did not exist. Skippers of these old schooners relied upon experience and coastal piloting, even though they were proficient at celestial navigation. They followed the shoreline, sailing "by guess and by God," and they "smelled their way through fog." When a hurricane happened upon them, they just rode it out. Not surprisingly, many sank, many were dismasted, and many became derelicts or were beached or stranded on treacherous shoals. The Coast Guard was kept busy, especially in the winter, searching for vessels in distress and towing derelicts or blowing them up to prevent them from becoming hazards to navigation.

Each year, starting in mid-November, winter cruising orders and assigned search areas for vessels in distress became the norm for Atlantic and Gulf of Mexico cutters. The cutters would depart home ports fully loaded with fuel, freshwater, and provisions. Their orders: not to return until spring, except to replenish supplies or in an emergency. Winter cruising was a strain on both men and cutters, so when the maritime radio became common, the cutters were instead placed on ready-alert status in their home ports, able to respond at a moment's notice.[2]

Thomas W. Lawson

After the turn of the century and continuing into the 1920s, steamships gradually replaced sailing schooners, except during World War I, when many of the latter were pressed back into service.

During the war, most foreign merchant ships were used for the war effort. Since the United States operated only 2 percent of the world's merchant fleet, an urgent demand was created for merchant hulls and crews.[3]

Steam and motor ships moved the trade routes farther offshore, away from shoals and the dangerous shoreline. However, they too were caught in winter storms and experienced many of the same perils, except the steamship added fire and explosion to the list of distress calls. As the search areas moved farther offshore, critical time was lost searching larger ocean areas for vessels in distress. Law enforcement, attempting to track and intercept contraband, experienced the same limitations caused by large search areas, as well as the ingenuity of smugglers hiding under cover of foul weather and darkness.

Prior to and during World War I, through mutual support and cooperation, Navy and Coast Guard aviators helped build each other in the cause of national defense. Events overseas foretold of hostilities that would erupt into a large European war in 1914. War-fighting capability, particularly for antisubmarine warfare against German U-boats, became an important part of the thinking in a developing naval aviation community. But how would the Coast Guard eventually employ aircraft in its own peacetime mission areas? What was the appropriate vision by which to leverage aviation

Wyoming

assets and improve operational efficiency? The new Coast Guard—formed by an amalgamation of the Revenue Cutter Service, the Lifesaving Service, and the Lighthouse Service in 1915—did not immediately seize upon the value of aircraft for either its old or newly gained missions and responsibilities. The Coast Guard had always been a seagoing service, and aviation had yet to prove itself. New eyes and great perseverance would be needed to overcome long-standing traditions and attitudes and the glacial inertia of the federal government.

1913

At the Burgess Company, improved instrumentation were installed in a new flying boat, the D-1, on March 31, including airspeed indicator, altimeter, chart board, compass, and inclinometer. A generator and radio were added at a later date.

The Secretary of the Navy differentiated between skills required for landplane and seaplane operations when he established the position of "NavyAir Pilot," with standards that required more than did international accreditation by the Federation Aeronautique International.[4]

Formal aeronautical engineering courses at a civilian university were advanced on June 12, 1913, when the secretary approved orders sending LT Jerome C. Hunsaker, USN, of the Bureau of Construction and Repair, to the Massachusetts Institute of Technology. Hunsaker's assignment was to establish an aeronautical engineering course within the

Department of Naval Architecture and conduct research and experiments for the design of airplanes and dirigibles. Because Europe was preparing for war, the future combatants were further advanced than the United States, and Hunsaker toured their aeronautical research facilities to expand his knowledge.[5]

On April 28, RADM Victor Blue, USN, of the Bureau of Navigation approved a plan for the Navy, Glenn Curtiss, and the Sperry Company to cooperate in developing and testing a gyroscopic stabilizer on a Navy flying boat. Flight stability was greatly improved when on August 30 Lieutenant (junior grade) Bellinger successfully tested a Sperry gyroscope stabilizer in C-2 at the Curtiss Hammondsport facility. This was the forerunner of the modern autopilot.[6]

Thereafter, under the supervision of Lieutenant Richardson, the first amphibian flying boat, the OWL ("over-water-land"), or E-1, was built at Hammondsport by modifying the hydroplane A-2. A-2's center float was removed and replaced by a flying-boat hull with three landing wheels. The OWL was successfully flown on October 5.[7]

U.S. Coast Guard Aviation Is Born

The Coast Guard had always been a seagoing service, and aviation had yet to prove itself. Elmer Fowler Stone graduated from the Revenue Cutter School of Instruction on June 7, 1913, completing an engineering curriculum and receiving a commission as a third lieutenant,★ U.S. Revenue Cutter Service (USRCS). On June 13, 1913, Third Lieutenants Stone and Norman Hall, a classmate, reported on board their first shipboard assignment, USRCS *Onondaga,* in her home port in Norfolk, Virginia. On board *Onondaga,* Stone was assigned to study the ship's steam machinery. Five months later, he qualified to perform the duties of an engineering officer and requested headquarters assignment as a line officer. On February 14, 1914, headquarters designated him a line officer of *Onondaga.*[8]

The Coast Guard's first aviator, 2nd LT Elmer F. Stone, emerged from a background typical of many turn-of-the-century people who had migrated from the simple life of the family farm to the rapidly advancing technology of the industrial city. He was born on a farm in Livingstone, New York, on January 22, 1887. His family moved in 1895 to a sheep farm in Norfolk, Virginia, where his younger sisters were born. Stone learned attention to detail, discipline, responsibility, and an ethic of hard work on the farm before graduating from high school in Norfolk.

In 1910, at the age of twenty-three, Stone qualified as a U.S. Revenue Cutter Service cadet, passing required examinations with higher scores than any other applicant that year.[9] He was appointed cadet on April 30 in the Revenue Cutter Service School of Instruction, the forerunner of the U.S. Coast Guard Academy.[10] His academy classmates gave him the nickname "Archie," which remained with him the rest of his life.

★Until the 1930s, U.S. service academies awarded only officer commissions, not formal higher-education degrees. Cadets and midshipmen at the military and naval academies and the Revenue Cutter School of Instruction completed engineering curricula and received commissions as second lieutenants, ensigns, or third lieutenants.

Ultimately, he was designated both naval aviator number 38 and Coast Guard aviator number 1. It was Stone in 1916 who had the insight to perceive the aircraft's ability to prosecute more efficiently the Coast Guard's various operational missions.[11] He was the leader in planning a Coast Guard aviation capability to search both for vessels in distress and smugglers avoiding tariff and custom duties while transporting illegal contraband.

Class of 1913, U.S. Revenue Cutter Service School of Instruction (Stone sitting far left)

On October 9, 1914, Stone was transferred to the USRCS *Itasca*. He was reassigned to *Onondaga*—now a U.S. Coast Guard cutter (USCGC)—in February 1915. Stone was coxswain of a boat from that vessel during a stormy rescue of seven shipwrecked seamen of the lumber-laden schooner *C. C. Wehrum* off False Cape, Virginia. A letter of commendation from the Assistant Secretary of the Treasury dated June 24, 1915, acknowledged his "skill and judgment displayed in affecting [*sic*] the more hazardous part of this work and in so managing the boat that the rescue was attended by no mishap whatever. The mere reading of their names and rates shows that this was a picked crew and their achievement shows that they were well chosen—and receives the special commendation of the Department."[12]

Next to the cutter's moorings in Hampton Roads was the Curtiss Flying School. Stone's and Hall's imaginations were set on fire watching seaplanes flying and maneuvering over, in, and around the port. The Coast Guard's vision of aviation operations was born. Stone, Hall, and later Carl Christian von Paulsen formed the triumvirate that was to pursue the formal founding of Coast Guard aviation.

Elsewhere near Hampton Roads, Glenn Curtiss had opened the Atlantic Coast Aeronautical Station on a twenty-acre tract on Boat Harbor Point, at the end of Jefferson

USRCS *Onondaga*

Avenue, Norfolk, on December 24, 1913. Located on the shoreline, the school operated both a two-hundred-by-three-thousand-foot runway and a seadrome that Curtiss's F Boats used to land and take off on water.

Curtiss had selected his close friend CAPT Thomas Scott Baldwin to run the school.[13] His titles of "Captain" and "Professor" were not official but honorifics adopted by civilian

Curtiss Atlantic Coast Aeronautical Station

exhibition balloonists in the late 1800s. The news media of the time continued using these colorful titles as they reported on the "adventurous spirit" of these daring men.[14]

Curtiss and Baldwin in 1934

A new war in Europe stimulated a need for a large and rapid ramping-up of trained aviators volunteering for service in the European militaries. The United States had not yet entered World War I. The Atlantic Coast Aeronautical Station provided a large training field for instructing Canadian and American volunteers joining allied forces in Europe and training civilians just becoming interested in flight instruction. Stone met and befriended many of the early aviators who were trained there. Some who eventually became notable were Eddie Stinson, William "Billy" Mitchell (later a general), Victor Carlstrom, and Vernon Castle. Mitchell was at the time a thirty-eight-year-old major in the Army Signal Corps, too old for Army flight instruction. Every Saturday night he traveled on his personal boat from his assignment in Washington, D.C., to the Curtiss school, returning to work by Monday morning. He paid all his travel and training expenses himself.[15] It was not until Mitchell obtained his flying license that the Army designated him an aviator.

The Navy had introduced the K Boat to the fleet in 1913, during maneuvers in the southern Atlantic as the first deep-V-hull flying boat. This was the first extensive use of aircraft with warships at sea. The K Boat's general performance was much improved over that of the flat-bottomed C-1 flying boat. The K Boat was refined by Curtiss to the F Boat, and later the MF Boat, which would be used extensively in 1914 as a training seaplane at the new Naval Aeronautic Station Pensacola training command.[16]

1916 Curtiss F Boat

All this activity stimulated the visions of CAPT Benjamin M. Chiswell, USCG, commanding officer of *Onondaga,* and Third Lieutenants Hall and Stone. Encouraged by Chiswell, in 1915 Stone and Hall met with Baldwin to discuss their idea of using aircraft to locate vessels in distress and shipwrecks that were obstructions to navigation. Baldwin offered the loan of a Curtiss F-type single-engine flying boat to test Stone's concept for aerial search and other useful tasks. The Curtiss "F Boat" was one of the first successful seaplanes yet designed and built. It had no navigation equipment on board and was used for offshore patrols only occasionally and within sight of land. The originality and passion of the two third lieutenants brought Captain Chiswell into the team, making it a powerful one. The experiment was so successful that it received an official blessing from the commandant of the Coast Guard.[17] Stone's successful tests also led to "Aerial Coast Guard activity officially funded by the Treasury Department." The sum of $1,500,000 was provided for flight instruction, and to lease and operate two types of Curtiss flying boats at the Atlantic Coast Aeronautical Station.[18]

1914

The year 1914 brought not only the outbreak of hostilities in Europe but also the establishment of aviation training at Pensacola, as well as additional aeronautical engineering and support capabilities. NAS Squantum, Massachusetts; Greenbury Point; and the Curtiss training facilities at Coronado, California, and Boat Harbor, Virginia, were considered redundant and were closed. On January 30, USS *Mississippi* (BB-23), under the command of LCDR Henry C. Mustin, and the armored cruiser USS *Orion* arrived in Pensacola, Florida, along with Lieutenant Towers, whose aviation unit transferred from Greenbury Point. Lieutenant Commander Mustin commanded both the battleship and the new

Pensacola Aeronautic Station. The new station had a complement of nine officers, twenty-three enlisted men, seven aircraft, and canvas tent hangars. Bureau of Medicine and Surgery circular letter serial 125221 added medical standards for aviators. Medical personnel were added on February 20, thereby establishing the discipline of naval aviation medicine.[19]

By the end of March, the growing number of aircraft and types required a new alpha–numeric designation protocol. The first letter now identified aircraft class, such as *A* for heavier than air, *B* for balloons, *D* for dirigibles, and *K* for kites. The second identified type of aircraft within a class: *B* for flying boats, *C* for combination land and water aircraft, *H* for hydroplane, *L* for landplane, and *X* for convertibles. The third character, a number, identified the numerical order of production in a class: A-1 would become AH-1, and C-1 would be AB-1.[20]

Aircraft Class	Type of Aircraft within Class	Numerical Order of Production
A heavier than air	B Flying Boats	AB-1 1st Heavier than
B Balloons	C Combination Land/Water	Air Flying Boat
D Dirigibles	H Hydroplane	AH-1 1st Heavier than
K Kites	L Landplane	Air Hydroplane
	X Convertibles	

The Bureau of Navigation approved a formal course of instruction on April 22 for student pilots and student mechanics at NAS Pensacola.

On April 20, 1914, naval aviation observed a major milestone and underwent the ultimate test—going to war for the first time. Within a day of receiving orders on the twentieth, Towers, three pilots, twelve enlisted men, and three aircraft sailed in USS *Birmingham* (CL-2) for Tampico, Mexico, and the Atlantic Fleet to participate in a looming conflict to the south. On April 21, Lieutenant (junior grade) Bellinger commanded a second detachment, which sailed on *Mississippi* with one pilot, three student pilots, and two aircraft. During an altercation known as the Mexican Crisis, President Woodrow Wilson approved the establishment of a military government in Veracruz, Mexico, in 1914 and in the Dominican Republic in 1916, and a military protectorate in Haiti in 1916. It was an exercise of "gunboat diplomacy" meant to protect the Panama Canal and its approaches. On April 25, Lieutenant Bellinger on AB-3 departed *Mississippi* to search Veracruz harbor for mines and scout the city. Again on April 28, Bellinger and ENS W. D. LaMont departed in AB-3 to photograph the harbor. May 2 saw the first air support for ground troops when Bellinger and observer LaMont reported the location of attacking enemy troops to U.S. Marines near Tejar.[21]

The Office of Naval Aeronautics was established on July 1, 1914, under the Division of Operations in the Secretary of the Navy's office. This was the first formal recognition of naval aviation. Another organizational change occurred on November 16, when command of the flight training school was transferred from the station ship at Pensacola to the newly designated Naval Aeronautic Station Pensacola. A new title, "Director of Naval Aeronautics," the officer in charge of naval aviation, was established on November 23. CAPT Mark L. Bristol, USN, became the first director.[22]

1915

This year continued the formalization of naval aviation, when on March 22 the title "naval aviator" replaced the title "NavyAir Pilot." Advances continued at a rapid pace.

On April 16, Lieutenant Bellinger made a successful catapult launch in flying boat AB-2 from Holden Richardson's catapult mounted on a barge anchored in Pensacola Bay. On June 1, the Navy awarded a contract to the Connecticut Aircraft Company in New Haven for its first lighter-than-air craft, a blimp designated DN-1. By July 10, NAS Pensacola had tested the first navigational sextant, using a pendulum to mark an artificial horizon. Since the pendulum was affected by gravitational anomalies during flight, the design was unsatisfactory, and a gyro-stabilized sextant was recommended. On July 22, the Director of Naval Aeronautics approved a recommendation from the commanding officer of NAS Pensacola that a standard suite of instruments be installed in all operational naval aircraft. The standard suite consisted of airspeed meter, incidence indicator, skid and sideslip indicator, barometric altimeter, compass, course and distance indicator, clock, sextant, engine tachometer, fuel gauge, oil gauge, and magazine camera.[23]

Perhaps the most important advancement in 1915 came on November 5, when Lieutenant Commander Mustin was successfully catapulted from USS *North Carolina* (ACR-12) while the ship was under way at eight knots in Pensacola Bay.[24]

Historical neglect by Congress of all military assets and personnel habitually follows the end of the nation's participation in a war, and this was certainly true from the end of the Civil and Spanish American Wars until 1912, when war clouds again were on the horizon. The Aero Club of America called for the establishment of the National Aerodynamical Laboratory to benefit both the government and private industry. The most Congress did, however, was establish the National Advisory Committee for Aeronautics (NACA) in 1915, as a last-minute rider to that year's naval appropriation.[25]

First successful catapult launch from underway ship

1916

On January 11, compasses modified from the British Creigh-Osborn design were sent by the Naval Observatory in Washington, D.C., to NAS Pensacola for testing. The compass became the naval aircraft standard throughout World War I. An aviation radio laboratory was established at NAS Pensacola when, on January 22, its commanding officer requested authorization from superintendent of the Radio Service to conduct radio experiments from aircraft. The Bureau of Steam Engineering ordered fifty radios to support aircraft radio experiments.

1916 was the year for advancements, with the navigational compass, establishment of radio communications between aircraft and ships, the invention of the radio direction finder, the entrance of the U.S. Coast Guard into naval aviation, the authorization of the first Navy ship to carry and operate aircraft, development of light metal alloys for aircraft construction, and establishment of a formal aircraft trial standard to test Navy aircraft.

In accordance with an agreement between the Navy and Treasury Departments on March 30, the Secretary of the Treasury notified the Secretary of the Navy that 2nd LT Charles E. Sugden, USCG, and 3rd LT Elmer F. Stone, USCG, were ordered to NAS Pensacola for pilot training.

The Chief of Naval Operations on May 30 requested the bureaus to develop gyroscope-based instruments for compasses, bombsights, and base lines (later known as turn-and-bank, or slip, indicators). On July 12, LT Godfrey Chevalier in AB-3 completed calibration of the catapult on board *North Carolina* when he was successfully catapulted from the ship while under way in Pensacola Bay.

On July 22, RADM David W. Taylor requested the Aluminum Company of America (ALCOA) to develop a lightweight alloy for fabrication of girders for zeppelin frameworks. On October 24 the Bureau of Steam Engineering requested the naval aircraft factory to develop radio-direction-finder equipment for aircraft. Capping the year, on November 30 two-seat, dual-control N-9 training hydro aeroplanes were delivered to the Navy by Glenn Curtiss.[26]

The furthest-reaching development in 1916 was formal establishment of standard procedures for conducting aircraft trials. These tests were to be used for contract acceptance of aircraft and for establishing an aircraft's flight safety performance before declaring an aircraft safe to fly. These aircraft trials would have a profound impact on aircraft development and officer-pilot careers over the next two decades.[27]

Coast Guard Enters Naval Aviation

Stone's successful initial test led to aerial Coast Guard activity officially funded by the Treasury Department. "$1,500,000 was provided to lease and operate seven different types of Curtiss flying boats at the Atlantic Coast Aeronautical Station."[28] Although the Curtiss F flying boat was Stone's preferred aircraft for continuing flights to further develop his concept of operations, among the seven leased aircraft was an early version of the BT flying boat. In 1915, and then again in 1917 and 1918, the basic BT flying-boat design was used by Curtiss to respond to Chiswell's request for a Coast Guard flying lifeboat (next page), and then again to respond to a contractual request for procurement by Rear Admiral Taylor for engineering design and production of the First Transatlantic Flight NC flying boats.

In order to conduct his experiments, Stone received flying-boat aerial and water operation instruction from Curtiss, the "master." Stone would receive his naval aviator Wings of Gold after additional formal instruction at NAS Pensacola that met standardized criteria required by all three sea services. Other naval aviators received aerial and water operation instruction only from Curtiss, Burgess, the Wright Brothers, or from the training command at Pensacola. Stone received instruction and experience from both. It could be argued that due to this additional training and experience on the water and in the air, Stone, as a new naval aviator, could be considered one of the top air and water pilots available to the Navy. This, along with a Curtiss recommendation, could have been the reason Stone would be assigned to the elite group of test pilots at the Bureau of Construction and Repair performing trials on new aircraft contracted by the Navy.

On March 21, 1916, *Onondaga* paid a port call at Washington, D.C. Captain Chiswell used this opportunity to lobby for Coast Guard aviation. He also entertained Glenn Curtiss, Byron R. Newton (the Assistant Secretary of the Treasury) and LTJG R. G. Thomas, USN (of the Navy Hydrographic Office, Norfolk, Virginia), on board *Onondaga*. Chiswell requested assistance from a Navy Construction Corps (predecessor of the Bureau of Aeronautics, or BUAERO, and later BUAIR) officer to design a flying motor surfboat: "Mr. Glenn H. Curtiss, at a luncheon with Mr. Newton on the Onondaga last Sunday, suggested that it might be practicable to convert a surfboat with a flying boat with wings and motor so arranged that they could be quickly eliminated when the boat lighted on the water and within a few minutes it would be, instead of a flying boat, an ordinary motor surfboat. If the lifeboat is better adapted, send lifeboat. He promised to think about it and I am going to try to encourage him."

This idea was not practicable, but Curtiss did design and construct his BT-1 "lifeboat" plane. The aircraft was a triplane flying boat with a short, boatlike hull, with flight-control surfaces mounted high on the aft end on tail booms.[29] It had a single engine driving twin, four-blade propellers. Later, in 1918, Curtiss would use an enlarged three-engine BT-1 design as the basis of his proposal to the Navy for the NC aircraft, which was to make the world's first transatlantic flight.

Subject: Training in aviation for officers of the Coast Guard Service
  1. It is gathered from your letter that you are in touch with officers of the Coast Guard Service who contemplate taking training in aviation. You are authorized to inform such officers that if the Captain Commandant of the Coast Guard Service will make a request on the Navy Department for an opportunity for the training

of his officers, the Department will be very glad to add two Coast Guard Officers to the class at Pensacola. A new class will be formed April 1st, and it would be advantageous if these requests should be received in time for the officers to take up the course on that date.

s/Josephus Daniels
SECRETARY OF THE NAVY DEPARTMENT

TREASURY DEPARTMENT

UNITED STATES COAST GUARD

COAST GUARD CUTTER
ONONDAGA   Potomac River, April 18, 1916.

My dear Hunniwell:

      If practicable, please mail me as soon as convenient plans, specifications and blue prints of a type of motor surfboat which you may regard as best adapted to the following:

      Mr. Glenn H. Curtiss, at luncheon with Mr. Newton on the ONONDAGA last Sunday, suggested that it might be practicable to convert a surfboat into a flying boat with wings and motor so arranged that they could be quickly eliminated when the boat lighted on the water and within a few minutes it would be, instead of a flying boat, an ordinary motor surfboat. If the lifeboat is better adapted, send lifeboat. He promised to think about it and I am going to try to encourage him.

      If it is possible to perfect something of that kind I believe it would be the biggest find for the Coast Guard of the century and might be the means of saving hundreds of lives. Maybe if you could hear them say nonchalantly that they are now building machines capable of lifting 20 tons, you would not be quite so skeptical as I believe you to be at present.

      Sincerely,

Chiswell letter to Hunniwell, Navy Construction Corps, April 18, 1916

Curtiss triplane lifeboat

Curtiss lifeboat without wings

The excitement and activity did not escape the attention of a young Navy Hydrographic Office officer at its Norfolk, Virginia, office. LTJG R. G. Thomas, USN, wrote to the Navy Department on March 21. When he received his answer Lieutenant Thomas showed it to Stone and Captain Chiswell, who immediately approved the request. Captain Commandant E. P. Bertholf, USCG, had approved the Navy's offer; Second Lieutenant Sugden and Third Lieutenant Stone arrived in Pensacola in time for class.[30]

While Stone was attending flight school at NAS Pensacola, Third Lieutenant Hall was also gaining unofficial aviation experience, at the Curtiss flying station on Hampton Roads. On May 6, 1916, Hall was the navigator on a Curtiss station H-10. The H-10, with pilots S. E. Crosswell and Phillip Utter, navigator Hall, and chief engineer Charles

Good set a distance record—178 miles in two hours fifty minutes and thirty seconds—from the school to a landing between Fort Carroll and Fort McHenry in Baltimore Harbor. A passenger, a Captain MacAuley stated, "We had a desperate battle with the winds off the mouth of the Patuxent River. At times we were brought almost to a standstill. For fifteen minutes we had this wind to contend with, and our progress was as slow as a snail. Finally we struck a free lane and shot forward at a 100-mile-an-hour clip." The story was sensational enough at the time to be featured in the May 7, 1916, *New York Times.*

After his promotion to second lieutenant, Hall, his eyesight precluding further training as a pilot, was ordered on October 28, 1916, to the Curtiss Aeroplane and Motor Company's factory at Hammondsport, New York, to study aircraft engineering.[31]

In addition to these aviation assignments, Coast Guard headquarters assigned CAPT Charles A. McAllister to the new position of Chief Engineer, Aviation Section.[32] Captain Chiswell's age prevented him from receiving orders to flight training at Pensacola.

It was Captain McAllister who drafted legislation introduced in the Senate to provide $1,500,000 to establish an "Aerial Coast Patrol within the Coast Guard." This legislation was revamped into the Navy Deficiency Act of August 29, 1916, which authorized ten Coast Guard air stations along the Atlantic, Pacific, Gulf of Mexico, and Great Lakes coasts; a Coast Guard aviation school; and an aviation corps consisting of ten line officers, five engineering officers, and forty enlisted mechanics. Congress did not, however, actually appropriate funds for them until 1924.[33]

ESTABLISHMENT.

101. THE ACT OF 29 AUGUST, 1916 (39 STAT. 600) ESTAB-IS QUOTED HEREWITH: "THAT FOR THE PURPOSE OF LISHMENT. SAVING LIFE AND PROPERTY ALONG THE COASTS OF THE UNITED STATES AND AT SEA CONTIGUOUS THERE-TO, AND TO ASSIST IN THE NATIONAL DEFENSE, THE SECRETARY OF THE TREASURY IS AUTHORIZED TO ESTABLISH, EQUIP, AND MAINTAIN AVIATION STA-TIONS, NOT EXCEEDING TEN IN NUMBER, AT SUCH POINTS ON THE ATLANTIC AND PACIFIC COASTS, THE GULF OF MEXICO, AND THE GREAT LAKES AS HE MAY DEEM ADVISABLE, AND TO DETAIL FOR AVIATION DUTY IN CONNECTION THEREWITH OFFICERS AND EN-LISTED MEN OF THE UNITED STATES COAST GUARD."

October 15, 1936, Coast Guard Aviation Instruction, Article 101, Navy Deficiency Act of August 29, 1916

First Coast Guard Aviation Group, NAS Pensacola

1917

While in aviation school at NAS Pensacola, Stone met and eloped with Myrtice Pace, daughter of Ashley "A.P." Pace, a lumber baron and the most influential man in town. The Pace family had moved from southern Georgia after purchasing a Pensacola lumber mill. During the early years at NAS Pensacola, Navy and city elite were very close, but A.P. did not give his consent for Myrtice to marry Stone, because he thought all aviators were "crazy, reckless daredevils." Since flying was a dangerous way to make a living, he thought, Stone would not be around very long to take care of his daughter. When the couple's first child, Marion, was born, old A.P. finally dropped his objection and became an adoring grandfather. Two years later, they had a son, Johnny.[34]

Myrtice had been sent to exclusive finishing schools for girls and was a very well educated woman, but when making a point she would use an old Georgia-cracker, cornpone accent and illiterate language. Once, at Sardi's in New York City, when she used her cracker-barrel talk, a local socialite was critical of her speech. Myrtice shot back, "Don't give me any of that fancy talk, honey, or I might have to conjugate you a verb!" Stone often adopted Myrtice's cracker-barrel language for emphasis.[35]

Stone completed aviation training on April 10, 1917, and was appointed naval aviator thirty-eight on the Navy's roster.[36] Authorization was also obtained to send an additional sixteen Coast Guard personnel to NAS Pensacola. At that time Coast Guard headquarters did not have a list of Coast Guard aviators, but that changed on March 30, 1920, when Stone was designated Coast Guard aviator number one. Only those officers actually engaged in flying at that time were put on the list.[37]

IN REPLY REFER TO

NO. 41-237

U. S. NAVY AERONAUTIC STATION,

Pe.   PENSACOLA, FLA.

April 10, 1917.

From: Commandant
To: Third Lieut. E. F. Stone, U.S.C.G.

Subject: Orders as Naval Aviator.

1. You are hereby designated as Naval Aviator and detailed for duty involving actual flying in aircraft, including balloons, dirigibles, and aeroplanes, in accordance with
an Act of Congress approved March 3, 1915 and Aug. 29, 1916.

2. Return these orders for forwarding to the Navy Department for confirmation.

J. L. Jayne

Pe. 41-237   1st endorsement   May, 3, 1917.

From: Third Lieut. E. F. Stone, U.S.C.G.
To: Commandant.

1. Received this date and returned.

E. F. Stone,

Pe. 41-237   2nd endorsement   May 3, 1917.

From: Commandant
To: Secretary of the Navy (Bureau of Navigation)
Via: Navy Department (Operations-Material).

1. Forwarded. The Department's approval of these orders
is requested.

2. Aeronautic Station letter No. 41-237 of even date ex-
plains the reason for issue.

J. L. Jayne

NAVY DEPARTMENT,

Commandant NAS Pensacola letter designating Stone naval aviator number thirty-eight

*The stage had been set, but sputtering funding caused false starts and hardships that would need to
be overcome by the dedicated men who believed in the vision.*

Coast Guard Transferred to Navy Department by Executive Order

When hostilities broke out in Europe in August 1914, the U.S. Navy was a small service,
its ships left over from the Spanish-American War and the Great White Fleet. American
technology and engineering for ships and aircraft lagged far behind those European
countries that had entered the war earlier, and both the War and Navy Departments
saw the need for a rapid and orderly expansion of the military services. Navy and Coast
Guard line officers were primarily academy graduates, educated in engineering and

physics curricula and trained for surface fighting ships. As the nation went to war, the Navy could not spare them for aviation training; they were needed to man the rapidly expanding battle fleets. From that point on, expansion of naval aviation was mostly accomplished with Naval Reserve commissioned officers, chief warrant officers, and enlisted personnel. It was not until ten months after the end of World War I, in September 1919, that the Navy convened its first postwar class of Navy, Marine Corps, and Coast Guard line officers at Pensacola.[38] The United States entered the war on April 6, 1917, just four days before Stone received his naval aviator Wings of Gold. The Army, Navy, Marine Corps, and Coast Guard were sadly lacking in war-ready personnel, assets, and pilots with training in engineering, mathematics, and physics.[39]

This rapid expansion of naval aviation was a time of unbounded enthusiasm, with heights of dreaming and scheming that have not been seen since. During World War I, naval aviation grew to 6,716 officers and 30,693 enlisted men in the Navy, and 282 officers and 2,180 enlisted men in the Marine Corps. The aviation inventory would include 2,107 aircraft, 15 dirigibles, and 215 balloons.[40]

To manage rapid growth, the Navy established and operated an aviation engineering support organization. The Navy did not know where to locate this new organization, so it was assigned to the Bureau of Construction and Repair at the Washington, D.C., Navy Yard. Testing support was provided by the Board of Inspection and Survey in the Bureau of Steam Engineering at the Navy Yard, and testing was conducted mostly at NAS Anacostia, NAS Hampton Roads, and the Naval Aircraft Factory in Philadelphia. Research was conducted by the Navy Research Laboratory (NRL) in Washington, D.C.[41]

On April 7, 1917, the Coast Guard was transferred to the Navy Department for the duration of the war by executive order. Coast Guard personnel were assigned to Navy units that were short of experienced personnel. In particular, Navy and Coast Guard aviator line officers, mostly academy graduates, were assigned to armored cruisers with aviation detachments, to special engineering programs in the Navy's Aviation Division, and to naval air stations in the United States and abroad.[42] Since Coast Guard officers had been ordered to aviation training from line-officer assignments on board ship, they were senior to new Navy Fleet Reserve pilots composed mostly of warrant officers and enlisted personnel fresh out of flight school. As a result, officer aviators not assigned to armored cruiser aviation detachments or assigned to special engineering assignments became commanding officers of naval air stations. Significant examples of those ordered to special assignments in 1916 and early 1917 were Navy officers Towers and Griffin and Coast Guard officers Stone, Parker, Hall, Donohue, Eaton, and Sugden.[43]

Towers and Griffin were assigned to the Bureau of Construction and Repair and to the Bureau of Steam Engineering, whose aviation engineering and test divisions would later become the Navy Department's Bureau of Aeronautics (BUAERO).

Lieutenant Stone, following a short assignment to the armored cruiser *Huntington*, was assigned to the Bureau of Construction and Repair as a test pilot with Towers

On September 7, 1917, the coveted naval aviator Wings of Gold we have today are assigned the official insignia worn on the left breast by all qualified naval aviators.

The first wings were issued to naval aviators number 1 to 282. Since they were formally issued, it was important to authenticate each winged insignia with an identifying number. Each winged insignia was engraved with the aviator's precedence number derived from completion date of flight instruction. The assignment of numbered naval aviator wings, therefore, led to creation of the naval aviator precedence list, or designated aviator number listing.[44]

and Griffin.[45] Stone would later be assigned as pilot of NC-4 on the first transatlantic flight and thereafter to development of catapults and the first aircraft carriers, *Langley, Saratoga,* and *Lexington.*

Lieutenant Parker, Coast Guard aviator number seven, was also in the first group of Coast Guard aviators graduated from NAS Pensacola in 1917. From there he was ordered to commission and command NAS Key West. In addition to conducting coastal patrols, this new air station trained over five hundred new Navy pilots. Later, from August 1918 to July 1919, Parker was commanding officer of NAS Rockaway Beach, New York.[46] (Prior to Parker's arrival, Lieutenant Stone had been temporary commanding officer at Rockaway.)[47] Following Parker's command at NAS Rockaway Beach, he was transferred to the NAS Pensacola training command, as Instructor-in-Charge of the Navy's new aviation ground school.[48]

LT Norman Hall, USCG, would become a senior inspector of materials for the design and manufacture of Navy NC flying boats at the Glenn Curtiss plants in Buffalo and Garden City, New York.[49]

LT Robert Donohue, Coast Guard aviator number two, would be assigned as commanding officer of NAS North Sydney, Nova Scotia, and later NAS Montauk, New York.[50]

The New Priority: Countering German Submarine Operations

Prior to U.S. entry in April 1917, World War I in the west was at a stalemate. American involvement meant a significant addition of allied troops, and more important, major new production capacity for war matériel. Since no aircraft was capable of flying across

The *Jersey Journal,* Black Tom Island explosion

the Atlantic, the only way to transport large quantities of war matériel to Europe was transatlantic maritime shipping.

Hostilities presented the nations allied against the kaiser's forces with a major problem. In spite of ongoing naval operations, German submarines were destroying a million tons of allied war matériel each month. Lost were vital supplies, troops, medical provisions, and the ships and crews needed for additional ocean crossings. Part of the problem was the destruction of war matériel produced in the United States and being shipped from ports along the mid-Atlantic and New England coastlines. German saboteurs, transported to the Atlantic coastline by clandestine submarines, were the cause. This was not insignificant. In 1914, German ambassador to the United States, Count Johann Von Bernstorff, and his staff officer Dr. Heinrich Albert led a group of saboteurs targeting New York Harbor and points in New England. One of its members, CAPT Franz von Rintelen, had perfected a "pencil" bomb, an incendiary device to ignite cargoes of ships at sea and coal being delivered to U.S. warships. A large ammunition depot, Black Tom Island, between lower Manhattan and New Jersey, was blown up by a pencil bomb. The explosion was so violent that shocks produced a 5.5 reading on the Richter earthquake scale, and no structures at the site survived the blast. Windows were blown out as far away as Times Square, and tremors were felt as far away as Philadelphia.[51]

LT Phillip B. Eaton, Coast Guard aviator number nine, would be assigned as commanding officer of NAS Chatham, Massachusetts. In the late spring and summer of 1918, the German navy increased U-boat submarine attacks on Allied shipping off the continental shelf of the East Coast. On July 21, 1918, the tugboat *Perth Amboy* and four barges were attacked off Cape Cod

HS-1 bomb drop off New England coast

by a surfaced German submarine, *U-156*. One R–9 float plane from NAS Chatham, piloted by Lieutenant Eaton and one HS-1L flying boat, piloted by ENS Eric Lingard, USNRF, attacked *U-156*. Eaton and Lingard both dropped Mark IV bombs. One hit *U-156*, and two landed close to its hull. No bombs exploded. Making a second run, the extremely frustrated Eaton threw a monkey wrench at *U-156*—it was the heaviest item he could reach. The captain of *U-156*, seeing the monkey wrench hit his deck and observing that none of the bombs had exploded, calmly remained on the surface, sank the remaining barges, then submerged and escaped. However, Eaton did prevent the tug from being sunk. An official investigation of the bombs suspected sabotage of the bomb's detonators by German intelligence officers transported by U-boat to New York shores. Lieutenant Eaton and Ensign Lingard would become the only U.S. aviators to bomb and strafe a German U-boat off the U.S. coast during World War I. At year's end, Lieutenant Eaton would become the commanding officer of NAS Montauk.[52]

In March 1918, HS-1 flying boats were shipped to France for antisubmarine patrol operations by U.S. naval air stations there. First Lieutenant C. E. Sugden, Coast Guard aviator number four, was the commanding officer of NAS Île-Tudy, in France. Sugden flew many antisubmarine patrols in the HS-1. NAS Île-Tudy was credited with sinking three German U-boats and was considered one of the most important air units on the French coast. When World War I ended, First Lieutenant Sugden was made a Chevalier of the French Legion of Honor.[53]

Returning from a fact-finding trip to Europe on September 4, 1917, technical members of the Bolling Commission recommended to the secretaries of War and the Navy that airborne antisubmarine warfare and European coastal patrol stations become the primary aviation focus.[54]

Increasing Industrial Capacity to Wage War

Prior to entering the war in 1917, U.S. industrial capacity and knowledge were inadequate to provide aircraft to both the Army and the Navy. To correct this deficiency, the year prior to entering the war Congress had authorized funding to staff and build NACA, a massive aeronautical research and development complex at Hampton, Virginia.[55] On November 15 a committee was established within NACA to focus on the development of light-metal alloys for aircraft production. Heading the committee was Constructor Jerome C. Hunsaker. It wasn't until May 17, 1917, that the Chief of Naval Operations made the first procurement request for fifty aircraft machine guns with synchronized firing (i.e., through the propellers) and for fifty machine guns with 360-degree, all-around firing capability. Because a rapid increase in the quantity of naval aircraft was expected, the previous method of identifying individual aircraft (such as AH) was discontinued by the Secretary of the Navy and replaced with "bureau numbers." This practice continues to this day. Lighter-than-air ships also expanded when on May 29, 1917, the Navy contracted Goodyear Tire and Rubber Company to train twenty airship pilots. By September the commanding officer, LT Louis H. Maxfield, of the Navy detachment at the Goodyear plant and ten students had completed training and were designated "Naval Aviator (Dirigible)," with aviator numbers 94 to 104. On December 7, 1917, the Secretary of the Navy authorized the first type of fighter aircraft. Built by Curtiss as the HA and designated the Dunkirk Fighter, the float plane was armed with dual synchronized machine guns forward and dual flexible machine guns in the aft cockpit.[56]

Since aviation development was too slow for Army requirements, the Signal Corps established in 1917 an aviation engineering and manufacturing command at McCook Field in Dayton, Ohio, where early development of the aircraft Liberty engine and propellers was done.[57] Many Liberty engines were installed in aircraft that Lieutenant Stone would flight-test for the Navy, including NC transatlantic aircraft.

On June 4, 1917, the Aircraft Production Board authorized construction of five Liberty engine prototypes, with both eight and twelve cylinders, from a design that could be mass-produced. The design had been developed by I. G. Vincent, employed by Packard Motor Car Company, and E. I. Hall, of Hall Scott Motor Car Company. The design was completed within days by the two engineers, sequestered in a Washington, D.C., hotel room. In less than six weeks, on July 4, the first Liberty aircraft engine arrived at the Bureau of Standards for testing. Packard assembled it from various parts pulled from manufacturing plants scattered from Philadelphia to Berkeley, California. On August 25 the engine passed a fifty-hour power test and was ordered into production. During the test it generated from 301 to 320 horsepower. On October 21, 1917, the first successful flight test of a twelve-cylinder Liberty engine was conducted on a Curtiss HS-1 flying boat at Buffalo, New York. This led to the adoption of both the Liberty engine and HS-1 aircraft as standard Navy equipment.[58]

On July 17, 1917, the Navy completed construction of the Naval Aircraft Factory, Philadelphia, on 760 acres at the Philadelphia Navy Yard. The aircraft factory had gotten

U.S. Army Signal Corps McCook Field, 1917 (total Army air assets)

McCook Field Propeller unit (all early wooden propellers were made here)

off to a fast start. War was declared April 6, 1917, ground was broken August 10, and the first aircraft, an H–16, was rolled off the line in late March 1918. Two weeks later, two H–16 aircraft would be ready to ship to England. On March 27, 1918, H–16 serial number A–1049 flew the first H–16 antisubmarine patrol in Europe. The H–16 was armed with two 230-pound bombs, one Lewis machine gun forward, two facing aft, and two amidships. Many Navy and Marine Corps test pilots, as well as Elmer Stone, would conduct aircraft trials at the Naval Aircraft Factory.[59]

USS *Huntington* (ACR-5) recovering R-6 torpedo float plane

Catapult Development

On July 12, 1916, LT G. de Chevalier had made a successful underway takeoff from an improved catapult on the armored cruiser *North Carolina*. Mare Island Navy Yard installed a catapult of the same type on the armored cruiser *Huntington* in April 1917. On April 26 *Huntington* conducted the first dead-load test for her scout-aircraft catapult at Mare Island Navy Yard. On May 28, *Huntington* arrived in Pensacola to take on board a seaplane and kite balloons for various experimental operations and evaluations from her deck.[60]

During their assignments to *Huntington,* 3rd LT Robert Donohue, Stone, and Chief Aviation Pilot (CAP) C. T. Thrun, all USCG, were part of a nine-man aviation detachment. Stone was attached to *Huntington* from July 2 to October 13, 1917. *Huntington* departed for Hampton Roads on August 1 to replenish, then sailed for New York, arriving five days later. On September 8, *Huntington* was assigned as guide ship for a convoy escorting six troopships to France, where Stone was to make several observation-balloon flights. Once in European waters, the convoy was turned over to U.S. destroyers, and *Huntington* steamed back to Hampton Roads. LTJG Marc A. Mitscher, USN, the senior aviator, had reported on board at Mare Island. As shown in ship's log, 3rd LT "Archie" Stone, 3rd LT "Jiggs" Donahue, and Lieutenant Mitscher were shipmates and knew each other well. (Mitscher would become a well-respected admiral and carrier task force commander in World War II.)

During this assignment Stone was involved in testing *Huntington*'s catapult. The catapult's car was generally lost over the side after launch, presenting a vexing technical problem.*

---

*Unfortunately, the problem was not solved, so aircraft and catapults were removed from all cruisers.[61] *Huntington*'s catapult was removed on October 13, 1917.

USS *Huntington* at anchor in Pensacola Bay, 1917 (note aircraft on stern catapult rails)

Enlarged view of kite balloon and observers, 1917 (note the personnel ladder and telephone line running to the ship)

Kite balloon lashed to deck

World War I: USS *Huntington* Curtiss R-6

Huntington's commanding officer, CAPT J. R. Robinson, did not appreciate an aviation detachment assigned to his ship. Without consulting anyone in the detachment, he filed a negative report concerning aircraft assigned to cruisers.[62]

Huntington aircraft on catapult

Huntington aircraft on catapult

Huntington aircraft departing catapult

Huntington aircraft departing catapult

The following are actual entries from USS Huntington's *logbook.*[63] *Ship's entries for material inspections, courts-martial, magazine inspections, and other routine entries are omitted. Note the first entry for December 1, 1916, where the ship's name is changed from USS* West Virginia *to USS* Huntington. *The commanding officer of USS* Huntington *was CAPT J. K. Robinson, USN; however, log entries were signed by the officer on watch. Log book entries have not been edited for grammar, capitalization of letters, or words added for clarity. The reader sees the log entries as they were written by the watch stander.*

UNITED STATES SHIP ....HUNTINGTON.......... .....FIRST RATE....... ...1.December,.1916..

REMARKS.

Commences and until 4:00 a.m.
    At 12:00 changed name of ship from U. S. S. West Virginia to U. S. S. Huntington. Hourly inspection of ship, conditions normal.

                                            Chief Gunner, U. S. Navy.

4:00 to 8:00 a.m.
    Routine inspection. Condition normal. Hoisted out racing cutter and hoisted in again during watch.

                                            Boatswain, U. S. Navy.

8:00 a.m. to Meridian.
    The Commanding Officer inspected living spaces and compartments below the main deck, except engine and firerooms. Magazine and smokeless powder samples inspected, conditions normal. Tested steering gear, both steam and hand, condition excellent. Lifted safety valves on boilers No. 15 and No. 16. Valve on No. 15 lifted at 265 pounds and reseated at 258 pounds; No. 16 lifted at 265 pounds and reseated at 260 pounds.

                                            Lieutenant (j.g.), U. S. Navy.

Meridian to 4:00 p.m.
    At 2:30 the Captain and P. A. Surgeon C. C. Kress, U. S. Navy left the ship to go ashore on duty. Field day.

                                            Ensign, U. S. Navy.

4:00 to 8:00 p.m.
    At 5:30 Captain and Medical Officer returned aboard.

                                            Ensign, U. S. Navy.

Page from USS *Huntington's* log, for December 1, 1916

6 July 1917, 4:00 to 8:00PM: "5:40PM aeroplane #20 blew up and caught fire. Sounded fire quarters. Fire was put out without damage except to aeroplane. At 5:42 sounded secure from fire quarters. At 5:48 shot aeroplane off track. It cleared the catapult satisfactorily and fell. Picked up car with steamer at 6:10."

10 July 1917, Meridian [Noon] to 4:00PM: "At 4:00 3rd LT E.F. Stone, U.S.C.G. returned to ship with torpedo."

11 July 1917, Meridian to 4:00p.m.: "At 3:30 3rd Lieutenant Robert Donahue U.S.C.G. from U.S. Naval Aeronautic Station reported on board for duty by order of the Navy Department No 71."

17 July 1917, 4:00 to 6:00p.m.: "At 4:30 fired seaplane car from catapult making a successful launching."

22 July 1917, 4:00 to 6:00p.m.: "The trailing edge of the left aileron of airplane A163 was slightly bent by Charles E. Neely (BM2c) due to carelessness while hoisting a boat without authority. Light, steady breeze from west south west."

28 July 1917, 8:00a.m. to Meridian: "At 9:45 stopped and maneuvered to launch seaplane. At 9:52 hoisted 1st motor sailer and 1st whaleboat to stand by with 3rd steamer for seaplane test. At 10:14 launched seaplane A-162, Lieutenant (j.g.) Marc A. Mitscher U.S. Navy in charge, successfully from catapult and hoisted same aboard at 10:43 after a satisfactory flight at test of the seaplane radio apparatus."

28 July 1917, Meridian and until 4:00p.m.: "Drifting—engines used as required to hold position for launching seaplane. At 12:20 launched seaplane A-164, 3rd Lieutenant Robert Donohue U.S.C.G. in charge, satisfactory flight. At 3:05 received on board one seaplane from Aeronautic Station Pensacola."

31 July 1917, 8:00a.m. to Meridian: "At 8:24 hoisted out seaplane #A-162 3rd Lieutenant Robert Donohue, U.S.C.G. in charge, and towed same ashore for compass adjustment. At 8:45 hoisted out seaplane A-164 Lieutenant (j.g.) Marc A. Mitscher U.S. Navy in charge and, after making a flight for a test of the seaplane radio apparatus, hoisted same aboard at 9:20."

31 July 1917, 4:00 to 6:00p.m.: "At 5:10 Lieutenant Marc A. Mitscher, U.S. Navy conducted radio tests with seaplane #165. At 5:17 Hoisted Seaplane #165 after completing test."

Later, in New York Harbor:

12 August 1917, 8:00AM to Meridian: "At 10:00 veered to 75 fathoms for purpose of getting ship in position for launching airplane. At 10:48 launched airplane #165 from catapult, Lieutenant Marc A. Mitscher U.S. Navy pilot, and Lieutenant (j.g.) Reginald S. H. Venable U.S. Navy observer. At 10:55 heave in on regular moorings—45 fathoms scope. At 11:30 airplane returned and was hoisted aboard."

14 August 1917, Meridian to 4:00PM: "At anchor: At 3:00 Coast Guard Cutter "Onondaga" stood out. At 3:40 seaplane #165, 3rd Lieutenant Robert Donohue, U.S.C.G. in charge, in coming alongside preparatory to being hoisted fouled #10 6" gun, damaging right wing tip and lower engine bed section."

Later, on convoy duty in North Atlantic:

9 September 1917, Meridian to 4:00PM: "At 1:40 seaplane #165 was hoisted out and made several flights. At 3:42 hoisted seaplane #165 aboard. Steaming as guide to convoy group, column formation, at standard speed."

9 September 1917, 4:00 to 8:00PM: "Steaming on left flank of convoy group for balloon practice on course 250 p.g.c. [per gyrocompass] (260 true). Standard speed 60 revolutions.

At 5:05 balloon ascended and was hauled down and secured on quarter deck at 5:07 to affect [*sic*] repairs."

9 September 1917, Meridian to 4:00PM: "Steaming as guide to convoy group column formation on zig zag courses. At 2:15 balloon ascended, 3:20 balloon hauled down."

12 September 1917, 8:00AM to Meridian: "At 9:14 passed British steamer on port hand distant 5,150 yards west bound. Inflated observation balloon and made ascension at 10:25 (altitude 600 feet). At 10:48 balloon reported steamer on port bow, not visible from mast head lookouts."

12 September 1917, Meridian to 4:00PM: "Steaming as guide to convoy group in double line formation, interval 1000 yards. . . . At 12:45 sighted smoke on starboard bow. At 12:45 went to torpedo defense quarters. Convoy changed course to left (lee side). At 12:47 sighted 4 funnel Two-mast cruiser hard on starboard bow. At 12:48 went to general quarters. At 12:54 exchanged recognition signal with British cruiser. At 1:18 secured from general quarters."

13 September 1917, 4:00 to 8:00AM: "Steaming as guide to convoy group in double line formation at 1000 yards interval ——— . At 4:40 sighted smoke of steamer bound opposite way and obscured in fog. At 5:45 observation balloon ascended. At 6:05 sighted U.S.S. *McCall* 4 points abaft port beam, distant about 6 miles."

13 September 1917, 8:00AM to meridian: "Steaming as guide to convoy group in double line formation as before ——— . At 8:10 observation balloon was landed on quarterdeck and secured. At 9:00 signaled U.S.S. *McCall* to come within hail. At 10:00 sounded general alarm and torpedo defense call. Sounded secure from torpedo defense at 10:27."

14 September 1917, 4:00 to 8:00AM: "Steaming as guide to convoy group in double line formation at 1000 yards internal on course ——— . At 4:57 dropped out of formation to left and rear of left flank to make a lee for observation balloon ascension. At 5:03 slowed to 1/3 speed and cast loose balloon gripes. Balloon rolled badly but finally ascended successfully at 5:10 to a height of 700 feet. Ordered full speed on engines to resume position in formation ——— . At 7:20 balloon observer reported smoke of steamer but could not distinguish same until 7:25 on account of haze."

The balloon stayed aloft for target practice into next entry.

14 September 1917, Meridian to 4:00PM: "At 1:50 put target over port quarter ——— . At 1:57 sent up kite with phone wire for balloon. At 2:15 set target adrift. At 2:30 put 2nd target over port quarter ——— . At 2:53 ——— kite connected to balloon. At 3:22 ceased firing. At 3:24 secured from drill. At 3:30 maneuvering to land balloon. At 3:47 landed balloon on quarterdeck."

16 September 1917, Commences and until 4:00AM: "Steaming as guide to convoy group in double ——— . At 1:14 sighted luminous streak in water greatly resembling torpedo wake heading towards bow from starboard beam and maneuvered to avoid same with full left rudder and full astern port engine. At 1:15 after ascertaining streak to be wake of a fish, set port engine to standard speed ——— to resume position in formation."

17 September 1917, Commences and until 4:00AM: "Steaming as guide to convoy grouping double line formation, 1000 yards interval on course ——— . Standard speed 57 revolutions per minute. Boilers in use #——— . Vessels composing convoy and their designated formation as follows. U.S.S. *Huntington,* U.S.S. *McCall* (left flank), U.S.S. *Duncan* (right flank), U.S.S. *DeKalb,* U.S.A.T. *Henry Mallory,* U.S.A.T. *Tenadores.* At 4:00 destroyer escorts were in position on their respective flanks and five of the six troopships in sight but out of formation and badly scattered."

17 September 1917, 4:00 to 8:00: "At 4:07 observation balloon made ascent to 600 feet altitude increasing altitude later to 775 feet. At 4:30 started zig-zag courses ——— ."

17 September 1917, 8:00a.m. to Meridian: "Steaming as before as guide to convoy group in double line formation 1000 yards interval on course as per plan #1 under boilers #5–# 16 inclusive. At 9:15 the observation balloon was forced down by a squall, capsizing and rolling over several times on its longitudinal axis. Stopped both engines and hauled in balloon at 9:25 losing about half of it in the operation. Patrick McGunigal (SF1c) jumped overboard and cut loose Lieutenant (j.g.) Henry W. Hout U.S. Navy who was caught under water in the balloon rigging. Neither man was injured."

18 September 1917: "Turned convoy over to European escort."

Returned to the United States

30 September 1917: "at anchor in Hampton Roads."

10 October 1917, Meridian to 4:00PM: "At 3:59 3rd Lieutenant Robert Donohue, U.S.C.G. was this date detached in accordance with telegraphic orders from Bureau of Navigation to report for duty at Naval Aeronautic Station Rockaway, Long Island, New York."

12 October 1917, 8:00PM to Meridian: "At 11:00 put rudder amidships. D. L. Bellew acting Assistant Master at Arms U.S.C.G. was this day transferred to report to the Commanding Officer N.Y. Div. U.S. Customs House in accordance with Bureau of Navigation telegraphic orders."

13 October 1917, Meridian to 4:00PM: "At 2:05 Third Lieutenant Elmer F. Stone, U.S.C.G. was detached from this ship and ordered to temporary command of the Merrell (C.G.C.) Air Station Rockaway, Long Island, New York."

Completing his assignment on *Huntington,* Stone was later awarded the Victory Medal with a Patrol Clasp in September 1918.[64] Stone would eventually be awarded the Aviation Clasp.

Navy Department General Order No. 482 defined criteria for the award, and sixteen individual Navy service clasps a quarter-inch wide by a half-inch long. The medal was authorized to be awarded to all in the naval service who served on active duty between April 6, 1917, and March 30, 1920, and those who served not less than ten days on shore in northern Russia or Siberia.

Stone's World War I Victory Medal

Each service clasp was developed for specific duties during the war. No one is permitted to wear more than one service clasp. Since only one service clasp can be attached to the medal's ribbon, a three-sixteenths-inch bronze star is worn on the service ribbon in lieu of multiple clasps.[65]

CHAPTER FOUR

First Transatlantic Flight NC Flying Boats—
Design and Assembly

1918

*T*he first serious effort to fly across the Atlantic was made by Rodman Wanamaker in 1914, "in the cause of science and the interest of world peace." The effort was preempted by the world war. Wanamaker, the son of a rich Philadelphia department store founder, convinced LT J. C. Porte of the British Admiralty and LT John H. Towers, USN, to fly the large three-engine flying boat America, designed and manufactured by Glenn Curtiss, on the expedition. The flying boat was purchased by the British and operated against German submarines. It is ironic that CDR Richard E. Byrd piloted Wanamaker's second America, an airship, across the Atlantic days after Lindbergh's historic solo crossing.

The first successful endeavor to fly across the Atlantic started nine years before Lindbergh's flight across the Atlantic, and prior to the end of the world war. Crossing the Atlantic in a fixed-wing aircraft, to many, was unthinkable and very dangerous. Two Navy officers share credit for the vision of an aircraft capable of transiting the Atlantic, Lieutenant Towers and RADM David W. Taylor, USN.

In 1914, Towers had been assigned to the office of the Chief of Naval Operations. In an internal memorandum, he contemplated an aircraft capable of transiting the Atlantic. He was ordered by the Navy Department to observe European aviation experiments and testing and report on the feasibility of a long-range seaplane project.[1] The European hostilities in World War I ended his observation travels.

In an August 1917 memorandum, Rear Admiral Taylor, chief of the Navy's Bureau of Construction and Repair, laid out a vision of antisubmarine warfare using large long-range seaplanes to bomb and disrupt German submarine operations. These aircraft would reach Europe without taking scarce ship cargo space; operate in most weather conditions from the ocean surface; and fly sixteen hours carrying considerable bomb loads. An early study indicated that the only practical aircraft route to Europe was by way of Newfoundland and the Azores. The new Liberty engine would make this possible.[2]

The first transatlantic flight was not a random act. A long-range aircraft that could fly from the United States to Europe was desperately needed, since merchant ships were scarce and could not be used to transport antisubmarine aircraft. Large projects such as this one involved risk, required major funding, and needed heavy political support. Jumping to a solution did not always answer the problem. The first step was to define the problem clearly, after which the solution would become obvious. This would lead to a well-thought-out plan, staffed by trained and experienced people, and culminating in a design for manufacturing or construction, together with an organization to carry it out.

The war ended on November 11, 1918, prior to the completion of the design and manufacturing of a long-range aircraft. The issue of enemy submarines sinking allied shipping and sabotage evaporated with the cessation of hostilities. During the ensuing postwar downsizing of the military, a new national priority emerged. For any nation-state, the demonstrated capability to travel long distances rapidly over oceans became a paramount consideration for global power projection in support of national objectives. A nation that achieved this potential would acquire greatly enhanced diplomatic influence.

The demonstration of a solution required the design of a long-range aircraft that could fly across the Atlantic. Many nations, and differing aviation modes, were competing to be the first to cross the Atlantic. Ever since the very first aircraft flight was made at Kitty Hawk, North Carolina, national pride had deemed it imperative that the United States accomplish the first aerial long-range Atlantic crossing. The London Daily Mail *offered a fifty-thousand-dollar prize to the first team to make the passage across the Atlantic successfully.*[3]

The Protagonists

During the war, Admiral Taylor had assembled an impressive team within the Aircraft Division of the Bureau of Construction and Repair to develop such a Navy aircraft.

LCDR Holden C. Richardson, USN

Earlier, in 1913, he had been the only person assigned to the bureau's first Aircraft Division. He was a 1901 Naval Academy graduate with an engineering graduate degree from Massachusetts Institute of Technology (MIT), specializing in hull designs. While assigned to the Aircraft Division, Richardson spent time at the Taylor Model Basin, in Washington, D.C., studying high speed, takeoff, and landing effects on seaplane hulls and float designs. At the age of thirty-eight, he became naval aviator number thirteen, specializing in aircraft maintenance and overseeing the design and construction of the six-thousand-pound 82-A seaplane.[4]

LCDR Jerome C. Hunsaker, USN

He relieved Richardson in 1913 when aviation divisions were also created in the staffs of Chief of Naval Operations, Bureau of Steam Engineering, and Bureau of Ordnance. Hunsaker graduated from the Naval Academy in 1908 and from the Massachusetts Institute of Technology (MIT) in 1912 with a graduate degree. While on Navy loan to MIT, he traveled to Europe and studied aviation research facilities. He returned to MIT in 1914 to establish a master's degree program in aeronautical engineering. While at MIT, he instructed such notable aviation pioneers as Donald Douglas, LeRoy Grumman, future Navy secretary Edward P. Warner, and Garland Fulton, the developer of rigid airships. He was not a naval aviator but was an aeronautical engineer with a commission in the Bureau of Construction Corps.[5]

LCDR George C. Westervelt, USN

He graduated from the Naval Academy in 1901 and was assigned to the Construction Corps in Seattle, Washington. While there, he assisted William E. Boeing in the design and construction of Boeing Aircraft Company's first airplane, the B&W, a single-engine twin-float biplane. Recognition of this accomplishment led to assignment as inspector of naval aircraft at the Curtiss Aeroplane and Motor Company facility in Buffalo, New York. For four months in 1917, he was a member of the Bolling Mission to study British, Italian, and French aircraft factories.[6]

LT Elmer F. Stone, USCG, and LCDR Norman B. Hall, USCG

Both graduated from the Revenue Cutter Service School of Instruction (later the Coast Guard Academy) in 1913. There they received training in engineering disciplines, physics, and sciences. Stone received flight instruction from Glenn Curtiss while assigned to USRC *Onondaga,* followed by Navy flight training at NAS Pensacola. He developed a concept of operations that would become Coast Guard aviation. Hall was assigned to aviation engineering training at the Glen Curtiss Aeroplane and Motor Company. Hall became the Coast Guard's first aeronautical engineer.[7]

LCDR Stanley V. Parker, USCG, and LT Eugene A. Coffin, USCG

Coffin graduated from the Revenue Cutter Service School of Instruction in 1910 and Parker in 1912, receiving academic training in engineering disciplines, physics, and science. Both received commissions as third lieutenants in the Revenue Cutter Service. Prior to attending flight training at NAS Pensacola, Coffin attended the Maryland School of Wireless Telegraphy at Baltimore and received his federal first grade operator's license. Both were part of the first group of Coast Guard aviators graduated from NAS Pensacola, as second lieutenants, in 1917. Parker, thanks to his service as commanding officer of NAS Key West and in training new Navy pilots, both in ground school at the Navy Aviation Training Command at Pensacola and in the cockpit, was well experienced to command the naval air station that would shake down the first transatlantic flight seaplanes. Parker would command, with Coffin as his executive officer, NAS Rockaway Beach, providing operational and logistics support for NC aircraft preparing for the first transatlantic flight. After receiving his wings at NAS Pensacola, Coffin was the commanding officer of new enlisted recruits at Pensacola. In December 1917, Coffin was transferred to NAS Montauk Point as a patrol plane pilot. While there, he also was in charge of developing the station's communications system. Drawing on his training and experience, Coffin trained NC seaplane personnel and NAS Rockaway personnel in the use and maintenance of aircraft and station radios.

Beginnings

In the late summer of 1917, Admiral Taylor had met with Hunsaker and Westervelt to assign development responsibility for a formal plan to implement his vision for a large, long-range seaplane. Westervelt expressed his opinion that such an aircraft was beyond that day's understanding of technology. The admiral would have none of it and directed both officers "to get some results!"[8]

Admiral Taylor sent a telegram to Glenn Curtiss, inviting him to join the team. Curtiss arrived for a Navy Department meeting on September 9, 1917, accompanied by William L. Gilmore and Henry C. Kleckler. They were briefed by Admiral Taylor on his concept of using long-range seaplanes to disrupt German U-boat operations.[9]

> Glenn Hammond Curtiss: A practical intuitive engineer, with naval aviation ties since the first shipboard takeoff in 1910 and the first shipboard landing in 1911; he was also the contractor for the first purchase of aircraft by the Navy. He trained the first Army aviator and naval aviator number one, LT Theodore G. Ellyson, USN. He also trained naval aviator number three, LT John H. Towers, USN, and LT Patrick N. L. Bellinger, USN, naval aviator number eight. Curtiss had been a contractor with the British government for mass production of "a large America type flying boat."[10]
>
> William L. Gilmore and Henry C. Kleckler: Both were Curtiss design engineers, with experience going back to the first Curtiss Hammondsport engineering and manufacturing plant.[11]

Curtiss was asked to put together a design proposal for an aircraft that would meet all the requirements. After working on the proposal in the Curtiss Buffalo plant, they returned on September 12 with two proposals based upon an expanded version of the existing design for the Curtiss BT-1 flying lifeboat, which was under development for the Coast Guard.[12] One was a very large triplane flying boat with five engines; the other was a similar large biplane flying boat with three engines. The proposed seaplanes had short hulls with tails carried high above the water on outriggers. Predicted performance characteristics computed for both seaplanes showed that the three-engine version satisfied the general requirements of the problem and could be built faster than the five-engine model, with a smaller risk of failure. Additionally, the five-engine version required hydraulic servos to overcome aerodynamic forces on flight-control surfaces.

Admiral Taylor preferred the five-engine version, but it was impractical. The smaller three-engine biplane design was chosen in view of its greater seaworthiness, weight saving, and arcs of gunfire. Curtiss designated this proposed aircraft the TH-1, with 3,370-square-foot wings capable of lifting 20,000 pounds.[13]

Responsibility for actual construction and modifications was assigned to CDR C. C. Westervelt (CC), USN, and LCDR Norman Hall, USCG, Inspector of Engineering Material (Aeronautical).[14] Lieutenant Commanders Hunsaker and Westervelt quickly started a preliminary investigation to assess construction of wing beams, struts, main subassemblies, proportions of wing areas, fin and control-surface areas, and the materials for important components. With a preliminary, general design defined, a procedure was established for developing detailed engineering drawings.[15]

A three-foot model of the preliminary design was constructed to scale and tested by Doctor A. F. Zahm in the wind tunnel at the Washington Navy Yard. His investigation of aerodynamic forces, from an airspeed of seventy miles per hour, determined configuration and area of tail surfaces to assure proper aerodynamic balance with regard to locations of the seaplane's center of lift relative to the center of gravity.[16]

Commander Westervelt was given direct charge of design development at Buffalo, under the supervision of Commander Hunsaker, of the bureau's design branch. Active work on the detailed engineering design began in early October 1917. Commander Richardson was assigned temporary additional duty in 1917, from service as the aircraft maintenance officer at NAS Pensacola to the Buffalo, New York, Curtiss factory. He would assist Westervelt and Hunsaker in determining types of fittings and types of construction for principal members of the wing and tail structures and for the hull and wing-tip floats.[17]

Richardson's and Hunsaker's critical review of the TH-1 design proved it to be grossly overweight, at 21,350 pounds. More horsepower and larger wing area for lift were needed. Another problem in the preliminary design was the eight-hundred-gallon fuel load necessary for a transatlantic crossing. The aircraft's weight grew to 25,000 pounds, further exceeding the wing loading, or lift, that could be generated by the preliminary wing design.[18]

Arriving on scene was the new Liberty low-compression, three-hundred-horsepower engine, and waiting in the wings was a high-compression, four-hundred-horsepower version. The engine was designed by two Packard and by Hall Scott Motors automobile engineers, Jesse G. Vincent and Edward. J. Hall. They had been brought together by the Department of the Army to design the All-American aircraft engine. After working only seventy-two hours in a room at the Willard Hotel in Washington, D.C., they developed a V12 engine with three hundred horsepower that Admiral Taylor renamed the Liberty engine. Within three months the prototype was produced and successfully tested. It became the standard, even though auto machinists needed additional training to meet the tolerances required.[19]

By November 1917 the design workload was starting to overwhelm the small Navy planning team. Completing the task would require all the resources of the bureau. Because the bureau was under enormous pressure for all types of aviation development to meet the demands of the war effort as well as needs of ship design and construction, dedication of the entire bureau's resources to any single project was impracticable. To complicate matters further, engineering design issues and the necessary solutions far exceeded in complexity any previously experienced by U.S. aircraft designers and manufacturers. New methods of structural design, materials, and construction were required.

The Navy concluded a production contract with the Curtiss Company in Buffalo for engineering services to complete design and manufacturing drawings for a thousand-horsepower flying boat. It was a combined Navy/Curtiss effort directed by the Bureau of Construction and Repair and performed by Curtiss engineers. The final design was to be owned by the Navy. The Bureau of Construction and Repair had direct oversight of the effort, including the Curtiss engineers. This did not sit well with Curtiss and his engineers; Curtiss wanted design freedom and ownership of the final design. He continued to call it the "Curtiss TH-1" design. The Navy, to make a point, changed the name to NC-1—N for Navy, C for Curtiss.

CDR John H. Towers, USN, naval aviator number three, assigned to the Office of Operations, Chief of Naval Operations, had also seen the value of flying NC aircraft across the Atlantic instead of using ships to transport the American version of the British Porte-Felixstowe flying boat, the F-5L (described below), and other aircraft, to Europe. Since the United States possessed only 2 percent of the world's merchant fleet, shipping large aircraft would displace important war materials. Towers had prepared a written proposal recommending that NC aircraft be the first to cross the Atlantic by air. He pointedly asserted that he had the background to lead such a flight. He was the senior naval aviator on active duty, and he had been studying problems and solutions associated with a transatlantic flight for many years, starting with participation in the 1914 Curtiss-Wanamaker Transatlantic Project. Ultimately, he requested command of the flight.[20]

Promotion of a transatlantic flight started prior to a Navy recommendation to the Secretary of the Navy for an aircraft capable of crossing the Atlantic. William H. Workman, representing the British Handley Page 0/400 twin-engine bomber, first started rallying interest in a transatlantic flight in the summer of 1918. The Aero Club of America assisted his publicity campaign.[21] Momentum built from there. Navy aircrews would end up competing with four teams of British pilots who were flying from a base in St. Johns, Newfoundland, one British team flying westward from Ireland, and a U.S. Navy dirigible, designated C-5.[22]

Competition to be the first to cross the Atlantic was fierce. Countries competed to develop the strongest capability for projecting strength beyond the oceans in order to exercise diplomacy as befitted world powers. Manufacturers competed to position themselves as world-class aircraft designers and producers—and individual aviators competed for the glory of being first.

Dirigibles were another possible option for the first transatlantic flight. The Navy had been developing dirigibles since April 1917, when the 175-foot DN-1 was built by Connecticut Aircraft Company. Dirigibles B-1 through B-20 were built by Goodrich Rubber Company between 1917 and 1919. Dirigibles B-1 through B-10 were 160 feet long, and B10 to B-20 were 167 feet. Maximum endurance was twelve hours. In the spring of 1918, Goodyear built ten 192-foot C-class dirigibles for the Navy. The C-5's new engines were modified to burn hydrogen from lifting bags as well as normal aviation fuel. This increased range and made C-5 capable of crossing the Atlantic without refueling from a ship.

Other in-house competition came in July 1918, when the first British Porte-Felixstowe F-5 boat was produced by the Naval Aircraft Factory in Philadelphia. This U.S. version, called the F-5L flying boat, was capable of direct flight via the Azores to Europe by adding fuel tanks and installing the new geared-down Liberty-engine.[23] However, the geared-down Liberty engine would not be in production for a year, so the F-5L would not be ready in time.[24]

The Competitors

Hugo Sundstedt, a Swedish aviator, had contracted with the William-Lewis Company in Newark, New Jersey, to design and manufacture a twin-float biplane for a transatlantic flight.[25] The Italian government was also contemplating entry into the competition. Even the French government hinted it would join the competition. Each nation wanted the prestige of competing in the first transatlantic flight.[26]

Sponsor	Aircraft Type	Manufacturer	Country of Origin	Pilot
U.S. Navy	NC seaplane	Glenn Curtiss	U.S.	Navy & Coast Guard
U.S. Navy	F-5L	Naval Aircraft Factory	U.K./U.S.	Navy
U.S. Navy	C-5 dirigible	Goodyear	U.S.	Navy
Private	Twin-float biplane	William-Lewis Co.	Sweden	Hugo Sundsedt
Undisclosed			Italy	
Undisclosed			France	
Private	Landplane	Sopwith	U.K.	Harry Hawker Kenneth MacKenzie-Grieve
Private	S.538 Shirl Torpedo Biplane Shamrock	Short	U.K.	Captain C. C. Wylie/Major J. C. Wood
Private	Biplane Raymor	Martinsyde	U.K.	Frederick P. Raynham C. W. Morgan
Private	Four-engine V/1500 Bomber	Handley Page	U.K.	Rear Admiral Mark Handley Page
Private	Vimy Bomber	Vickers Aircraft, Ltd.	U.K.	Arthur Whitten-Brown/ John Alcock

Flight Operational Requirements

Aircraft range and fuel requirements would be determined by flying distance, aircraft weight, and engine and propeller efficiency (which determined aircraft speed and fuel consumption).

These parameters constituted an engineering problem. Forming an understanding of necessary logistics to support the flight, such as basing, navigation, and weather information, would require on-site evaluations.

To study problems associated with a transatlantic flight and develop an operational plan to achieve such a flight, the Navy convened a board consisting of CAPT John T. Tompkins, USN, Commander Towers, and LCDR Godfrey Chevalier, USN.[27]

Four routes were studied:
- Newfoundland to Azores to Portugal
- Newfoundland to southern Greenland to Ireland
- Newfoundland to Iceland to Ireland
- Brazil to French West Africa.

The parameters of the study encompassed:
- Aircraft range and reserve fuel requirements
- Navigation requirements
- Communications requirements, air-to-air and air-to-surface
- Weather reporting and forecasting requirements
- Survival gear and rescue requirements.

Ultimately, the Newfoundland to Azores to Portugal route was deemed the best.

Scouting the Route

LT Richard E. Byrd, USN, commanding officer of NAS Halifax, Nova Scotia, was ordered to survey Newfoundland's east coast for a suitable seaplane operation harbor.[28] Meanwhile, the Navy's 1st Marine Aeronautic Company had been flying antisubmarine warfare operations from Punta Delgada, in the Azores, since early 1918. The commanding officer was directed to provide information concerning the adequacy of harbor facilities for seaplanes there and in Horta, on the island of Fayal.[29]

Lieutenant Byrd's Newfoundland survey, taken in the summer of 1918, recommended basing NC aircraft at Avalon Peninsula's Cape Broyle, but there were big weather swings at Avalon, and ice floes were blown from Greenland and Labrador during the spring. A summer survey could be very misleading. Lieutenant Commander Bellinger and Lieutenant Stone were ordered to survey St. Mary's Bay and Trepassey Harbor in Newfoundland, and they departed Boston on March 26, 1918, on board the destroyer USS *Barney*.

Upon arrival, they found St. Mary's Bay blocked by eight-foot-thick pancake arctic ice floes. Following a brief stay in Halifax Harbor to wait for the wind to change and blow the ice away from Newfoundland, *Barney* sailed on a dangerous voyage to Placentia Bay. During this part of the voyage she dragged anchor. Her anchor chain broke and she began drifting overnight in treacherous ice floes. Bellinger and Stone had traveled overland to Trepassey, now free from ice floes, and were waiting for the ship there.[30]

Their report to Towers stated that Newfoundland and its waters were marginal for both seaplane and ship operations except when good weather conditions and favorable winds happened to exist. St. Mary's Bay was too deep, St. Johns was too small, and Placentia was open to the sea and not a safe anchorage. Trepassey Harbor was the best of the poor choices.[31]

Piecing together Lieutenant Commander Richardson's 1917–19 files from the National Archives, the Bureau of Construction and Repair, the Bureau of Steam Engineering, and the Secretary of the Navy's and Chief of Naval Operations' aviation divisions provided a rich narrative of the give-and-take between Navy and Curtiss engineers during the design phase of the NC-1 airplane.[32]

NC-1 design began in 1917. Due to advances after NC-1 design, NC-4 differed slightly from the first three seaplanes.

Building a Team

Commander Towers had many major issues to resolve, especially the flight route, which depended upon engine configuration and fuel capacity and consumption. These variables were, in turn, dependent upon engine type and propellers selected. Tower's leadership team, assembled to assist with these and other developments, comprised the following officers, with associated functional areas:

LCDR R. E. Byrd, USN—navigation equipment and methods preparation

LCDR G. deC. Chevalier, USN—airplane crews, overhaul crews, repair crews, handling crews for base ships and stations

LT R. F. Barratt, USNRF—aerography

Maj B. L. Smith, USMC—equipment and supplies

LCDR A. C. Read, USN—equipment and supplies

LCDR R. A. Lavender, USN—radio and intercommunication

CDR H. C. Richardson, Construction Corps (CC), USN—experiments

LCDR P. N. L. Bellinger, USN—operations and executive duty

LCDR S. A. Kraus, USN—engineering

LT G. S. Murray, USNRF—propellers

LT R. S. Wentworth, USN—radiators

LT J. L. Breese, USNRF—engines and auxiliaries

CDR J. C. Hunsaker, (CC), USN—Bureau of Construction and Repair representative

LCDR G. Fulton, (CC), USN

CDR A. K. Adkins, USN—Bureau of Steam Engineering representative

LCDR H. T. Dyer, USN.

Aircraft Design Advances

On December 7, 1917, Admirals Taylor and Griffin of the Bureau of Steam Engineering jointly recommended to Secretary of the Navy Josephus Daniels that Navy aircraft be the first to fly the Atlantic, prior to the target date of summer 1919.[33] The Army Air Corps did not have any aircraft capable of such a long flight.[34] By December 21, 1917, the design had progressed enough in reducing risk to justify the secretary in approving construction of four NC-1-type seaplanes. The request included stipulations that such work would not interfere with other war-effort demands, since all aircraft manufacturers were already overburdened.[35]

NAVY DEPARTMENT,
WASHINGTON, D.C.
December 21, 1917.
To: Bureau of Construction and Repair and Bureau of Steam Engineering.
SUBJECT: Three Engine Flying Boat Proposed.
1. *The Bureaus are directed to prepare a requisition as recommended in their joint letter of 7 December 1917.*
2. *The construction of these seaplanes shall in no way interfere with the production of aircraft to meet the program already laid down, nor with the development and construction of special types of aircraft as recommended by Commander Naval Aviation Forces Abroad.*

/s/ JOSEPHUS DANIELS.

Navy Secretary Document   **4-1**

In 1917, Lieutenant Commander Westervelt, who reported directly to Lieutenant Commander Hunsaker at the Bureau in Washington, was the on-site officer in charge of Navy airplane development and design at the Curtiss Buffalo plant. CDR Arthur K. Atkins, of the Bureau of Steam Engineering in Washington, D.C., was responsible for design and development decisions on engines and devices powered by electricity, such as radios. LCDR Harold W. Scofield assisted him on-site in Buffalo.[36]

During the early stages progress was slow, since many studies and tests were needed, and many versions were discarded. Many design details could be determined only by testing subassemblies to destruction. To carry out the actual engineering design, the seaplane was divided into its main subassemblies. All ideas, whether from Curtiss employees or the Navy, were pooled for final decisions. Main subassembly details were distributed to members of the design team. It took time to sort through all the comments and suggestions by the Navy and Curtiss engineers, and comments often stimulated heated arguments. When design arguments could not be resolved at the Buffalo plant, they were not resolved by Curtiss but sent to Lieutenant Commander Hunsaker at the bureau in Washington.

One example of a difference in opinion was Richardson's disagreement with Curtiss engineers over the design of the tail and tail structure. It was a very complex mechanical, aerodynamic, and structural engineering problem. Strict attention was necessary to avoid eccentric loading. Especially difficult was resolution of the mechanical stresses on the stern-post fittings, since no less than thirteen tail-structure members transmitted loads to these fittings. The upper-wing hinge also supported the upper-tail spar, so it too was a difficult engineering design problem. Richardson removed his objection only after a model was constructed and analyzed through destructive testing. To his credit, Richardson fully supported the design once it was proven. He drew upon his experience with development of the 82-A aircraft to solve the balancing of elevator, rudder, and ailerons.[37]

When a subassembly design was considered complete, Curtiss engineers computed dimensions and prepared stress diagrams, as well as other structural engineering diagrams. In turn, Bureau of Construction and Repair representatives Mr. Hubbard and Ensign McCarthy reviewed these documents. Critical subassemblies were further reviewed for approval by the Bureau of Construction and Repair, in Washington. Once components and subassemblies were test-fitted together, many had to be modified, replaced, or discarded and redesigned. Many designs approved in the early phase had to be discarded as more detailed studies were completed.

On top of all this activity, a major design change was initiated when horsepower from the developing Liberty 12-cylinder engine was measured at only three hundred horsepower. The original 26,000-pound design had been based on a thousand-horsepower power plant. The three-engine design provided only nine hundred horsepower, necessitating an aircraft reduced to 22,000 pounds.[38] Wind-tunnel tests were conducted again on the final design of the NC-1. They indicated a strong travel of the center of lift fore and aft, according to change in aerodynamic angle of attack (the angle between the direction of wind before passing over the airfoil and the chord line of the airfoil). The original design had the center of gravity (CG) located 37 percent of the chord length back from the leading edge of the wing's chord. The seaplane's first weight and balance measurement identified the distance as 47 percent. This was alarming, since no single subassembly could be moved to change the seaplane's CG. Wind-tunnel tests and aircraft trials later showed that balance could be maintained only as long as the wing's angle of attack was held to eight degrees nose-down. One of the flight characteristics noted was the tendency of the NC aircraft to stall when in choppy or rough air, because the aircraft's stall speed would vary as a result of the CG's constantly changing relative to the center of lift.[39]

Original NC-1 Design[40]	
Weight empty	13,000 pounds
Weight loaded	22,000 pounds
Airfoil	R.A.F. Number 6★
Span, upper wing	126 feet
Span, lower wing	94 feet
Wing chord	12 feet
Gap between wings, engine section	13 feet 6 inches
Gap between wings, outer wing posts	12 feet
Total wing area including ailerons	2,380 square feet
Length overall	68 feet, 3 1/2 inches
Beam	10 feet
Height, keel to top of skid boom	24 feet 5 1/8 inches
Hull length	44 feet 9 inches
Wing-tip float length	9 feet

Original NC-1 Design[40] (continued)	
Height	25 inches
Beam	20 inches
Weight, each	79 pounds
Buoyancy, each	1,600 pounds
Tail surface, upper stabilizer	164 square feet
Lower stabilizer	104 square feet
Upper elevator	140 square feet
Lower elevator	100 square feet
Two vertical stabilizers	80 square feet
Two outer rudders	35 square feet
Two center balanced rudders	35 square feet
Engines	
3 Liberty, 300 brake horsepower, Low-Compression, total horsepower 900	
Speed	80 knots
Upper-wing dihedral	0°
Lower-wing dihedral	3°
Final NC-4 Design[41]	
Weight empty	15,874 pounds
Weight loaded	28,000 pounds
Airfoil	R.A.F. Number 6★
Span, upper wing	126 feet
Span, lower wing	94 feet
Wing chord	12 feet
Gap between wings	12 to 13$1/2$ feet
Total wing area including ailerons	2,380 square feet
Length overall	68 feet 5$1/2$ inches
Height	24 feet 5$1/8$ inches
Hull length	45 feet
Engines	
4 Liberty, 400 brake horsepower, High-compression, total horsepower 1,600	
Speed	80 knots
Upper-wing dihedral	0°
Lower-wing dihedral	3°
Total fuel capacity	1,891 gallons
Oil tank capacity	160 gallons
Full load speed, maximum	74 knots
Full load speed, minimum	58 knots

★ R.A.F.: abbreviation for Royal Aircraft Factory.

Note: Values not shown on the above NC-4 list are the same as shown on the previous NC-1 list.

The enlarged BT-1 hull that Curtiss had proposed for NC-1 came under critical review. Lieutenant Commander Richardson was concerned that high-speed laminar flow of water along the hull would cause the hull to squat and generate a stern wave large enough to wash over the elevators. He also thought efficiency could be improved by eliminating the stubby bow and turned-up stern. Richardson took models of the original hull shape and the modified shapes to the Taylor Model Basin for tests. The model tests confirmed Richardson's predictions, and the hull was redesigned with a straight stern and without the second step. (A step is a sharp droop in the hull's keel downward used to break surface tension suction holding the aircraft down during takeoff.) Hull drag was reduced 20 percent with stern straightening and an additional 30 percent by eliminating the second step. Additional changes included replacing the normal basket-weight construction with longitudinal-type framing, similar to the hull of the British-developed H-16 aircraft. Weight estimates were too high, so the hull weight was reduced by two hundred pounds by changing the keel material from white oak to Sitka spruce and by eliminating the rabbet joints at the keel.[42] On completion of his temporary additional duty assignment at Buffalo, Lieutenant Commander Richardson returned to NAS Pensacola.[43]

A new production contract was awarded on January 8, 1918, designating the Curtiss Garden City plant as the Navy's remaining agent for design, drafting, and manufacturing (but not complete manufacture) of the aircraft. It was a "cost plus 10 percent profit contract." There were so many novel construction features that a fixed price could not be determined.[44] The Curtiss Buffalo plant was excluded from NC production, since its purpose was mass production of aircraft for the British. Engineers from the old Hammondsport plant, oriented toward innovation and design, staffed the Garden City plant.[45] Manufacturing had to be moved from Buffalo to Garden City, on Long Island. The move was accomplished by express train over a single weekend.

Multiple potential causes for delays required close monitoring. Spruce lumber was widely used in building aircraft during this period. The main sources of Sitka spruce were the states of Oregon and Washington. At the beginning of the war, labor strife in these two states jeopardized the war buildup for manufacture of aircraft. The U.S. Army became an arbitrator in the labor disputes with the loggers, in an attempt to keep spruce stocks on par with what was needed.[46] Yet another obstacle presented itself: the Garden City plant was too small, so the Navy constructed a building large enough to assemble two NC aircraft at the same time.

In February 1918, Secretary Daniels approved the Taylor and Griffin NC seaplane recommendation made in December and gave it double-A priority. He assigned Commander Towers to lead the NC design and production effort. The target departure was to be from Newfoundland, not later than May 14, 1919, enabling the crew to take advantage of the light from a full moon, since the flight would end after sunset.[47] The horizon could not be seen when flying at night over water. This could cause disorientation and inability to maintain upright and level flight. Instruments and procedures for "blind flying," or Instrument Flight Rules (IFR), would be developed much later.

The Navy team assigned to oversee construction and modifications to seaplanes was made up of the superintending constructor of aircraft, CDR C. C. Westervelt, USN, and the inspector of engineering material (aeronautics), Lieutenant Commander Hall.[48]

The Garden City plant was still limited in space and assembly personnel, so the Navy broke the overall design into subassemblies and contracted other companies to assemble them in parallel with each other, to shorten overall production time. Fuselage hulls for the four aircraft, for example, were divided among three contractors to be constructed simultaneously. The hull of NC-1 was to be built by the Curtiss Garden City plant, to speed production of NC-1. Curtiss engineers were not happy with Richardson's new ten-foot hull beam. They were sure the beam would be revised and made wider, and so, without Navy permission, they added an extra plank in the hull of NC-1 so flanges could be added later.[49] Hulls for NC-2 and NC-3 were to be built by boatbuilder Lawley & Sons of Boston, and the hull for NC-4 by Herreschoff of Bristol, Rhode Island.

This division of hull building among several subcontractors led to considerable variations in weight from the 2,400-pound hull design. Boatbuilders prefer robust construction, and their hulls were 200 to 425 pounds heavier than the design called for. This added weight would represent a loss of 1.6 hours of flying time for NC-2, 1.2 hours for NC-3, and 1.8 hours for NC-4, with a design fuel load.

The Curtiss Garden City plant manufactured nacelles and major gasoline system components.[50] Other subcontractors included:

- Automobile body manufacturer Locke Body of Manhattan, New York—struts, wings, and tail subassembly
- Albany Boat Company of Watervliet, New York—wing floats
- Pigeon-Fraser Hollow Spar Company of Boston—tail booms
    - ALCOA, Pittsburgh, PA—aluminum fuel tanks Unger Brothers & Company of New Jersey,
    - Brewster Body Company of New York and Beaver Machine Company of Newark, New Jersey—metal fittings
- Ford and Packard Motor Companies of Detroit, Michigan—Liberty engines.

Transporting NC-1's wings and the tail assembly from the Locke Body Company, at 453 East 56th Street in Manhattan, to the Curtiss Garden City plant on Long Island was a major feat. The wing assemblies were too large to fit on the flatbed trucks of the time. In addition, if the wings could have been loaded on them, the trucks could not have negotiated the Brooklyn Bridge and the traffic-laden, narrow Manhattan streets. Large horse-drawn wagons normally used to transport theater scenery were loaded with wing and tail assemblies. In August 1918, during the quiet of late night, they made their way with red warning lights hung on each loaded wagon. A Navy officer in an automobile, waving a red lantern to warn oncoming traffic, led the procession of wagons. Another

Navy officer, also waving a red lantern, brought up the rear to keep traffic from trying to pass the wagon convoy. This process was repeated for the NC-2, NC-3, and NC-4 seaplanes in turn.[51]

Final assembly of each NC flying boat was made from subassemblies, built by the many subcontractors, at Garden City. Form, fit and function checks, and inspections were made at the plant, and corrections were made when subassemblies did not fit together properly or minor adjustments were necessary.

As the operations base for the new seaplanes, the Navy selected NAS Rockaway Beach, which had established at the beginning of the war on ninety-four acres of leased land on Jamaica Bay. It was an operating base for HS-2 aircraft and for hangaring dirigibles. NAS Rockaway was chosen because, prior to and during the war, New York City was the focal point for aircraft design and manufacture. Rockaway was also chosen for its close proximity to the Curtiss Garden City plant and because it was an excellent site for aircraft trials and other operating tests.

None of the Navy's air stations, including NAS Rockaway, had hangars large enough to house NC-type seaplanes. A hangar 110 feet by 165 feet was constructed for two of these large aircraft. Because of their size, a special marine railway inclined at fifteen degrees and carriages were constructed on ramp, to launch and haul out the aircraft. Since only two NC flying boats could be hangared at one time, the other two would ride at anchor in the bay or be parked on their carriages on the ramp apron.[52]

Final reassembly for operational use and for aircraft trials was to be accomplished at NAS Rockaway.[53] It was therefore necessary to transport wing and tail assemblies from the Garden City plant to Rockaway. It was carried out in the same manner as transport from subcontractors to Garden City.

All the strict Navy oversight had caused Curtiss engineers to lose interest, slowing engineering design and drawings production to a snail's pace by the summer of 1918. The Curtiss engineers' morale had been further lowered by the implementation of the major design change reducing aircraft weight from 26,000 pounds to 22,000 pounds. This change required extensive recomputation of dimension details, the discarding of many engineering drawings, and the scrapping of some of the completed subassemblies.[54]

Admiral Taylor was not happy! First, Taylor again dispatched Lieutenant Commander Richardson from NAS Pensacola for temporary additional duty at Garden City. His job was to "stir things up." Second, he wrote a letter on July 6 to Glenn Curtiss expressing his disappointment at the lack of progress. He stated that his disappointment was so great he would transfer the total contract to the new naval aircraft factory in Philadelphia unless Curtiss "made it his personal business to impress upon the members of your organization that this is the most important single piece of work which has been entrusted to them, and I am expecting you to stand behind this work and bring it to a successful conclusion."

This was a strong statement, one that Curtiss knew Taylor could back up. The Navy had long built ships within its own yards, so it was not without precedent for the NC-1 to be designed and manufactured at the Naval Aircraft Factory. This would have a major negative impact on the Navy work of all aircraft design and manufacturing companies. Curtiss snapped to attention and "tightened ship" at Garden City. NC-1 took nine months to complete assembly for the twenty-one-mile overland wagon and truck transport to NAS Rockaway Beach, New York. It stood fully assembled at NAS Rockaway on September 1, 1918.[55]

Weight estimates continued to show that the design was too heavy. High-tensile strength, heat-treated steel fittings replaced brass and other metals, resulting in considerable additional weight reduction. But the use of high-tensile, heat-treated steel also caused delays, since uniformity with fittings produced from flat steel plate was difficult to achieve. Mechanical engineers tended to be very conservative in selecting metal types for details. Without strict oversight, they would specify the highest-grade steel when mild steel would suffice. This would become a significant problem, generating delays for repairs and alterations during redesign. What should have taken hours now took days.

Tensile and shearing forces on metal fittings presented a serious problem. Normal methods used by aircraft manufacturers were abandoned, replaced by those used by bridge designers. All forces passing through a joint passed through a common center. As in a pin bridge, all the forces were applied to a large hollow bolt at the center of the wingspan. The hollow bolt reduced weight without losing tensile or shear strength.[56]

As the aircraft engineering design began to take form, major subassemblies and models of the seaplane itself were tested in the wind tunnel. Performance was measured and compared with the original engineering studies and estimates.

The hull bottom was a double-plank V with one keel step, similar to those on wing-tip floats on smaller seaplanes. The hull was divided by five bulkheads into six watertight compartments, with watertight doors. The forward compartment had a navigator and lookout compartment for the commanding officer. The pilot's cockpit was located in the next compartment. It had tandem side-by-side controls and flight and engine instrumentation. Next was the crew's compartment for those on watch or sleeping. Then came a compartment for gasoline tanks, attended by a mechanic; the last compartment was for the radio operator and his equipment. Both the keel and planking were Sitka spruce. Two spruce girders laced with steel wires provided longitudinal strength. A layer of muslin was glued between the two layers of planking for watertight integrity.[57]

The main wing spars were spruce, box-shaped, hollow structures. Each truss was designed like a bridge, with continuous cap strips of spruce, corresponding to the upper and lower cords of a bridge truss, tied together by an internal web system of vertical and diagonal pieces of spruce. The ribs were twelve feet long but weighed only twenty-six ounces each. An innovative, newly designed, hinged leading wing cap housed control cables for ailerons and flaps. This eliminated wind resistance from cables rigged in the wind stream. Wing struts were also of the spruce box-type design. To prevent bowing of struts under compression forces, a system of steel cables was attached at midpoints. To reduce wind resistance, the struts were shaped like fish, with sharp leading and trailing edges. Steel wires were used for diagonal wing bracing.[58]

The tail design was unique to this aircraft. The vertical stabilizers looked like a biplane with vertical wings. The surface area was actually twice as large as the biplane wings of a U.S. Army single-seat fighter of that day. The tail structure was supported by three hollow,

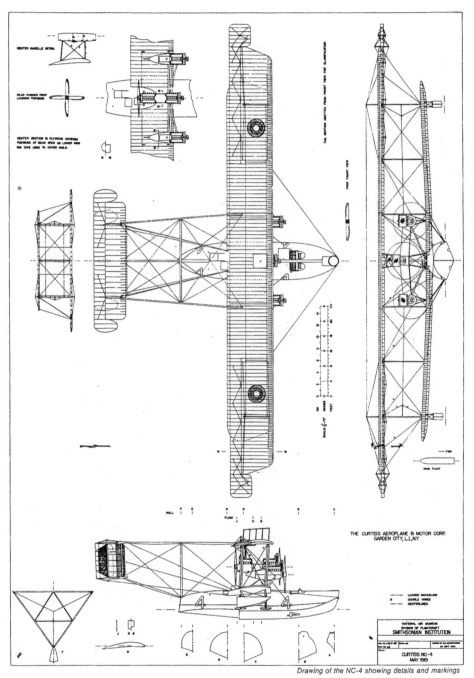

Drawing of the NC-4 showing details and markings

Engineering drawing of NC seaplane final design

box-shaped, spruce booms braced with steel cables. The tail remained above, clearing high-breaking seas and offering a clear range of fire aft from a machine gun.[59]

Wind-tunnel tests for the careful balancing of flight-control surfaces and control cables threaded over ball-bearing pulleys were necessary steps to reduce forces to the point that only one pilot was needed to fly the seaplane.[60]

For the first time in aircraft construction, aluminum fuel tanks, using sheet aluminum and welded seams to further reduce aircraft gross weight, were used The empty ninety-one-gallon gasoline gravity tank and nine two-hundred-gallon gasoline tanks were half the weight of the same number of empty traditional steel or copper tanks with the same capacity.[61]

Communications would be maintained by a radio with two-hundred-mile range. A radio-telephone would be used to communicate within the aircraft formation in flight. The radio's useful range was twenty-five miles.[62]

The NC aircraft were hybrids of aircraft and sailing-ship rigging and sails technology. Each had a wood hull rather than a fuselage, and the rigging wires resembled the shrouds of a sailing ship. The 126-foot wingspan was the size of some later modern airliners. Indeed, the aircraft's cramped crew quarters, creaking wooden structure, and the wind whistling through wire rigging and doped-silk covered wings would be reminiscent of a ship under sail on a long transatlantic crossing.

CHAPTER FIVE

First Transatlantic Flight NC Flying Boats Shakedown

1918–1919

Getting seaplanes on the ramp, ready to complete the first transatlantic flight from Newfoundland to Portugal, required considerable planning, flight performance testing, and adjustment to aircraft design and configuration. After all, the NC flying boats were designed and manufactured in only a year's time.

From August 1918 to April 5, 1919, the commanding officer of NAS Rockaway Beach, New York City, was CDR Stanley V. Parker, USCG. NAS Rockaway Beach's executive officer was LT Eugene A. Coffin, USCG. Coffin was chosen for his training in radio and telegraphic communications. Prior to the Navy's picking the seaplane crews for the first transatlantic flight, NAS Rockaway personnel were responsible for support, maintenance, and aircraft line crews for NC-1-type seaplanes. Stone was assigned to NAS Rockaway as the air station seaplane officer.

All of NC-1's subassemblies arrived at NAS Rockaway from the Curtiss Garden City plant in the latter part of September 1918. Final assembly was completed within one week's time, and preflight checks were immediately begun. The seaplane was equipped with small-diameter propellers and three low-compression, three-hundred-horsepower Liberty engines. Weight and balance measurements showed her empty weight to be 12,956 pounds, just under the designed 13,000-pound empty weight.[1]

The NC-1's preflight tests were completed, and, with a gross weight of 16,930 pounds, LCDR Holden Richardson, USN, copilot LT David McCulloch, USNRF, Machinist Philo Danly, and Curtiss Company engineers Van Sicklen and George Robinson flew the first NC-1 aircraft trial on October 4, 1918, almost one year from the design's beginning. Several high-speed runs were made to get the feel of the aircraft prior to getaway. The flight reached only fifty feet and was thirty seconds in duration. The flight test showed that the horizontal stabilizer's forces were too small and that she flew as though tail-heavy. The stabilizer's angle relative to the wings was reduced, and the next aircraft trial was much improved. Six more flights were flown the same day, totaling 4.6 minutes. The aircraft's maximum gross weight of 22,000 pounds, as specified in the design, was eventually flown successfully.

NC-1's water-work performance exceeded predictions from the model-basin tests earlier. The deep-V hull acted as a shock absorber when contacting the water. This was true from high-speed landings to slower-airspeed, full-stall landings, as well as for landing on swells of moderate height. In the next three months, NC-1 underwent thirty-six flights comprising twenty-eight hours of total flight time.[2]

Flying tests on NC-1 for radiators, propellers, fuel consumption, radio communications, and pilot instruction continued, resulting in many changes that improved the seaplane design. During these flight tests, the Bureau of Steam Engineering developed improved propellers, and, at its research laboratory at the Washington Navy Yard, perfected carburetor adjustments on a newly improved high-compression Liberty 12-cylinder engine. Performance output was increased from three to four hundred horsepower.[3]

Still using the three low-compression, three-hundred-horsepower engines, a round-robin flight was flown by Lieutenant Commander Richardson and crew from November 7 to 9 from NAS Rockaway Beach to NAS Anacostia, near Washington, D.C., to NAS Hampton Roads, Virginia, and returning to NAS Rockaway Beach. The center NC-1 engine had to be hand-cranked to start, but the two outboard engines were retrofitted with Bijur electric-started motors. The general public saw her for the first time.

The flight's beginning at Rockaway Beach was not a smooth one. There were cantankerous engine starts. Shifting tidal sand covering the launching ramp to a depth of over a foot had to be removed by hand-shoveling. In addition, a center-engine radiator leak required engine shutdown, and an unplanned off-shore landing occurred on eight-foot swells at Barnegat Inlet, New Jersey. After radiator repairs, a refill with seawater, and a seasick crew, the flight continued to Washington. The mechanics must have eventually gained confidence in the aircraft, since one of the pilots found them sleeping in the center compartment when he was going to the stern on an inspection. Upon its arrival at NAS Anacostia, a news article in the *Washington Evening Star* nicknamed the NC-1 "Nancy 1," and from then on reporters referred to the four seaplanes as "Nancy boats." Richardson's crew remained overnight at NAS Anacostia and at NAS Hampton Roads before starting the next legs of the flight.

The aircraft behaved exceptionally well throughout the flight. The pilots were often able to fly long distances with hands off the controls. Without changing airspeed with elevator movement, they were able to gain and reduce altitude with only power adjustments.[4] The first instrument flight in the NC flying boat was tried on this flight. Lieutenant McCulloch operated the rudder, looking at compass readings while keeping his head in the cockpit so he could not see outside. Richardson flew, visually maintaining airspeed, altitude, and level flight. This flight test showed that as long as the aircraft remained level, compass readings were reliable. In a bank, however, compass readings were unreliable; the indicated heading stayed steady even though the aircraft was turning. It became evident that in a fog, with reduced visibility, or at night without a visible horizon, it would be quite possible for the seaplane to enter a steep bank without the pilot realizing it unless an instrument was developed to indicate the airplane was in a bank and turning.[5]

NC-4 on cross-country flight from NAS Rockaway to NAS Anacostia to NAS Hampton Roads and return to NAS Rockaway

World War I ended with the Armistice on November 11, 1918. Funding, personnel, and equipment were drastically cut, and the wartime antisubmarine warfare mission for NC seaplanes ended. The ASW mission had, however, laid the groundwork for a sea-power demonstration that would become the first transatlantic flight.

Tests showed NC-1 had great lifting capability with its three low-compression Liberty engines, but it was underpowered and would eventually be fitted with four of the new high-compression Liberty 12-cylinder engines. On November 27, 1918, NC-1 made a world-record-breaking flight for the most people carried—fifty-one total. The 22,028-pound aircraft took off with forty-eight passengers, pilots Richardson and McCulloch on board, and a machinist mate second class who stowed away in the fuel-tank compartment. NC-1 flew a thousand yards at an altitude of fifty feet.[6] A week later, NC-1 flew from NAS Rockaway Beach to Montauk Point, Long Island, and returned to Rockaway Beach, starting the flight with a 22,141-pound gross weight.[7]

NC-1 with fifty passengers and crew, which set a world record

Following the world-record-breaking flight, the three NC-1 engines were replaced with the new improved propellers and with the new high-compression four-hundred-horsepower engines. Getaways at a gross weight of 24,700 pounds were easily accomplished. When the engines were changed out, a new electric engine-starter was also installed, allowing the pilot to start any engine from the cockpit. To increase engine efficiency, the center engine was replaced with a "pusher" instead of a "tractor" propeller arrangement. Since hostilities had ended, the machine gunner's cockpit was removed from the top wing of NC-1 and NC-2. It became evident that the seaplane could carry a much larger gross weight if the engine horsepower could be increased.[8]

Prospective navigation legs were investigated for a first transatlantic flight, and it soon became evident the increased fuel load needed for the crossing would require an increase in gross weight to 28,000 pounds. An engine placement and mounting redesign would be required to achieve higher-gross-weight performance, using a fourth engine to compensate for the added weight. The Curtiss Company recommended a four-Kircham-engine configuration, but these power plants were not yet sufficiently tested. The new down-geared Liberty engine had not been developed sufficiently for use. The high-compression Liberty engine was chosen over the Kircham and the down-geared Liberty. NC-2 would be the first to be fitted with three tractor propellers on three high-compression Liberty engines with new streamlined nacelles. NC-1 was still being used to collect data with the original three engines. NC-2 was now designated NC-2-T.[9]

Commander Towers reported the findings of a February 16, 1919, design review in a letter to Commander Hunsaker and in a confidential memorandum relaying the meeting's minutes. Representatives from the NAS Rockaway Operations Aviation command, the Bureau of Construction and Repair, and the Bureau of Steam Engineering were present.[10]

> The NC-1 was tried out last fall with small diameter propellers and low-compression Liberty engines, and performed in accordance with its design characteristics. If at that time high compression engines, which developed more power, and provided suitable propellers had been available the design performance, would have made the Trans-Atlantic Flight appear more favorable, and no consideration would have been given the complete change of power plant involving the use of 4 engines. It is this change of power plant, which has caused the trouble now.
>
> If suitable propellers and radiators had been determined last Fall and Winter from trials of the NC-1 which has had some 50 hours flying, the present boats would have been several weeks advanced.[11]

The first discussion was on the subject of the type of engines:

- *Liberty engine, direct drive, low compression*
- *Liberty engine, direct drive, high compression*
- *Liberty engine, geared drive, low compression, and*
- *Liberty engine, geared drive, high compression.*

"The Bureau of Steam Engineering stated that ample numbers of direct drive high compression engines were available—and gear drive engines will not be available until May 1st."[12]

Decision: "Use Liberty engines with direct drive and high compression."

The next subject discussed was the question of engine arrangements:

- *Two tractors and a center pusher (as now installed in NC-2).*
- *Twin tandem, consisting of tandem engines in each wing.*
- *Single tandem, center installation with single engine in each wing.*

Decision: "Go ahead with twin tandem installation in NC-2."

Decision: "If sufficient time remains after the completion of fuel consumption and propeller tests on NC-1, install the center tandem single engine wing arrangement in that seaplane with the idea of using this aircraft, so fitted, on the flight, if the test proves the arrangement may have been adopted as standard."[13]

Decision: "Remove the pilot's nacelle and place the pilots in the hull."

Decision: "No tests be made on NC-4, there to be embedded in this seaplane such arrangements as prove satisfactory in the tests of the other seaplanes."[14]

After both NC-3 and NC-4 were changed to match NC-2-T's configuration, they were the only two aircraft stored in the NAS Rockaway Beach hangar when not in use or during foul weather. This proved to be unfortunate for NC-1. While she was at anchor, about midnight during March 1919, a heavy squall line passed Jamaica Bay. The fierce wind blew directly up NC-1's stern, destroying the aileron, the control column, and one elevator control horn. The only good news was that the damage revealed a serious defect in the control-column assembly, which had been assembled incorrectly by Curtiss workers. The NC-1 was out of commission for two weeks.[15]

NC-1 was returned to service late on April 1 and was moored overnight just off the seaplane ramp. A storm warning had been issued at noon but was not received until 1800, the end of the workday. Ramping NC-1 was not possible at the time; the wind was already too strong, and washed-up sand covered the marine railway on the ramp. She remained at anchor overnight. The storm raged into a sixty-knot gale during the night, and NC-1's anchor began to drag. About 0200 the anchor caught on the end of the ramp and held. Heavy seas were running from the northwest onto the beach. The port (left) wing-tip float hit the ramp. Surging wind and seas caused violent rolling motions that broke off the float and set it adrift. Spars for the lower wing at the outer strut were also broken.

NC-1 capsized, rolling over on her left wing until the wing touched the bottom of the bay. In that condition, she rode out the gale for two days without sinking. The gale reached ninety-one knots at one point. The outer portions of the lower wing's spars were adrift, and the overhang of the upper wing was unsupported. The intermediate struts held, and two wing tip floats were secured under them. That is how she rode out the storm.[16]

After further tests, NC-2-T, as anticipated, could not get off the water at a gross weight of 28,000 pounds. A new 1,600-horsepower configuration using four high-compression four-hundred-horsepower Liberty engines allowed getaway, or takeoff, at that weight. The four-engine configuration placed all engines between the wings. One engine was mounted with a tractor propeller on each side of the centerline. The two remaining engines were mounted in tandem, one behind the other, on the aircraft centerline. The front centerline engine was equipped with a conventional tractor propeller, and the rear centerline engine utilized a pusher-type propeller. This configuration concentrated weight near the centerline, allowing easy maneuverability in the air.[17]

An April 5, 1919, memorandum signed by Commander Towers (shadow box below) described activities and decisions made on the 2nd by Towers, Westervelt, and Richardson.

NAS Rockaway seaplane ramp blocked with washed-up sand

NC-1 after the storm at low tide showing the port lower wing panel destroyed and upper wing tip damaged

They reviewed the status of all NC aircraft relative to a May 1 flight to Newfoundland in preparation for the transatlantic flight. They agreed that NC-1 repairs would probably take until the end of May. NC-2-T required many changes, and a May 1 departure was not possible. NC-3 and NC-4 would be launched prior to May 1.

Commander Towers memo of 5 April 1919

"It has been suggested however, that alterations be made in program substantially as follows, which should, with good luck, make 3 boats available to fly May 1. The proposal is to continue trials with NC-2 as she is now rigged and get as much information as possible from her. In the meantime, alter the hull and power plant installation of NC-1, which have not been damaged by the storm, to be similar to that decided on as most suitable for NC-3 and 4.

"During the period the NC-2 is under trials these changes in NC-1 may be proceeded with. Upon completion of NC-2 testing, the damaged port lower wing of NC-1 will be replaced by taking the corresponding parts from NC-2.

"This should have the effect of putting the NC-1 in commission by the first of May with the proper power plant arrangements, leaving the NC-2 as a partly stripped boat, NC-1, 3 and 4 would be ready to fly on May 1."[18]

The storm damage to NC-1 had stopped its critical tests, but propeller and radiator tests held back the final conversion of NC-2 for so long that rebuilding NC-1 was necessary. NC-2 trials had revealed flaws in the engine plate radiators. They were weak and excessively heavy. A honeycomb radiator design replaced the plate type, and the forward radiator on the tandem engine was lowered about eight inches for additional cooling air flow.

Repairs to NC-1 included conversion to NC-2-T's and NC-3's three high-compression Liberty engine configuration. The original unstreamlined engine nacelles were retained. During NC-1's rebuilding, NC-2 returned to service, and propeller and radiator tests resumed. The radiator changes proved satisfactory.[19]

Tests continued until NC-1 was ready to receive NC-2's wings to make it a complete seaplane. All wings had been assembled at the Garden City plant, and new ones could not be made prior to the scheduled departure date, since the subcontractor had destroyed the wing-panel fabrication jigs. The decision was made to use wings from the sacrificial NC-2.

These were too heavy but were necessary for testing fuel consumption. NC-3 and NC-4 were still in production at the Garden City plant. The departure date slipped to May 4.[20]

A gross weight of 23,800 pounds dictated that NC-1 could not make a getaway from the water but that it could sustain flight once airborne. (Later, with improved propellers and three high-compression engines, a getaway could be made with a gross weight of 24,000 pounds.)[21]

NC-3 was assembled and ready for aircraft trials before NC-4, and the resulting trials indicated that 28,000 pounds was the maximum takeoff weight on getaway with four direct-drive, high-compression Liberty engines. Final weight of an empty NC flying boat, with topped-off radiators and fixed instruments and equipment, was 15,874 pounds. The disposable weight remaining for crew, supplies, ordnance, freight, fuel, and oil was 12,126 pounds. No ordnance or freight would be carried on the transatlantic flight. A five-man crew weighed 850 pounds, oil 750 pounds, and gasoline 9,650 pounds.[22]

In the middle of April 1919, transfer of NC-1-type seaplane oversight activity had been ordered from the Bureaus of Construction and Repair and of Steam Engineering to NAS Rockaway, and on April 21 Commander Towers received orders to proceed there and command Seaplane Division 1 for the first transatlantic flight.

First Lieutenant Elmer Stone's abilities for flight-testing seaplanes, engineering, and navigation skills had received the notice of others in the Navy. A March 19, 1919, Bureau of Construction and Repair memorandum confirmed the request of CDR G. Fulton, USN, and Commander Towers that Lieutenant Stone was to be assigned to "test the NC type of seaplanes preparatory to the Trans-Atlantic Flight."[23] The Navy Department issued orders to First Lieutenant Stone, dated April 21, 1919, to detach to "proceed to such place as the NC Seaplane Division One may be—for duty in connection with the Trans-Atlantic flight."[24]

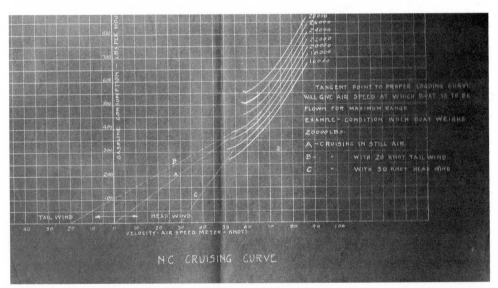

NC fuel consumption data obtained from NC-2

The project was now becoming an operational matter as manufacture of NC-1 neared completion. As a tenant command located at NAS Rockaway, the NC-1 team at NAS Rockaway included:[25]

CDR J. H. Towers, USN	Division Commanding Officer
CDR H. C. Richardson, (CC), USN	Experiments
LT D. H. McCulloch, USNRF	
LCDR D. N. L. Bellinger, USNRF	Operations
LT E. F. Stone, USCG	
LT L. T. Barin, USNRF	
LCDR M. S. Mitscher	Personnel
LTJG A. F. Dietrich, USNRF	
LCDR R. E. Byrd, USN	Navigation
LTJG W. Hinton, USNRF	
LCDR A. C. Read, USN	Material
ENS R. A. Talbott, USNRF	
LCDR R. A. Lavender, USN	Radio and Communications
LT Eugene A. Coffin, USCG	
ENS H. Sadenwater, USNRF	
ENS H. C. Rodd, USNRF	
LT J. L. Breese, USNRF	Power Plant Installation and Operation
ENS B. Rhodes, USNRF	
Boatswain's Mate L. R. Moore, USNRF	
CMM C. S. Rhodes, USN	
CMM C. I. Kesler, USN	
Mach. Rasmus Christensen, USNRF	
Mach. E. H. Howard, USNRF	
LT R. S. Wentworth, USNRF	Radiators
LT G. S. Murray, USNRF	Propellers

When Towers reported on board NAS Rockaway, numerous flight tests were being made with F-5L boats as well as the NC seaplanes. F-5L boats assisted in testing the new radio-communications equipment, new radio-direction-finding equipment, and flight inclinometers.[26]

Many setbacks resulted from hasty decisions and hasty work to meet the May 1 deadline. In addition, the NAS Rockaway hangar was not heated, and cold conditions slowed work.

NC-2's wings were easily adapted to NC-1, but bad luck continued to plague both seaplanes and schedule. Since the third week of April, Navy and Curtiss crews had been working twenty-four-hour days on two twelve-hour shifts. On Sunday morning, May 4, final details were being worked out for a Newfoundland departure on the next day. Chief Machinist's Mate Rasmus Christensen, NC-1's engineer, had been up since 0200 and his work performance was probably compromised by fatigue. NC-1 was still in the hangar. He interrupted work on NC-1's starboard radiator to fuel her from drums on the hangar deck. The electric motor on the fueling pump caught fire. The hose pulled free from NC-1's fuel tank and spilled burning gasoline onto the hangar deck, torching NC-1's starboard wing.

reau of Supplies & counts
    Navy Departme
Washington, D.C. 1 July 1919
Paid mileage $19.60   21
From Washington, D.C.   NAVY DEPARTMENT 32   5891-151
To   Rockaway, N.Y.   WASHINGTON   N-3/Le
     C.P.BENNETT   5892   April 21, 1919.
     Lieut. (pay corps) U.S.N.

            To: Commander
                John H. Towers, U.S.N.
                Office of Naval Operations,
                    Navy Department.
                (Chief of Naval Operations)

            SUBJECT: Detached Office of Naval Operations,
                      Navy Department; to duty as Commander
                      of NC Seaplane Division One.

            1. You are hereby detached from duty in the
        office of Naval Operations, Navy Department, and from
        such other duty as may have been assigned to you; will
        proceed to such place as the NC seaplane Division One
        of seaplanes, that will make the Trans-Atlantic
        Flight, may be, reporting to the Commandant of that
        Naval District, and assume command of that Division
        when they are placed in commission.

            2. As Commander of the NC Seaplane Division One
        of regularly commissioned seaplanes, your status
        will be the same as Commander of a Division
        of sea-going ships of the Navy.

            3. Your designation as a Naval Aviator remains
        in force until specifically revoked.

                            (signed) Franklin D. Roosevelt
                                     Acting.

        Copy to:
            Op (av)
        -
                        1st Endorsement
                    Office of Naval Operations (Aviation)
                        Washington, D.C.
                                          April 22, 1919.

            1. Delivered; detached.

                            (Signed) John S. Fulton, Jr.
                                     By Direction.
        -

Commander Towers' orders to command NC Division 1

In a mere six minutes, the starboard wing of NC–1 was hopelessly burned and the lower elevator and part of the lower stabilizer of NC–4 were damaged.

It was fortunate that Lieutenant Stone was in the hangar working late on NC–4. Under his direction, he, Christensen, and others extinguished flames and prevented total destruction of the NC–1 starboard wing, and most likely the entire seaplane. Departure for Newfoundland was delayed until May 8 due to weather and to allow parts from NC–2 to be cannibalized to replace those burned on NC–1 and NC–4.

Monday, May 5, was a real morale buster. That afternoon, ENS Hugh J. Adams and Chief Machinist Mate Harold B. Corey, during a flight in an HS-2, turned too steeply, stalled, and crashed into a dirigible gas generator. Both were killed. That same evening, two sailors from NAS Rockaway were severely injured in a vehicle accident.

NC-2's port lower wing had been used earlier to replace NC-1's storm-damaged wing. Now, the undamaged starboard wing from NC-2, removed and stored after the storm, would be restored to NC-1's starboard side. The following morning, NC-1 was ready for aircraft trials. During the trial, the starboard wing felt heavy. Investigation revealed that NC-2's wing and aileron had one square foot more wing area than NC-1's, giving it more lift force on the starboard wing. This condition caused uneven lift forces on either side of the seaplane.

A heated argument erupted over how to correct the problem. The solution finally chosen was to reduce aileron surface by trimming the aileron taken from NC-2, adjusting the wing tip, and placing ballast in the wing-tip float. Time was running out, and, even by working all night, there was not enough time to paint the trimmed aileron.[27] Congratulations for a quick repair were received from Assistant Secretary of the Navy, Franklin D. Roosevelt.[28]

From a pilot's perspective, the final equipment configuration was very thorough. Each pilot was issued a compass, inclinometer, headgear, and transmitter for internal communication. The codesignated commanding officers/navigators (CO/NAV) were issued a boat compass, special drift indicators, chronometers set to Greenwich mean time (GMT) and Greenwich sidereal time, hack (or stop) watches for recording celestial sights from sextants, the *Navy Hydrographic Office Nautical Almanac*, plotting sheets, charts and chart boards, navigation tables, and plotting instruments. The CO/NAV was also issued headgear and a transmitter for internal communication, and there was a special circuit to communicate by radiotelephone with the other NC aircraft and with ship stations. One helmet and internal transmitter was provided for each aircraft's engineering crew.

The central instrument panel had a combination lateral and longitudinal inclinometer, airspeed indicator, altimeter, tachometers, and an oil-pressure gauge for each of the four engines. Inclinometers were simple, with bubbles in curved glass tubes that would show angular pitch up and down, as well as angle of bank. They were difficult to use in rough air. *Turn and bank indicators and artificial horizons did not yet exist.* Engine switches and voltage regulators were positioned within a diagram, on a panel between the two pilots, showing which supported each engine. Electric engine-starter pulls were positioned on a panel behind, and between, the pilots' seats, and engine throttles were on the deck between the pilots. A master engine-cutoff switch for all four engines was located on the deck below the instrument panel. A turn indicator on the deck, in clear view of both pilots, was located on the aircraft's centerline. Each aircraft compartment had electric lighting.[29]

Propeller testing ran right up to the deadline. The Olmstead propeller was the most efficient of those tested, but the only existing spare propellers had to be shipped by destroyer to Newfoundland, in case they were needed there.[30]

The three seaplanes were finally ready for their departure flight, but bad luck continued to plague the crews. Just prior to departure, Machinist's Mate E. H. Howard, USNRF, caught his right hand in the rear propeller of NC-4, severing it from his arm. Chief Machinist's Mate E. C. Rhodes, USN, replaced him. Howard, concerned that the morale of the NC crews would be affected by his bad luck, walked three hundred yards to sickbay without help for medical treatment. Following treatment, he returned and hollered to his commanding officer, "I'm all right, sir! I hope there's bad weather for two weeks, for if there is, I'll make the trip with you yet!"[31]

NC-4 at NAS Rockaway Beach ready for departure

CHAPTER SIX

First Transatlantic Flight

1919

Just eight years before Lindbergh's flight across the Atlantic, and immediately prior to the end of World War I, crossing the Atlantic in a fixed-wing aircraft was very dangerous and generally unthinkable. The distance was just too long, aircraft instrumentation and navigation were too primitive, and weather reporting and forecasting were negligible. However, World War I stimulated rapid advancement in aircraft design, aerial navigation, and weather reporting and forecasting. Airplanes were built that could fly farther, stay aloft longer, and carry more. Several war-production aircraft were so advanced that flight across the Atlantic was nearly possible.

Ready, Set, Go!

There were five different nations competing to be the first to fly across the Atlantic Ocean. The U.S. Navy alone had three aircraft competitor teams within its ranks. A Swedish civilian pilot and four competitive British pilot teams were poised to fly east from a base in St. Johns, Newfoundland, and one British team planned to fly westward from Ireland to Newfoundland.[1]

The first Navy competitor aircraft's final power-plant design was not ready before the race. It had been identified back in July 1918, when the British Porte-Felixstowe F-5 boat was produced by the Navy's new aircraft factory in Philadelphia. The U.S. version of this aircraft was called the F-5L flying boat. Adding fuel tanks and installing untested geared-down, high-compression Liberty engines (yet to be produced) would have made direct flight via the Azores to Europe feasible. The F-5L was eliminated early in favor of NC flying boats.[2]

The second Navy competitor arose from brother naval aviators assigned to the new twin-engine U.S. Navy C-5 dirigible. Support equipment and hydrogen cylinders had been transported to St. Johns in the cruiser USS *Chicago,* arriving May 10, 1919. U.S Navy lighter-than-air pioneers LT Raymond F. Tyler, LT A. D. Preston, ENS Scott E. Peck, and their commanding officer, LT Charles G. Little, were on board *Chicago* as C-5's support crew. The dirigible was scheduled to fly from NAS Cape May, New Jersey, to St. Johns. It would then fly nonstop from St. Johns to Ireland. The airship was 196 feet long, with a 42-foot diameter, and was powered by two 120-horsepower Union engines; its maximum range could span the Atlantic. One engine's carburetor was designed to burn hydrogen instead of venting it into the atmosphere during flight.

The third Navy competitor was the NC seaplane, built by Curtiss.[3]

Barely in Navy service for a month, C-5 departed NAS Cape May for NAS Montauk, Long Island, New York. C-5 was commanded by LCDR Emory W. Coil, whose copilots were LTJG John B. Lawrence and ENS David P. Campbell; the flight engineers were LTJG Marcus H. Easterly and Chief Machinist's Mates T. L. Moorman and H. S. Blackburn. On C-5's arrival at NAS Montauk on May 8, full support was provided by the air station's commanding officer, LT Robert Donahue, USCG (Coast Guard aviator number three). C-5 departed Montauk for Newfoundland on May 14. After a harrowing flight through rough air and fog, including the experience of a compass failure in the fog, C-5 arrived at Pleasantville, near St. Johns. After losing her compass, C-5 had followed railroad tracks to navigate.[4]

Lieutenant Little and a hundred sailors from USS *Chicago* moored the airship, using a three-wire mooring system. A twenty-five-knot wind was blowing, creating lift on the airship and making it hard to control. By midafternoon, wind had increased and two mooring lines had parted and been replaced. As wind speed continued to increase, the airship became uncontrollable. Unable to power up and get airborne for safety because the engine carburetors were in pieces for cleaning, Lieutenant Little and a crewman, in the airship's cab, were attempting to deflate the hydrogen envelope through the ripping panel, which was a piece of balloon fabric that could be torn, or ripped apart, in order to collapse—or deflate—the dirigible in an emergency. Additional manila mooring lines had been attached, but as Lieutenant Little, having failed to open the ripping panel, and the crewman leaped out of the cab, the airship broke loose. C-5 climbed an estimated two hundred feet, plummeted, and then disappeared toward the Atlantic. The British freighter *Clan Davidson* later observed C-5's debris three hundred miles out to sea. C-5 was eliminated from competition.[5]

The NC flight crews would compete against at least five teams of British pilots.

In the spring of 1919, Lieutenant Commander Bellinger and Lieutenant Stone were in Halifax Harbor, in the course of their seaplane-basing survey trip in Newfoundland. While in Halifax they learned that the freighter *Digby* had disembarked there navigator Kenneth MacKenzie-Grieve, pilot Harry Hawker, and their Sopwith landplane in Placentia, Newfoundland. Bellinger and Stone called on board *Digby,* whose captain told them the Sopwith's crew had a cocky confidence that they would be the first to fly across the Atlantic to Europe. Bellinger and Stone quickly departed Halifax in USS *Barney* (DD-149) and then traveled overland to Trepassey Harbor, Newfoundland, to complete their survey.[6]

C-5 departing NAS Cape May, New Jersey

Another British competitor comprised Major J. C. Wood, navigator Captain C. C. Wylie, and their modified Short N.1B Shirl torpedo biplane. The new version was designated a "Short S.538" and named *Shamrock;* it had a large (four-hundred-gallon) belly tank. Wood and Wylie's strategy was to fly from Ireland west to the Americas. On April 18, when they were ferrying *Shamrock* from England to Curragh, Ireland, the engine experienced a vapor lock and failed midway. They ditched *Shamrock* in the sea short of Ireland. *Shamrock* was salvaged, but corrosion from saltwater was so bad that the aircraft could not be rebuilt in time. Thus *Shamrock* too was eliminated from competition.[7]

Raymor was a Martinsyde biplane flown by British pilot Fredrick P. Raynham and navigator C. W. Morgan. The aircraft was ready for shipment, and they were itching to go.

The freighter *Digby* departed England on April 15 with yet another competitor. Rear Admiral Mark Kerr and Handley Page intended to fly the Atlantic in a four-engine V/1500 bomber. All unnecessary equipment had been removed to reduce weight.[8]

Vickers Aircraft, Ltd., prepared a converted Vimy bomber for shipment to Newfoundland from England on the freighter *Glendevon*. Two Royal Air Force (RAF) officers, Arthur Whitten-Brown and John Alcock, were to crew the Vimy.[9]

There were several other British competitors also preparing aircraft for shipment to Newfoundland.

NC crews at NAS Rockaway during NC Division 1's commissioning muster

Since the freighters *Digby* and *Glendevon,* transporting the crated aircraft *Raymor,* the V/1500 bomber and the converted Vickers Vimy would not arrive in Newfoundland until mid-May, all the British competitors except Hawker, MacKenzie-Grieve, and their Sopwith would be too late.[10]

Hugo Sundstedt, a Swedish aviator, had contracted with the William-Lewis Company in Newark, New Jersey, to design and manufacture a twin-float biplane named *Sunrise* for the first transatlantic flight. Unfortunately for Sundstedt, *Sunrise* crashed during a flight exhibition at the Bayonne, New Jersey, Yacht Club on March 27. She was damaged beyond repair and, therefore, eliminated from competition.[11]

Rushing Too Much Causes Errors and Delays
The last straggler, NC-4, completed assembly at NAS Rockaway and rode the marine railway down the ramp into Jamaica Bay on April 30, 1919. Its first flight was on May 1.[12]

On Saturday morning, May 3, Seaplane Division 1's personnel were mustered. With NC-1, NC-3, and NC-4 as a backdrop, Commander Towers formally commissioned the flying boats and made crew assignments.[13]

Many of the same men who had flown early aircraft trials together were assigned key crew positions for the NC transatlantic flight. The original four NC aircraft commanding officers and navigators were Commander Towers, NC-1; LCDR Marc A. Mitscher, NC-2; LCDR Patrick N. L. Bellinger, NC-3; and LCDR Albert C. Read, NC-4.

Cannibalization and loss of NC-2 caused a shuffling of the crew assignments, shrinking the crews from four to three, for three seaplanes. The final NC crew assignments were as follows:[14]

NC-3

Commander, navigator, and NC Division 1 commander, CDR John H. Towers, USN

Pilot, CDR Holden C. Richardson, USN

Copilot, LT David H. McCulloch, USNRF

Radio officer, LCDR Robert A. Lavender, USN

Engineer, LTJG Braxton Rhodes, USN

Engineer, Chief Boatswain's Mate Lloyd R. Moore, USN

NC-4

Commander and navigator, LCDR Albert C. Read, USN

Pilot, LT Elmer F. Stone, USCG

Copilot, LT Walter Hinton, USNRF

Radio officer, ENS Herbert C. Rodd, USNRF

Engineer, LT James L. Breese, USNRF

Engineer, Chief Machinist's Mate E. C. Rhodes, USN

NC-1

Commander and navigator, LCDR Patrick N. L. Bellinger, USN

Pilot, LCDR Marc A. Mitscher, USN

Copilot, LT Louis T. Barin, USNRF

Radio officer, LTJG Harry Sadenwater, USNRF

Engineer, Chief Machinist's Mate Rasmus Christensen, USN

Engineer, Chief Machinist's Mate C. I. Kesler, USN.

CDR John H. Towers, USN

CDR A. C. Read, USN

Dr. (Commander) Hunsaker in his memoirs states:

The big boats had dual controls and the two aviators sat side by side and worked together on the controls which required strong effort at times. Read was a relatively small man, and he chose Stone because of his size and strength. The two were a good team. Stone had experience with flying boats, which were notoriously difficult to keep from stalling in rough air or at reduced speed. Stone also had experience in bad visibility weather. Stone had been a test pilot and knew how the crude instruments of the day could give indications contrary to the reliable "seat of the pants" signals of acceleration. On the eighteen hour flight of the NC-4 to the Azores, Reed's [*sic*] function as a navigator required him to stand in the forward cockpit. Stone was in fact the chief aviator with Lieutenant Hinton sitting beside him as a partner.

Two of the most significant factors in NC-4's success proved to be radio communications and radio direction finding. Installation of radio equipment was completed just two days before departure on May 6. No flights could be made to test the equipment, only ramp checks. A wind-driven radio generator was mounted to catch both the airstream and the wind driven from the center tandem engines. The NCs each had a continuous-wave transmitter, a skid fin antenna, a radiotelephone, and a long-line antenna that could be reeled in and out to various lengths, depending on the radio wavelength selected.[15]

LCDR Patrick N. L. Bellinger, USN

Marc A. Mitscher, as a captain, USN, in later years

Ensign Rodd's NC–4 radio position

NC–4 moored at NAS Rockaway

NC-4 moored at NAS Rockaway

All times reported during the NCs' flight to Trepassey Harbor, Newfoundland, are
Eastern Standard Time. Since there are slight variations in times in the participant's
reports, those from Ensign Rodd's radio logs are used, since he had access to
transmitted time checks with the U.S. Naval and Greenwich observatories.

NC-1 and NC-3 had taken early-morning flights on May 8 to check their readiness and
had returned. It was 0930 when Commander Towers said, "Well, boys, let's go!" Witnesses were
limited to a small gathering of newspaper reporters, relatives, and the Navy ground crew as
NC-1, NC-3, and NC-4 prepared to depart NAS Rockaway for Trepassey Harbor. Bellinger,
prone to grandstanding, told the reporters, "With the help of God, and in spite of the devil . . .
we'll get there." One dignitary, CAPT Noble E. Irwin, USN, Division Chief, Naval Aviation,
in the Office of the Chief of Naval Operations (CNO), distributed four-leaf clovers to the
crews. Each crew was provided with sandwiches and coffee. At 0957 NC-3's engines roared
to life, and she was lowered down the marine railway into the bay. As Towers in NC-3 taxied
out into Jamaica Bay, NC-1 and NC-4 quickly followed, and by 0959 all three boats had been
launched. The three boats taxied on the bay, warming and testing their engines.

At 1002 NC-3 was airborne, followed by NC-4 at 1003 and NC-1 at 1004. NC-3 flew
west toward Roamer Shoal Light until NC-1 and NC-4 could take their positions. All
three joined in a very loose V formation, with NC-4 in left echelon on NC-3.[16]

NC-1, NC-3, and NC-4 taxi for takeoff on first transatlantic flight

Ensign Rodd operated NC-4's radios. He had taken Towers's advice and, for comfort, had placed bath sponges over the earpieces in his helmet. NC-1 reported that NC-4 had a good spark and good communications; NAS Rockaway replied, "Good luck! Signed Wise, Jones, Parks, and the rest." These were the men who had worked so hard the previous two nights installing NC-4's radios. At 1027 all three boats were in communication with each other, and at 1040 Rodd unreeled his trailing long-line antenna. At 1050 an important message from London was received by the three aircraft: Admiral Knapp reported that the British Air Ministry had offered Scilly Islands Air Station for repairs and refueling. It also promised that all facilities at Plymouth would be available as needed.

Many stations sent good-luck messages, and NC-4's radio direction finder functioned normally. At 1300, communication was established with Station 1, the destroyer USS *McDermut*. One hundred miles off Cape Cod, four destroyers were stationed fifty miles apart to assist the NC aircraft. Station 1 sent a good-luck message from the Assistant Secretary of the Navy, Franklin D. Roosevelt.[17]

NC-4 was slightly heavier than the other two boats and had to be flown slightly faster to maintain a stable cruise speed. Lieutenant Stone's flight mottoes were "Speed is control" and "Power plus the aircraft's attitude equals performance." Passing Montauk Point at an altitude of 2,300 feet, NC-4 was ahead of the pack, and Lieutenant Stone flew a large circle to fall into left echelon position again on NC-3. After four hours and fifty-one minutes of flight from NAS Rockaway, the NC formation passed Highland Lighthouse, Cape Cod, heading offshore for Cape Sable.[18]

At 1350 Chief Machinist's Mate Rhodes noticed that NC-4's aft engine, one of the two tandem center engines, was burning an excessive amount of oil. Spare oil was becoming scarce. He notified Lieutenant Breese, and the two engineers shut down the engine. Station 1 came into view at 1405. NC-4 continued on three engines but fell behind the formation and disappeared from sight of NC-3 and NC-1, passing Station 1 at 1418.[19]

Continuing on to Halifax at ninety-five miles per hour, NC-1 and NC-3 flew through squall lines and rough air for three hours. Richardson reported "vicious squalls coming down the gullies and over the head line giving us a battle to keep right side up and on our course. McCulloch and I in the NC-3 had our hands full, and towards the end of the run I developed a cramp in my right hand."

The pilots of both NC-1 and NC-3 found it difficult to fly the unwieldy aircraft in rough air. Both pilot and copilot in each of the two seaplanes were physically required on the flight controls to maintain control. Gusts caused both aircraft to lurch, and their wings would unexpectedly drop to either side, placing the aircraft in steep banks to alternate sides. This flight condition continued all the way to Trepassey Harbor. Commander Richardson later reported that he was satisfied with NC-3's flight performance in the squall. He, of course, still had a visual horizon for orientation. Richardson might not have been so satisfied had the quick wing drops to unusual flight attitudes, and perhaps stalls, occurred inside a cloud in rough air.[20] This event is noteworthy since Lieutenant Stone would later experience the same dangerous phenomena flying through fog and rough air on the leg to Horta, Fayal Island, the Azores.

NC-1 experienced aileron control problems in the starboard wing, which had been transferred from NC-2-T. There had not been time available to test the wing's rigging after installation. The starboard wing wanted to fly lower than the port wing. Mitscher subsequently corrected the problem at Halifax Harbor by pouring eighty pounds of water into the port wing tip float. He figured if the weight was too much, the volume of water could be adjusted at Trepassey Harbor. It worked!

NC-4's bad fortune continued. Flying on only three engines, it was about halfway to Station 2, USS *Kimberly*, when a crankcase water-jacket seal spewed water and steam from the forward center tandem engine. With both center tandem engines now shut down, NC-4 was forced to descend. Ensign Rodd quickly reeled in the trailing long-line antenna so he would not lose it should a water landing become necessary.

Stone landed the seaplane offshore at 1445 in moderate to heavy swells. His skill at landing seaplanes in heavy seas once again saved an NC. An open-sea landing at night would have been even worse, and would be a very demanding operation, since height above water while approaching touchdown is difficult to determine. Compounding the danger, the horizon is difficult to discern, since the black horizon blends in with the black sea. Lieutenant Commander Read calculated the celestial position with his sextant. The seaplane had to taxi eighty miles, on two outboard engines, to reach NAS Chatham, Massachusetts. Taxiing offshore into the night was a dangerous and harrowing experience. Since the radio windmill generator required center engine operation for adequate airflow to turn its little propellers fast enough, Ensign Rodd was not able to contact any unit to report NC-4's difficulty; however Rodd could hear Bar Harbor, New York, and other stations trying to contact him and asking other ships and aircraft if they had seen or heard from NC-4. These communications continued into the early morning hours.

Very concerned, NAS Chatham's commanding officer, LT P. B. Eaton, USCG, had launched two HS-2 aircraft to search for NC-4, but they were not radio equipped and did not locate the seaplane.

1919 NAS Chatham, Massachusetts

1919 approach from seaward to NAS Chatham

The radio generator was not the only equipment that depended upon wind-driven propellers to function. The fuel system also had a slipstream-driven fuel pump that moved gasoline from the main fuel tanks to a ninety-gallon gravity tank that in turn fed all four engines. During the long taxi to Chatham the outboard engines quit from fuel starvation, startling the crew. Hand-pumping fuel to the gravity tank allowed the engines to be restarted and water-taxiing to be resumed. By 0620 NC-4 had passed Nanset Light, and by 0710 it was at the Chatham channel entrance. Rodd could hear NAS Chatham calling the destroyer stations, notifying them that Coast Guard Station 40 had sighted NC-4. Safe from further problems, NC-4 made Chatham's seaplane ramp at 0735. Except for the sudden duel engine stoppage, the all-night taxi on the open sea had gone remarkably smoothly. The news media dubbed NC-4 "Lame Duck," and the nickname stuck until her landing in Lisbon.

The center engines were disassembled and examined at NAS Chatham. With a drop in oil level due to high consumption during flight, the oil had thickened and would not pass through the strainers. Lack of lubricating oil had caused the forward engine bearings to burn out and a connecting rod to break. The oil strainers were removed and cleaned, and the forward high-compression Liberty engine was replaced with a spare of the only type available, a low-compression Liberty. Oil consumption was, as a result, no longer a problem. In addition, a carburetor jet had clogged with rubber from poorly designed gasoline joints. The carburetor was disassembled, cleaned, and reassembled. To top it off, improper installation caused an engine starter to fail. The starter was replaced.[21]

By May 10 NC-4 was again ready to fly, but foul weather would keep her on the ground.

Meanwhile, both NC-1 and NC-3 arrived in Halifax, Nova Scotia, on May 8—NC-3 at 1858, NC-1 at 1958. The engineers on both NC-3 and NC-1 inspected their engines and found cracks in one of NC-3's Olmsted propellers and two of NC-1's. Though only three of the eight original propellers were cracked, spare propellers stored on board USS *Baltimore* were used to replace all NC-1 and NC-3 propellers; the five original propellers that were not cracked were stored on board as emergency spares. Spare propeller hubs were also needed. Richard Byrd, who had been the commanding officer of NAS Halifax in 1918 before it was transferred to the Canadian government, recalled that spare propeller hubs required for Olmsted propellers were stored there. The Canadians were happy to give Towers the hubs.[22]

More than two hours before reaching Halifax, the NC-3 crew had noticed that fuel gauges reported only two hours of fuel remaining. As the flight continued it had become obvious that the gauges were stuck, so they were corrected in Halifax. All that was left before both aircraft could depart Halifax was replacing their broken engine starters, which had stripped gears, and fueling from USS *Baltimore,* moored astern, one at a time.

Both were ready to depart Halifax for Trepassey the morning of May 10. NC-1's engines roared to life, but one of NC-3's engine starters again stripped a gear. After waiting about a half-hour, Towers ordered NC-1 to proceed on to Trepassey, figuring NC-3 would catch up after repairs were made. NC-1 took off at 0847, flying out of sight over McNab Island at an altitude of five hundred feet. With a new starter installed, NC-3 departed at 0901 and encountered air that was quite bumpy. Commander Richardson found that the muscle strain from fighting rough flight conditions on the way to Halifax had made his "arm muscle bound and sluggish to react on the controls."[23]

Thirty-five miles out from Halifax, near Egg Island Light, NC-3's rear center tandem engine oil pressure failed. Richardson made an offshore landing in moderate seas. Chief Boatswain's Mate Moore's inspection of the engine revealed a clogged oil strainer and cracks in one of the newly replaced propellers. Oil strainers would have to be removed again from all three NC aircraft, and engineers would have to inspect all engines and their strainers once more. NC-3 was forced to turn back to Halifax and to *Baltimore* for a replacement propeller. All four engines were still used, with the rear center tandem engine throttled back to avoid the propeller drag that would have occurred with a dead engine.

After landing at Halifax, the NC-3 crew found that all *Baltimore*'s spare propellers had been swapped out after their arrival from Rockaway. However, one of the five original propellers was swapped from the center tractor-tandem engine to the starboard outboard engine. The center engine acquired one of NC-3's undamaged original Olmsted propellers. NC-3 was airborne again at 1246, only to find that it would have a rough ride and strong crosswinds all the way to Trepassey.[24]

Observing many icebergs during their approach, NC-3 arrived off Trepassey at approximately 1800, Eastern Standard Time, and maneuvered for a landing into the wind. As the seaplane starting to descend for landing, Commander McCulloch was forward in the navigator's cockpit talking with Commander Towers when a sudden strong downdraft forced the port wing down violently. Richardson used full aileron, but nothing happened. He added full rudder, but the seaplane still did not right itself. Richardson had "to go down after the wing [that is, descend sharply to recover control]. This maneuver was successful." In the time it took to say "What the heck is going on?" McCulloch was back in the copilot's seat, trying to help.

The descent continued the bumpy ride. One air ripple was so rough that it bounced an engineer in the rear compartment off the deck several inches, along with the box he was sitting on. Only thirty feet above Mutton Bay, approaching Powel Point Lighthouse, NC-3's pilots fought to a landing into the wind. After taxiing "on the step" (at high speed) into the harbor, wrestling with violent wind downdrafts to keep the starboard wing from digging into the water, and occasionally bouncing into the air in wind gusts, they moored NC-3, nested alongside NC-1 with the seaplane tenders USS *Prairie* and *Aroostook*.[25] NC-3 had landed at Trepassey Harbor at 1931 on May 10, NC-1 at 1541. NC-1 and NC-3 were now put through complete inspections and engine overhauls, consisting of cleaning and lubricating, removal and cleaning of critical parts like carburetors, and inspecting parts that had previously failed, like fuel-line joints.

On May 11 both seaplanes were refueled and made ready to fly, but maintenance problems, weather, and sea conditions prevented departure until the 14th. This delay would permit NC-4 to "fly with the pack" on the first transatlantic flight. During this delay,

Towers, Richardson, Bellinger, and Mitscher made several survey flights in a single-engine Curtiss MF seaplane that was carried on board *Aroostook*. These flights would acquaint them with local prevailing wind and sea conditions without consuming precious NC flight time or wearing their own equipment unnecessarily. Due to cold weather and icy nights, special steam lines were rigged from the sterns of *Aroostook* and *Prairie* and from the oil tanker *Hisko* to heat the oil tanks of both NC seaplanes, so the oil would not congeal and cause damage on subsequent engine starts.[26]

NC-1 and NC-3 attracted newspaper reporters, who had no place to stay overnight, since all hotels were full. The inventive reporters rented a railroad dining car with cots and converted it into a dormitory. A sign painted on the railcar's side read, "NC-5."[27]

Back at NAS Chatham, on May 14, the weather having improved, NC-4 was airborne at 0810 for a test flight. Landing at 0818 to inspect propellers and to clear an oil line, she was airborne again at 0907 It reached Halifax at 1310 and left at 0853 the next morning for Trepassey Harbor, where it arrived at 1759, May 15. While at Halifax, a second NC-4 engine starter and the forward center engine tachometer shaft failed, requiring replacement. The turn-off valve to the primer had been carelessly left open, an engine cylinder had filled with gasoline, and during engine start the full cylinder fired with such force that a tooth broke on the starter gear. Poor installation caused the tachometer shaft to fail. In addition, the aluminum gasoline-pump pipe to the gravity tank had split due to vibration and excessive pump pressure.[28]

As we have seen, weather and maintenance work delayed NC-1 and NC-3 from departing ahead of NC-4. Towers thought "weather was so uncertain that we felt that we could not afford to wait for NC-4 if good weather should turn up first." But now NC-4 had arrived, and all three seaplanes were in Trepassey Harbor. NC-4 received a new engine. New Paragon and Lang propellers arrived on board the destroyer USS *Edwards,* and all three seaplanes were outfitted with the new oak propellers. The metal tips on NC-4's Olmsted tractor propellers and on the Olmsted pusher propeller had cracked a quarter of the way to the propeller hubs. By the end of the transatlantic flight, the new oak Paragon tractor and Lang pusher propellers had not cracked, proving that oak propellers were best for water work and wet rainy flights.[29]

The morning of May 16, the seaplanes had each been fueled, with 1,600 pounds of gasoline in the tanks. A strong wind blew across the harbor, and in the afternoon it hauled around to the south, making sea and wind conditions reasonably favorable. NC-1 and NC-3 taxied around to keep engines warm; NC-4 was having trouble starting its center engines. Not wanting to wait longer, NC-3 made three getaway attempts but was too heavy for liftoff. By then NC-4 had all engines running and was taxiing to keep engines warm. Commander Towers made a difficult decision to leave behind NC-3's Lieutenant (junior grade) Rhodes, with five gallons of drinking water, the emergency CG 1104 radio transmitter, and a chair, transferring all to a speedboat in order to lighten the seaplane. (He would later regret leaving the drinking water and emergency radio.) While NC-3 was reducing weight, NC-4 took off for a short test of her new engine. When NC-4 too

NC-4 with Olmsted propeller

experienced difficulty breaking the surface, Breese threw two large cans of lubricating oil overboard. She returned to land and waited for NC-3 to be ready to fly.

Off at Last!

It was 1736, May 16, and at last favorable weather and sea conditions prevailed for getaways from Trepassey Bay to start the world's first transatlantic flight. Towers had planned from the start to take advantage of a full moon the night of May 14 for the flight, but on May 16 the moon was still nearly full. The course was laid out from Trepassey direct to Horta, on Fayal, or to Ponta Delgada, on San Miguel Island, in the Azores, and then on to Lisbon, Portugal, and Plymouth, England. The aviators were enthusiastic, but the flight had many dangers. All three seaplanes would undergo frightening and precipitous moments.

Observing all the people waiting to witness the getaways, one would have thought the entire population in the Trepassey area had turned out. The seaplane's engines roared, and after extra-long takeoff runs the seaplanes got airborne as the sun was setting: NC-3 at 1806, NC-4 at 1807, and NC-1 at 1809.

Washington, D.C., Weather Bureau forecasters and the local forecaster on *Aroostook* predicted overcast cloud layers, clearing rainstorms upon arrival at the Azores, and a following tailwind. The forecasters recommended "Go!"[30]

NC–4 departing Trepassey Bay

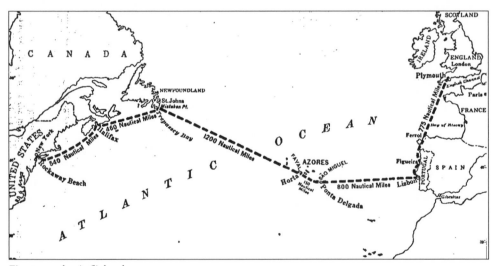

First transatlantic flight plan

Seven mother ships had been positioned to act as tenders. Each tender had Rockaway-trained NC maintenance crews and spare parts on board. Although the seaplane crews did some maintenance work, most was accomplished by the tenders' trained personnel.[31]

Halifax, Nova Scotia	USS *Baltimore* (CM-1)
Trepassey, Newfoundland	USS *Aroostook* (ID-1256)
	USS *Prairie* (AD-5)
Horta Fayal, Azores	USS *Columbia* (CA-16)
Ponta Delgada, Azores	USS *Melville* (AD-2)
Lisbon, Portugal	USS *Rochester* (ACR-2)
	USS *Shawmut* (ID-1255)
Plymouth, England	USS *Aroostook* (proceeded there once NCs departed Trepassey)

Twenty-one U.S. Navy destroyers were stationed fifty miles apart between Mistaken Point, Newfoundland, and the Azores. Every fourth destroyer was equipped to gather and report information on weather and sea conditions. Each destroyer had a station number in sequence, starting from Mistaken Point. Each ship could fire star shells from its three-inch guns, had searchlights to point up into the sky, and displayed lighted numbers on its deck corresponding to its station number. As the seaplanes passed overhead, the destroyers would point their searchlights into the wind and turn toward the next-numbered station.

The battleships USS *Utah* (BB-31), *Florida* (BB-30), *Wyoming* (BB-32), *Texas* (BB-35), and *Arkansas* (BB-33) were positioned along the Trepassy-to-Azores track—two to the north, two to the south, and one off the coast of Ireland. They also reported weather and sea conditions. The navigation, weather reporting, and communications assistance provided by all these ships were to be among the big reasons for the success of the NC aircraft (though counting on them too much would lead to relaxation of attention to detail). NC-4's eventual successful crossing would be greatly enhanced also by the effective use of radio communications and direction finding by the seaplane's radio operator, Ensign Rodd.[32]

> From this point on, all times reported will be based on a Greenwich Mean Time, or GMT.

Flying low, in "aerodynamic ground effect," in a very loose V formation, the three seaplanes headed across Mutton Bay for Mistaken Point and then climbed to six hundred feet. Again the pilots fought rough gusty air. Ahead the visual horizon was hazy as darkness fell. Passing over a large iceberg, the formation broke, and NC-4, on a course well to the north of NC-3, passed her. NC-1 continued to follow NC-3 but was slowly overtaking her.

As a deep-red sun set behind heavy cloudbanks at 2215 GMT on May 16, the seaplanes passed Mistaken Point and changed course for the Azores. Fifteen miles from Mistaken Point they passed the reserve destroyer USS *Greer*, on transatlantic Station 1. The air remained turbulent, and a heavy overcast hid the horizon to the south, but the horizon was clear to the north. Fifty miles out, star shells fired from the destroyer on Station 2 were seen.

Radio communications were established. After passing Station 2 the seaplanes climbed to an altitude of one thousand feet to find smoother air and better visibility.

Conditions a thousand feet above the sea were better. Turbulence was still rough, and visibility was poor, but communications were good. NC-3's navigation lights were turned on, but their circuit was shorted out from earlier salt spray, and the lights immediately failed. Soon after that, the seaplane's interior light circuit failed. It was bad enough that no one on board NC-3 had flown NC seaplanes at night before, but now the pilots could not see the compass or other flight instruments on the instrument panel. Luminous paint on instrument numbers was supposed to shine in the dark, but the glow lasted only about five minutes unless a flashlight was shined on them to brighten them again.

NC-4, with its faster airspeed, was having difficulty staying in formation and clear of NC-3's tail assembly. Very soon after passing Station 3, NC-4 passed so close to NC-3's starboard side that the two seaplanes nearly collided. NC-3 could see NC-4's bright navigation lights, but NC-4 could see only NC-3's dark shape and feel the turbulence as it passed. Stone turned hard right on Read's direction, and that was the last time they saw NC-3 airborne.

Passing Station 6, Read could still see NC-1's navigation lights astern and made the decision to go it alone. As the NC-1 crew was looking for Station 5, it saw a white light flashing dead ahead. Chief Boatswain's Mate Moore was waving a lantern from NC-3's aft hatch to prevent a collision. NC-1 decided to proceed independently. All three seaplanes were now on their own.[33]

An almost full moon rose at 0300 GMT on May 17, and NC-1 and NC-3 were passing numbered ship stations so routinely that the crews grew careless, and as they became tired they relaxed their vigilance. Having easily determined their positions from the destroyers, they did not keep positions obtained by celestial-navigation fixes and annotated on their charts as current as they should have. NC-1's and NC-3's radio-direction-finder (RDF) equipment was not usable.

RDF, celestial navigation, dead reckoning, and destroyers used as beacons were all that was available to help them find their way. If destroyer station sightings and direction finding were taken away, all that would be left to navigate by were the moon, stars, sun, and dead reckoning. Should a heavy overcast preclude seeing celestial objects, the seaplane would be lost, unless it had a current, accurate position and a current wind-drift calculation with which to start a dead-reckoning navigation plot. NC-4's celestial navigation was more up to date than those of the other aircrafts, and, thanks to Ensign Rodd's very capable use of NC-4's radios, they still had very good RDF capability.[34]

Weather and events were about to worsen. Instead of improving conditions, daybreak brought many more problems. Fog, rain, and rough air intensified, obscuring the sun, horizon, and ocean surface and making flight more difficult. As NC-4 was passing destroyer Station 13, at 0625 GMT on May 17, NC-1 radioed NC-4 asking if it had heard from NC-3. Two minutes previously, at 0623, NC-3 had passed Station 13. A short time later NC-3 was heard requesting a weather report from Station 16. Conditions became more difficult for NC-4 upon reaching Station 15. Between Station 15 and the Azores, as NC-4 maneuvered to stay clear of rain squalls, fog obscured the horizon and reduced visibility. Station 16 was the last destroyer NC-4 sighted on this leg to the Azores, due to fog and rain.

The Sagas of NC-1 and NC-3

Both NC-1 and NC-3 were now lost in the fog. Between Stations 17 and 18, NC-3 was in trouble, far off course in fog. When NC-1 passed Station 17, the seaplane's chart showed it fifteen miles north of the ship's reported position. Was the ship's navigation or NC-1's off by fifteen miles?

NC-1 was, in fact, unknowingly, two hundred miles northwest of Fayal Bank, off Corvo. As it turned out, neither NC-1's nor NC-3's radio direction finders would function, because of ignition interference from the two center tandem engines, located directly over the RDF equipment. NC-3's and NC-1's radio officers were in a hurry prior to departure from NAS Rockaway. They installed their RDFs in a quick and easy installation place. Ensign Rodd understood the ignition interference problem with high-frequency radios and instead installed NC-4's RDF outboard, away from the center tandem engines. Celestial navigation was out of the question, with clouds obscuring the sky.

Shortly before passing Station 17, Ensign Rodd on NC-4 heard NC-3 communicating with Ponta Delgada. NC-4 did not see Station 17, but she received a radio report that she had passed the station at 0745 GMT on May 17. At 0931 GMT, Station 17 advised NC-4 that NC-3 had called with a "rush" message that was too weak to understand. This was the last message received from NC-3.

The Loss of NC-1

An hour before noon, Bellinger ordered pilots Mitscher and Barin to climb NC-1 to 3,200 feet to obtain visual flight conditions above the fog.[35] After two hours without locating any destroyer stations or seeing the ocean surface, Bellinger ordered his pilots to descend again in an attempt to regain visual conditions under the clouds. NC-1 broke out of the clouds only seventy-five feet above the sea's surface. No ships were in sight.[36]

Bellinger decided to land and shut down the center engines so RDF could be used. Fog and tired eyes had deceived the NC-1 crew into believing the sea was running at only ten feet. Landing at 1310 GMT on May 17, they found seas running at least twenty feet, or forty feet from trough to crest. In addition, there was a strong crosswind blowing parallel to the swells. They could not get airborne again unless the wind and seas moderated. They could not know that they were a mere forty miles northeast of Flores.[37]

NC-1 buried its bow deeply in a wave, breaking wing struts and tail beams. The wing panels filled with seawater, and it became necessary to slash the wing's fabric to drain it. Bilge pumps could not stay ahead of the water pouring into the hull, and all hands had to bail to keep ahead of it. Fortunately, after NC-1 had drifted backward with her nose into the wind for five hours, a lookout on the Greek steam freighter *Ionia,* out of Newport News, Virginia, and bound for Gibraltar, sighted the downed aircraft in the distance at

1800 GMT, just as fog closed in. The steamer began a search pattern and located NC-1, put a pulling boat over the side, and recovered the crew at 1820, just before dark. *Ionia* resumed course for Gibraltar. *Ionia* did not have a marine radio, but after the NC-1 crew told the master who they were and that the U.S. Navy was searching for them, it was not difficult to convince him to transport them to USS *Columbia* at Horta.

Ionia took NC-1 in tow, but after only two hours the line broke and the seaplane drifted in the high seas. The destroyer USS *Gridley* arrived on the scene, but the NC crew remained on board *Ionia* while *Gridley* stayed with the drifting NC-1, planning to attempt a tow at daybreak. The destroyer USS *Fairfax* arrived the following morning and relieved *Gridley*. The next day, at 1940 GMT, when *Fairfax* tried to tie a towline on NC-1, the seaplane capsized, broke up, and sank from sight.[38]

NC-1 in tow by pulling boat from USS *Fairfax*

NC-3's Plight

At noon on May 17, NC-3 had been looking for Station 15. Towers was sure that he was substantially south of the intended track and turned north. Having climbed to get on top of the fog, NC-3 was now at 4,300 feet. It descended two thousand feet through a hole in the clouds to a flight path beneath them. Before descending, the crew had seen Station 14 ahead, firing star shells, but now the destroyer was invisible. For an hour they tried to obtain RDF bearings, but nothing worked, and they had only two hours of fuel remaining. They were in the same situation that NC-1 faced: the only choice was to land on the open sea and try to obtain an RDF navigational fix.

Hitting the first swell hard, the seaplane "porpoised" and skipped on a couple of wave tops before slowing to a stop. On landing at 1330 GMT on May 17, the center forward engine struts buckled, flying wires slackened, the aileron wires became very slack, the hull leaked, a hull truss wire broke, and several longitudinal frames buckled and cracked. Aircraft damage and eight-to-twelve-foot seas—sixteen to twenty-four feet between trough and crest—precluded a getaway from the surface. A ground swell added four to five feet to the wave heights. No one responded to NC-3's radio calls, but it did manage to obtain a RDF bearing on *Columbia*. The crew heard a radio report that NC-1 was also down with a damaged wing and that destroyers were searching for her, and another that NC-4 had landed at Horta and was alongside *Columbia*. Shortly thereafter Towers fixed NC-3's position at forty-five miles southeast of Horta.[39]

NC-3 was riding comfortably, with improvised sea anchors made of canvas buckets holding her bow into the wind and seas, and the crew was alternating two-hour watches so men not on watch could get some rest. NC-3 was drifting tail first toward the island of Horta. Taxiing on the outboard engines was out of the question, since it would push the aircraft, causing the bow to dig into the swells and damage the hull further. The only choice was to sail and drift. The crew wished they had the CG-1104 emergency radio voice transmitter they had left behind at Trepassey to save weight.

Shortly before 0800 GMT, the port lower wing's rear edge caught a wave and dug into the sea, carrying away, or breaking, the wing all the way from the rear spar to its trailing edge. As the wind and seas continued to increase, the lower elevator continued to dig into the sea, each time damaging the hull. Damage to the wing got worse, and Towers made the decision to cut the damaged portion free. Seas were steadily growing in height. At approximately 0800 Commander Richardson was awakened by "a noise which sounded like the hull breaking in two. The lower elevator was caught in a wave wrenching the tail surfaces badly, and the noise I heard was the whipping of the control column."

Climbing cross swells occasionally broke over the lower wing. When they receded, water sucked at the cloth, making a sound like a rattling tin roof. The seas steadily broke the wing's ribs, one after the other, causing the wing's cloth to sag and creating big bowls to trap and hold water. This was a danger that could capsize the seaplane. The wing's cloth had to be sliced.

At 1130 GMT on May 18, the situation worsened. The port wing-tip float broke and floated away, its loss threatening to capsize the seaplane. The crew started sending SOS signals on their radio and flew the national ensign upside down as the international distress signal. No one heard or saw them.

All members of the crew took turns standing on the starboard wing to keep the ship upright, pumping water out of the hull, tightening wing-tip float wires, and cutting away new wing damage. About 1200 GMT the crew sighted a slope of land belonging to Pico, a seven-thousand-foot volcanic mountain, the highest point in the Azores. Using a bearing to Pico and taking a sun line using the sextant, Towers fixed their position forty-five miles southeast of Pico. Towers discarded any idea of a water taxi and chose to sail to leeward tail first, with a following wind, on a course north of San Miguel. They would spend another night at sea in fifty-foot seas and forty-five-knot winds. At sundown the crew discovered that keeping a man on the starboard wing to prevent capsizing was no longer necessary.

By 0600 GMT the next day the wind had hauled around and was blowing NC-3 off course. The best the crew could do was to hold a southeasterly heading, which would take them south of San Miguel, widely missing it. Luck prevailed, and the wind shifted so they could resume an easterly course toward the island. Chief Boatswain's Mate Moore sighted San Miguel at 1023 GMT, and the NC attempted to contact USS *Columbia* on the radio. Although the operator could hear USS *Baltimore* in Halifax, no one heard him. At about 1600 it became apparent to NC-3's crew that they could make it to Ponta Delgada sometime near 1800.

After two days and nights, they drifted within sight of land. As they got closer, objects became clearer. They could identify the lighthouse, a radio station, a sugar factory, houses, and trees. Just as they saw Ponta Delgada's breakwater, the starboard wing-tip float carried away and had to be cut loose. Towers stationed a man on what was left of each wing to balance the seaplane. The men walked in and out as balance conditions continuously changed with the seas. Confident of maintaining the seaplane's balance on the sea, they started the two outboard engines. The engines vibrated badly, but enough power was available for NC-3 to taxi into the harbor. It passed the breakwater with three men on the wings.

As NC-3 was entering Ponta Delgada Harbor at 1625 GMT on May 19, the destroyer USS *Harding* steamed toward them "with a bone in her teeth"—that is, at high speed—and bore down on the seaplane. Nonetheless, the NC-3 crew's pride told them to arrive under their own power, not towed by a destroyer. They rushed to correct the national ensign from a distress signal to right side up, indicating normal cruising. Towers flashed a message on the Aldis lamp for the destroyer to "stand close by as we run in under power." After fifty-two hours and 205 miles on the ocean, NC-3's flight was over.[40]

NC-3 off port side of USS *Harding*

Damaged NC-3 moored in Ponta Delgada Harbor

The Saga of NC-4 and Success

To retrace the time line again, NC-4, a little more than two hundred miles from Corvo, the westernmost island in the Azores, climbed to stay out of fog. As the seaplane approached three thousand feet, Hinton was on the flight controls. Rough air jolted the seaplane, and one wing dropped rapidly causing a steep bank, the compass spinning as the seaplane fell rapidly into a spin through gray, heavy fog. Taking control of the seaplane, Stone recognized, from his experience as a Navy chief test pilot, that the aircraft was in a stall and spin. With only a faint sun glimmering through the fog for a reference point, he recovered from the stall and spin, resuming normal flight at 1,200 feet and climbing to an altitude above the clouds and into sunlight. Once again, as during the hangar fire at NAS Rockaway, Stone's experience and quick reactions had prevented the catastrophic loss of NC-4.

Stone remarked of the stall and spin after the flight: "This did not last for any length of time, only about thirty seconds—we got out of it quick!"[41]

At 0945 GMT on May 17, NC-4 ran into heavy fog just as Station 18 radioed Station 19 that it had passed. At 1030 GMT, Ensign Rodd radioed Stations 19 and 20, asking if they had fog. Station 19 reported thick surface fog, and 20 reported mist. NC-4 was flying between fog and clouds at 3,400 feet, and Read wanted to descend if it was clear at the surface. At 1113 GMT, NC-4 requested weather conditions from Station 21, which replied with surface conditions: visibility ten miles, wind 220 degrees. Station 21's RDF bearing from NC-4 was twenty-five degrees left of the seaplane's heading. The RDF bearing on

As you will recall, NC-1 and NC-3 had experienced the same difficulty maintaining aircraft control in rough air between NAS Rockaway and Trepassey Bay.
During NC seaplane design development, wind-tunnel tests predicted a strong
travel of the center of lift (CL) fore and aft according to changes in aerodynamic
angle of attack, the angle between the direction of wind before passing over the
airfoil and the chord line of the airfoil. The original design had the center of gravity
(CG) located 37 percent of the way back from the leading edge on the wing's
chord. Initial actual aircraft weighing and balance calculations identified the distance
as 47 percent. Wind-tunnel tests and aircraft trials later showed that balance could
be maintained as long as the wing's angle of attack was held to eight degrees nose
down or speed maintained at approximately ninety miles per hour.

Dr. Hunsaker had cautioned in his design memorandum, "These flying boats are
notoriously difficult to keep from stalling in rough air or at reduced speed."[42]

Station 21, plotted on Read's navigation chart, told Read that NC-4 would pass south of
Corvo and make landfall at Flores.

At that time only two hours of fuel remained. Read saw an opening in the fog, and Stone
descended to 1,500 feet, just below the cloud layer. A few more breaks in the fog revealed
the sea, and Read saw a tidal rip, indicating they were getting close to a shoreline. On
closer examination, Read determined that the tidal rip was really Flores's southern shore.
Read ordered Stone to make a turn to the right to parallel the shoreline and avoid high
terrain inland. Lieutenant Commander Read later remarked, "As we rounded a point a
peaceful farmhouse came into view in the midst of cultivated fields on side hills. That scene
appeared to us far more beautiful than any other ever will."[43]

Read set a course for Ponta Delgada, 250 miles away. To stay clear of clouds and fog,
Stone continued descending, holding just below the clouds. Racing the fog bank to Horta,
Stone had now descended to twenty feet off the ocean surface and passed the next station
at masthead height. When they missed the next station, it became evident that they could
not reach Ponta Delgada that day. Working his navigation chart for a dead-reckoned course
to Fayal Island, Read had Stone change course southward toward Fayal and *Columbia*. The
island came into view, and they flew in rough air down the coast to Horta's narrow harbor.
Read's navigation had to have been correct, since the harbor terrain was too high and
narrow to allow the seaplane to turn around. But it was in fact at Horta where Stone made
a smooth landing at 1325 GMT.

Reaching Horta, Fayal, and *Columbia*, NC-4 had completed a fifteen-hour, thirteen-
minute flight from Trepassey. NC-4 moored behind *Columbia*, with emotions running high.
The ship's crewmen were waving their hats and cheering NC-4's crew. There were also
those who, in their exuberance, did not think. Several motor launches, with crews jumping
for joy, ran at high speed toward NC-4. One did not stop or shear away from NC-4 in time
and bumped the seaplane, punching a hole in the hull. Lieutenant Commander Read was
livid that someone would think so little of their great sacrifice that they would not stand

clear out of respect. On the other hand, Read was grateful they had arrived safely and had achieved their great goal.[44]

The riskiest part of the transatlantic flight was now behind the NC-4 crew, and its success was a "shot in the arm" for the Navy during a time of postwar downsizing and cutbacks in military spending. Transit of the Atlantic Ocean by air demonstrated the continued relevance of the Navy's ability to project power abroad. This was a very important capability in the new, changing world of U.S. diplomacy, with its aim to protect trade routes to the expanding global markets in Europe, Africa, the Middle East, and the Pacific Rim.

While at Horta, Lieutenant Breese replaced the semirotary auxiliary water hand pump with a standard bilge pump. On the flight from Trepassey to Horta, the center flat-sided oil-tank baffle plate seams had begun to split, and the split had increased with time. Repairs to the tank's seams and carburetor jet cleaning were required at Horta. Close inspection of NC-4's propellers revealed that no cracks or splits had resulted from the ocean crossing.[45]

May 20 SITREP (Situation Report)

Fifteen and one-half hours from departure from Trepassey, NC-3's flight was over. Of the three seaplanes, NC-3 had arrived first at Ponta Delgada but was in no shape to fly farther. NC-4 was in Horta, delayed by weather from flying to Ponta Delgada. NC-1 had sunk from sight. In the afternoon visibility improved, and in less than two hours NC-4 flew to and landed at Ponta Delgada. NC-4's crew was met by the governor, the mayor, and a large local population.

Two Waiting in the Wings

NC-4 still had not arrived in Europe. She would not have completed a transatlantic flight until she reached Portugal, and three competitors were nipping at her heels. At 1538 local Newfoundland time, Hawker and McKenzie-Grieve lifted off for Ireland in their Sopwith, *Atlantic*. They would experience much the same weather as the NC seaplanes, but worse yet, they would experience an in-flight engine failure. They managed an engine restart at one hundred feet above the sea but were out of engine cooling water, with an overheating engine. They ditched *Atlantic* into the sea midway to Ireland. The two men were rescued by the Danish freighter *Mary*. *Atlantic* had been eliminated from competition.[46]

At about 1630, on May 18, in Newfoundland, Raynham and Morgan attempted takeoff in their Martinsyde biplane, but a wind gust pushed heavily on her side. Her landing gear collapsed, causing a crash. The Martinsyde too was eliminated from competition.[47]

Waiting in the wings were Rear Admiral Kerr and Handley Page, with their Handley Page V/1500 being assembled at Harbor Grace, and the just-arrived Vickers Vimy bomber being uncrated for assembly at St. John's. Two Royal Air Force officers, Arthur Whitten-Brown and John Alcock, were to crew the Vimy.[48] They did not know that the NC-4 had arrived at Ponta Delgada.

Racing to the Finish Line

The May 26 weather forecast for the morning of May 27 between Ponta Delgada and Lisbon was a go! A "first-light" getaway was planned for the morning. Everyone thought the takeoff would be easier than at Trepassey, since the fuel load for NC-4 was two thousand pounds lighter, enough for eight hundred nautical miles, plus reserve. But the early morning getaway was to prove as difficult as at Trepassey—only, a too-heavy seaplane was not the problem.

Heavy seas rolled into the harbor from a storm offshore, and the outboard port engine carburetor jets clogged with shredded rubber gasket material from fuel-line joints. It took two hours to change out the carburetor, and then NC-4 was airborne, at 1017 GMT, May 27, bound for Lisbon, with Stone at the controls. Instantly, Read had Rodd transmit a message to Admiral Jackson on Ponta Delgada, thanking him for his hospitality.

In Lisbon, the cruiser USS *Rochester,* flagship of RADM Charles P. Plunkett, USN, had prearranged to sound her steam whistle when NC-4 was airborne from Ponta Delgada. Her whistle now blasted loudly, announcing to all of Lisbon that NC-4 was on the way.[49]

The Navy had stationed fourteen destroyers, numbered one to fourteen, for the eight-hundred-nautical-mile, ten-hour leg to Lisbon. *Rochester* also stationed a detail in Lisbon's central park, the Parca do Commercio, on the bank of the Tagus River. The men set up a large blackboard that showed NC-4's progress toward Lisbon. On board the seaplane, Lieutenant Stone's handwritten marginal note on a chart showing destroyer stations, as reprinted in the Curtiss Aeroplane and Motor Corporation 1919 publication *The Flight across the Atlantic,* said, "Journey went very well from here on."

NC-4 overflew Station 1 at 1112 GMT, and Rodd reported strong signals from destroyers as far away as 350 miles. Two minor problems made the flight more interesting. Passing Station 4, NC-4 was eight degrees off course to the south, and between Stations 7 and 9 it flew through scattered rain squalls. NC-4 had an ordinary ship's compass, mounted on two sets of gimbals. Investigation now showed that the bouncing getaway in heavy seas at Ponta Delgada had bumped the compass off its gimbals, causing the eight-degree error. After the crew replaced the compass on its gimbals, no further problem was observed.

The crews from NC-1 and NC-3 arrived in Lisbon by ship several days ahead of NC-4. The American minister at Lisbon planned a formal ball, and the Majestic Club a formal dinner for the NC crews, but after several days they could wait no longer, and the ball and dinner were held for the men of NC-1, NC-3, and Portuguese navy and aviation officers.

At 1720 GMT the flagship sent a message from Rear Admiral Plunkett to Lieutenant Commander Read: "Fine work, come along." At 1739 GMT, Read spotted the westernmost point of land in Europe, the Cabo da Roca lighthouse. When NC-4 passed Station 13 at 1835 GMT, *Rochester* requested its estimated time of arrival in Lisbon. Read had Rodd send, "Expect to arrive about eight o'clock GMT. Please have searchlight on water trained into the wind." They had finally passed Station 14.[50]

On May 27, at approximately 2045 GMT, NC-4 came into view of the crowd at Lisbon. Stone approached straight up the Tagus River to the harbor, made a wide circle to the south and then a gentle glide on final approach to a landing.

As she was landing, at 2101 GMT, the flagship and Portuguese warships fired a twenty-one-gun salute. Ship whistles blasted, and the crowd cheered. NC-4 taxied to a mooring astern of her mother ship.

NC-4 landing on Tagus River, Lisbon, Portugal

NC-4 moored behind mother ship

Little did Hawker and MacKenzie-Grieve know that NC-4 would land on the Tagus River in Lisbon before they could even leave Newfoundland. They were eliminated from competition.[51]

Lieutenant Commander Read and his crew were greeted by Commander Towers as they boarded *Rochester*. There they were greeted also by Rear Admiral Plunkett and the rest of NC-1's and NC-3's crews, the Portuguese minister of marine, the American and British ministers, and many other Portuguese naval and army officers.

Rochester's Marine band struck up the "Star-Spangled Banner" as all came to attention and saluted. A spotlight illuminated the NC crews. The Portuguese government held a reception for NC-4's crew on board *Rochester* with a Portuguese hundred-piece band. All U.S. and Portuguese warships in the harbor had "dressed ship," with their signal flags displayed from bow to stern. Even though NC-1 and NC-3 had not completed the journey, the Portuguese government on May 27 decorated everyone in all three crews with its highest medal, the Order of the Tower and Sword.[52]

Criteria: The Military Order of the Tower and Sword is Portugal's highest award. It is awarded for exceptional and outstanding deeds of heroism and to reward outstanding acts of abnegation and sacrifice for Portugal or mankind. This award was established by King D. Afonso V in 1459. It is traced from the ancient Order of the Sword, an order of chivalry.

The first transatlantic flight—forty-four hours and thirty-six minutes, and 3,308 nautical miles—was a grand accomplishment. It would be eight more years before Charles A. Lindbergh would cross the Atlantic.

With little notice in Lisbon, but enthusiastic coverage in England, Hawker and MacKenzie-Grieve arrived in London on May 27. After World War I, England needed some heroes. The British press went overboard, with gushing columns of type. The British government struck a special medal for Hawker and MacKenzie-Grieve for their attempt.[53]

Stone's Portuguese Order
of the Tower and Sword

The crew of the NC-4, in Lisbon. Left to right: Chief Machinist's Mate Edward H. Howard, USN, engineer; LT James L. Breese, USN, engineer; LTJG Walter Hinton, USNRF, copilot; LT Elmer Stone, USCG, pilot; LCDR A. C. Read, commanding officer and navigator, NC-4. Missing from photo is ENS Herbert C. Rodd, USN, radio officer.

One of the humorous occasions in Lisbon is shown in the photograph opposite. Lieutenant Commander Read looks sternly at Lieutenant (junior grade) Hinton, while Lieutenant Stone looks on with a smile. Hinton wears his naval aviator wings beneath his service ribbons, when his prized wings were supposed to be worn above them. Read is not happy.

Another humorous event occurred after landing in Lisbon, immediately after all the official festivities. Working long hours and sharing dangerous moments together, Lieutenant Stone had befriended Chief Machinist's Mate Rhodes. Both thought it appropriate to blow off tension and celebrate by visiting as many of Lisbon's bars that night as they could. Lieutenant Commander Read did not approve of liquor and was a temperance man. Besides, he had planned a morning departure for Plymouth. So Read sent the shore patrol to town to haul them back.[54]

First Across, Now on to Plymouth

Plymouth, England, was planned as the end point for the NC transatlantic flight, even though "the Atlantic was crossed" when NC-4 landed at Lisbon. It was the three-hundredth anniversary of the *Mayflower*'s departure from Plymouth for the New World, and for the first transatlantic flight from the United States to land at Plymouth would be seen as a powerful declaration to the world.

After NC-4's arrival in Lisbon on May 27, activity was concentrated on preparing her for the Plymouth flight. No major maintenance was required, but fabric had loosened from the lower horizontal stabilizer ribs, as had also occurred at Horta due to failure of the fabric lacing. Being a stickler for detail, Lieutenant Stone removed tape strips, secured the fabric, and replaced the tape. He also noticed that the trailing edge of the wings between the hull and outboard engines had partially loosened and been torn from the spars by water spray on getaways. The cup strips and rib webs were broken. No repairs could be made.

Gasoline feed pipes for the two outboard engines were air bound after every overnight layover. This condition was caused by the position of the strainers between the cylinders, resulting in an inline inverted siphon. Vents were depicted on the seaplane's engineering drawings, but in the rush to be first across they had not been installed. Tape and fairings on braces for wings and struts from the hull to the lower wing had been partially carried away by water jetting through them on getaway at Ponta Delgada and from mooring buoys. Stone covered them with electrician's friction tape.[55]

On the morning of May 28, *Rochester* was getting under way for Plymouth, with Towers and the other NC crew members on board. *Rochester* would arrive in Plymouth around noon on the 30th.[56]

Hinton requested to fly the getaway from Lisbon, since Stone had made all takeoffs and landings. At 0529 GMT on May 30, NC-4 made its getaway down the Tagus River, then made a wide half-circle turn, flying back upriver at a low altitude for a news-media photography opportunity and a farewell to the citizens of Lisbon. It cleared the shoreline at 0555 GMT, and at 0612 Read had Rodd send a message to USS *Shawmut* for forwarding to the American minister: "Request you express to all heartfelt appreciation of commanding officer and crew of NC-4 for wonderful welcome. Read."[57]

Destroyers were again stationed, this time between Lisbon and Plymouth. Stations A through E were deployed along the shoreline between Lisbon and the western tip of Spain. Stations 1 through 5 were deployed from offshore of the northwest corner of Spain to just short of Brest, the westernmost point of France.

About two hours into the flight, near Figueira, Portugal, the crew saw cooling water leaking from the outboard port engine water jacket. They could not allow for the radiator to run low of water and cause the engine to overheat and seize up. At 0723 GMT, NC-4 landed on the Mondego River at Figueira. Inspection revealed a very minor leak.

Breese and his engineers repaired the leak "by pumping in a can of radiator antileak into the water system." Low tide bared sandbars, blocking the river and forcing a delay in departure until high tide, 1338. Since they could not now make it to Plymouth before dark, a decision was made to land at Ferrol, Spain. They arrived with a smooth landing at Ferrol at 1647 GMT; there USS *Harding* met them to act as a tender.[58]

At 0627 GMT on May 31, NC-4 departed Ferrol for Plymouth. As she approached Brest, haze, mist, and low clouds required the seaplane to descend to two hundred feet. The crew missed sighting several destroyer stations as a result of low visibility, but communications with them remained strong.

Passing Brest, NC-4 flew over land, making a wide circle over the city, and then took a heading for Plymouth. Navigation was not a problem. Flying out of the mist, with Plymouth off her bow, NC-4 made a westward circle to see ship locations and the position of their tender and mooring buoy. With an easy glide, Stone landed NC-4 inside Plymouth Harbor's Cattewater at 1325 GMT.[59]

Plymouth Harbor was in formal naval dress to welcome the NC-4 crew; all naval vessels had dressed ship. Mayor J. B. Brown had proclaimed May 30 a holiday, so red-white-and-

National Archives photograph of famous painting of NC-4 in full color

blue bunting was on city buildings and the Stars and Stripes were everywhere. The Royal Air Force was prepared to send a flight of three Port/Felixstowe F-2A flying boats to escort NC-4 to Plymouth. Thousands of citizens turned out to see NC-4 land. Flying out of the haze at 1,500 feet, NC-4 arrived at 1419 GMT, escorted by the three British aircraft. Read asked Stone to circle Plymouth Harbor as ships' bells rang, whistles blasted, and flares fired. NC-4 had flown eight hundred miles on the Lisbon-to-Plymouth leg, for a total transatlantic flight of 3,936 nautical miles, or 4,526 statute miles, and a flight time of fifty-two hours thirty-one minutes.

Stone taxied to the mooring buoy, and Read turned NC-4 over to a group of USS *Aroostook* machinist's mates. Read and his crew boarded *Rochester*'s captain's gig, bound for the flagship. Admiral Plunkett arranged for a Marine band to play as the NC-4 crew formed a reception line to greet a very long line of visitors before departing for *Aroostook*.

Shower, Shave, and Shine

Finally on board *Aroostook,* on which they had left clean uniforms at Trepassey, the NC-4 crew cleaned up and put on fresh uniforms in preparation for ceremonies ashore.[60]

Admiral Plunkett met the crew in his barge, which they boarded for transport to Plymouth's Barbican Monument and the city's greeting ceremonies. They disembarked on the stone stairs leading to the monument commemorating the Pilgrims' departure point

Lord Mayor Brown's welcome at Plymouth, England

for the New World. The crew was greeted by Mayor Brown, dressed in ceremonial garb—a long crimson robe trimmed with fur, a gold chain necklace, wig, and cocked hat. Three mace bearers and the city's clerk also wore wigs.

The mayor proclaimed:[61]

Plymouth is always a point of historic interest to Americans. The memorable sailing of the Pilgrim fathers from this spot, though comparatively unnoticed at the time, was an event which has proved to be a point in history of immeasurable interest. Mainly out of that small beginning a mighty people has sprung up, and today, in most dramatic fashion, their descendants have crossed back to us in a way never dreamed of by our forefathers, and equaling in scientific development and daring the greatest imaginings of Jules Verne. Your flight today brings our two great countries together in the warmest fellowship, Gentlemen, I salute you and welcome you to England.

Admiral Plunkett and NC crews en route to Grand Hotel

At the conclusion of the ceremony, Admiral Plunkett and the NC-4 crew were driven to the Grand Hotel for lunch.[62]

The next morning, June 2, Admiral Plunkett and all the NC crews took the train to Paddington Station in London, then to the Royal Aero Club, and on to Hendon Field for an impressive air show. After three days in London, the three NC crews were ordered to

French NC-4 commemorative medal by Morian

Paris, France, to meet the U.S. Navy CNO. From there the CNO took the three NC crews to the French Ministry of Marine and then to meet President Woodrow Wilson, who was attending the World War I peace treaty negotiations.

President Wilson told them, "The entire American nation is proud of your achievement. I am glad to see you and to shake your hand, and I am glad to give you my warmest congratulations. I am happy to be able to say, personally, how proud I am of all of you. The whole of America and the Navy is most proud of your achievement."

While at the Ministry of Marine, the French government presented individuals of the NC-4 crew with a one-of-a-kind silver commemorative medal.

Criteria: French silver piece commemorating NC-4 aviators for the first transatlantic flight.

The same day, back in England, June 5, Major General J. E. B. Seely, the British House of Commons Undersecretary of State for Air, held a luncheon for the NC crews. A number of high-ranking notables were there, men from governments and industry as well as many aviation enthusiasts. Included among them was the Prince of Wales and MacKenzie-Grieves, who sat next to Lieutenant Commander Read.[63]

Four days later, on June 9, Commander Towers and the NC-4 crew reported to the British Air Ministry. The officers were decorated with the Royal Air Force Cross (AFC), and Rhodes was decorated with the British Air Force Medal (AFM) for noncommissioned personnel.[64] Only service ribbons were presented, since the awards were so new the medals themselves had not yet been struck.

From London, all were returned to Paris for a week's leave to rest and relax. Following that leave they boarded USS *Zeppelin* for a return voyage to New York, where they were treated to a ticker-tape parade.[65]

On November 11, 1920, Armistice Day, Assistant Secretary of the Navy Roosevelt, standing on the steps of the Navy Department, decorated the NC crews with the Navy Cross for "distinguished service in making the first successful Trans-Atlantic flight."[66]

> Criteria: Awarded to a person in the naval service who distinguishes himself or herself by extraordinary heroism not justifying the award of the Medal of Honor. To warrant this distinctive decoration, the act or the execution of duty must be performed in the presence of great danger or at a great personal risk.

By the end of 1919 the British had struck medals for the AFC and AFM awarded earlier, and the Prince of Wales desired to properly present the medals.[67]

> Criteria: The Royal Air Force Cross was instituted in June 1918 as a variant of the Victoria Cross. It was awarded to officers and warrant officers for courage or devotion to duty while flying, though not in active operations against the enemy. It was not officially named, as other officer's medals were. During World War I, approximately 680 were awarded. During World War II, approximately 2,000 were awarded. Generally there are no citations in the *London Gazette,* although there could be indications of the nature of the recipient's service which had led to the AFC being awarded. Since 1993, this medal has been awarded to all qualifying RAF ranks.

Lieutenant Novell and Bernt Balchen on New York's Broadway for New York's reception of the first transatlantic flight aviators

Above: Franklin D. Roosevelt, on the Navy Department steps, decorating NC crews with the Navy Cross

Left: Stone's Navy Cross

Right: Stone's British Royal Air Force Cross awarded June 9, 1919, by the Prince of Wales

In reply refer to No.

NAVY DEPARTMENT
OFFICE OF NAVAL INTELLIGENCE
WASHINGTON

APN:CMM

September 25, 1919.

From: Director of Naval Intelligence
To: First Lieutenant Elmer Stone, U.S.C.G.

1.   It is the intention of the Prince of Wales, while he is in Washington in November, to present certain officers, with British Decorations, which have not yet been conferred upon them. At this time me will present over again any British Decorations which have been sent to Officers of the Army and Navy, provided the officer is present at the ceremony and will send back to this office his decoration several days beforehand in order that it may again be presented.

2.   It is not the intention of the Department to order any officer to Washington for this purpose. Please indicate your desire in this matter, as it is merely intended by the Prince of Wales to present the decorations over again only in case the officer so desires.

3.   Please indicate your wish and also if you know of any officer who has received the British Decoration, that may not be a matter of record, it will be very good of you if you will convey this information to him.

A. P. Niblack

Navy Intelligence letter of September 25, 1919

Eleven years later, on May 23, 1930, President Herbert Hoover awarded a specially struck Congressional Gold Medal to the crew of the NC-4.[68]

President Hoover presenting Congressional Gold Medal to individuals of NC-4 crew

Miniature Medal Criteria: On April 25, 1935, Congress authorized a miniature medal, one and a quarter inches in diameter, for wear on the uniform. This medal is identical to the full-sized medal except for its size and that it is worn suspended from a ribbon. The ribbon consists of five stripes of equal width in red, white, blue, green, and red. Red, white, and blue are the colors of the United States; green and red are the colors of Portugal.

Above: Special Congressional NC-4 Service Ribbon

Left: Special Congressional NC-4 Medal

On August 23, 1919, Stone received a written commendation from Assistant Secretary of the Navy Roosevelt:[69]

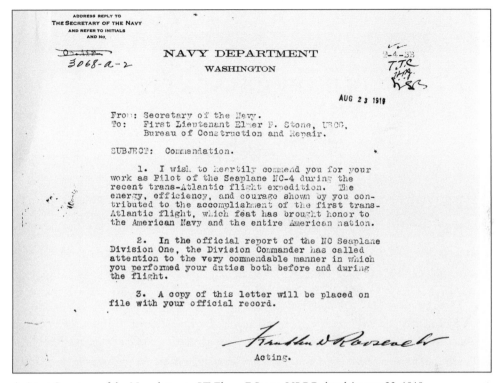

Assistant Secretary of the Navy letter to LT Elmer F. Stone, USCG, dated August 23, 1919

Personnel of NC-4. Left to right: copilot LTJG Walter Hinton, USNRF; commanding officer LCDR A. C. Read, USN; pilot LT Elmer F. Stone, USCG

CHAPTER SEVEN

Evolving the Naval Aviation Test Organization

1913–1926

*N*avy operational and technical resources and capabilities were organized by bureaus, headed by admirals and organized by major operational or technical capability. Examples were the Bureau of Ships (BUSHIPS), the Bureau of Ordnance (BUORD), and the Bureau of Navigation (BUNAV). Bureaus reported to the Chief of Naval Operations at the Navy Department. In 1913, naval aviation was so new that no bureau had yet been established to manage aviation resources and

RADM William A. Moffett, first chief of BUAERO, in cockpit

its programmed growth. Instead, a new organization was established with only one aviator-engineer, LCDR Holden C. Richardson, USN, in the Aircraft Division of the Bureau of Construction and Repair at the Washington Navy Yard. Later, in 1917, more aviators with engineering disciplines were assigned. The division's director was CAPT William A. Moffett, USN. Aircraft testing was assigned to a new Board of Inspection and Survey in the Bureau of Steam Engineering. Both the division and board were composed of experienced test pilots that were Naval and Coast Guard Academy graduates grounded in engineering, physics, and mathematics. These same early test pilots would become the senior leaders in the Navy, Marine Corps, and Coast Guard who developed aviation capabilities within their services and whose leadership would later influence the outcome of a second world war.

Much later, on July 12, 1921, the two organizational structures (engineering and flight test) would merge, by act of Congress, to become the Bureau of Aeronautics (BUAERO, later BUAER), and Captain Moffett would be promoted to rear admiral on July 25 of that year. The same act of Congress predicated Rear Admiral Moffett's assignment as chief upon his qualification as an "aircraft pilot or observer" within one year of appointment. The first qualification requirements for Naval Aircraft Observer were promulgated on March 22, 1922, and Rear Admiral Moffett qualified on June 17. Navy Uniform Regulations in 1922 required naval aviation observers to wear the same insignia worn by naval aviators, except the right wing and shield were removed and an O was superimposed on a fouled anchor. The office of Aviation Operations was relocated to a division under the CNO.[1]

1922 naval aviation observer wings (breast pin)

On October 6, 1917, the Secretary of War authorized the Navy use of part of the Army landing field at Anacostia, in the District of Columbia. Approval included erection of two seaplane hangars and ramps on the Anacostia River. By January 1918, NAS Anacostia had been commissioned as a base for short test flights and to provide maintenance for seaplanes on test flights from NAS Hampton Roads, Virginia.

On October 16, the Navy Department assigned 3rd LT E. F. Stone to "temporary command at NAS Rockaway, New York until arrival of a regularly designated Commanding Officer, then you will report to that officer for duty as that Station's Seaplane Officer."[2] For the next eight months, Stone flew seaplanes and amphibians assigned to Rockaway. At the time, NAS Rockaway was an important facility for naval aviation's seaplane development and growth, and Stone's capabilities did not go unnoticed by the Aviation Division of the Bureau of Construction and Repair. On May 15, 1918, he received orders for a change of duty station, to report to Captain Moffett, director of the Aviation Division of the Bureau of Construction and Repair at the Washington Navy Yard.[3] His duties were to travel "between Washington, D.C., and such places within

NAS Anacostia, 1918

a radius of 500 miles thereof, and Miami, Florida, as may be necessary in connection with inspection and trials of sea planes."[4]

Changes in duty assignments were quickly followed by changes in rank. On June 7 Stone was promoted to second lieutenant and on July 1 was promoted once again, to first lieutenant (equivalent to the Navy ranks of lieutenant and lieutenant commander, respectively). Later in the war, the newly established Coast Guard converted from the USRCS rank and rate structure to that of the Navy. Stone became a temporary lieutenant commander on September 25, 1919.[5]

One of Stone's aviation pioneer friends was Army captain Eddie Rickenbacker, the leading world war "ace," with twenty-six aerial combat victories. Rickenbacker had invited Stone and his family over for dinner one evening when Stone's son, Johnny, blurted out to the famous ace, "Captain Rickenbacker, how many Huns did you shoot down?" Captain Rickenbacker was pleased with the question and said, "Johnny, I've written a book about it, and I'll give you a copy that will tell you all about it."

The book, *Fighting the Flying Circus,* about the air war in France, had been published in 1919. It described America's primitive aircraft and flying at twenty thousand feet above sea

McLoughlin's *Aces of the Air*

level, at fifty degrees below zero Fahrenheit, with no oxygen equipment. He wrote in the flyleaf of Johnny's copy, "To my little friend Johnny, may you always have good fortune." Sadly, Johnny did not receive the promised good fortune; he died of meningitis two years later.[6]

Rickenbacker's respect for Stone and Coast Guard aviators was further expressed by his introduction to the book *Aces of the Air,* published by McLoughlin, Inc., of Springfield, Massachusetts, in 1930.

When the world war ended, Congress directed a reduction in military forces. The Navy was limited by law to only six air stations with seaplane squadrons within the continental United States. It was useful for the Navy to give to the Coast Guard its air stations at Morehead City, North Carolina, and at Cape May, New Jersey. Should a new war emerge, the Coast Guard would be transferred to the Navy Department, and these two air stations would effectively enlarge the number available to the Navy for seaplane operations. Additionally, these two air stations were located next to the major shipping routes from the eastern United States to the English Channel and the Mediterranean Sea.

Within the military, reductions in rank and enlisted rates were also initiated. On September 2, 1921, came an order for all Coast Guard officers to be returned to their permanent ranks.

NAVY DEPARTMENT

OFFICE OF NAVAL OPERATIONS

WASHINGTON

In reply refer to Initials
and No.

PNLB-BB

April 7, 1921.

MEMORANDUM.

SUBJECT: Personnel Situation in Technical Bureaus.

1.   It is believed that the failure in the progress of development of Naval Aviation is due to the present
organization and the limited personnel attached to the
aviation sections of the technical bureaus.

2.   It is believed that in the endeavor to push
the tactical operations of aircraft and utilize what was
available, progress in development has been neglected,
and at this stage it is believed that the development
should be pushed to a much greater extent, even at the
expense of tactical operations.

3.   To take steps to remedy the situation, the
following is recommended to be done immediately:

Assign Naval Aviators of the regular line, who
have had sufficient experience in the operation of aircraft, to the bureaus, as follows:

5 Naval Aviators to the Bureau of Ordnance.
3 Naval Aviators to the Bureau of Engineering.
3 Naval Aviators to the Bureau of Construction
                             and Repair.
3 Naval Aviators to the Naval Aircraft Factory.

April 7, 1921, memorandum on naval aviation growth

Stone reverted to lieutenant.[7] It would not be until April 21, 1924, that Stone would be a temporary lieutenant commander again.[8]

Reduction in force within naval aviation resulted in a 12 percent cut in active-duty personnel, including many aviators who had been involved in developing capability and growth. Reductions also had the effect of stifling personnel advancement, and by April 7, 1921, the Navy Department's Office of Naval Operations was concerned about "failure in

The Development and Impact of
Early Flight Testing
on Naval Aviation

NAS Anacostia, 1932

the progress of Naval Aviation." Reorganization and priority changes would be necessary to provide progress and operational capability. In 1926, a Flight Test section was established at NAS Anacostia. In those days, NAS Anacostia consisted of only a dirt-and-grass field with a large double hangar that opened on the west side to a seaplane ramp on the Anacostia River for seaplane and amphibian aircraft testing. The air station was the home command for aircraft trials (i.e., flight tests).[9]

Not much was known about aircraft stability in the early days. Proper operational configuration, which determined weight and balance, was critical to meet contractual requirements and to assure the aircraft's stability under operational conditions. Yet it was "fly, try, and then fix and fly again," followed by a careful analysis after every event. When an aircraft was delivered for acceptance testing—or "aircraft trial," as the tests were known—it was completely inspected to be sure there were no defects and to ensure that it was ready. It was then instrumented and loaded with weights to simulate various equipment, armament, and ammunition. General testing covered handling and stability at high speed, cruising speed, and low speed, and at various altitudes; rate of climb; service ceiling; a dive to terminal velocity (power off); spins and recovery, with and without power; ordnance delivery, release of bombs in dives at various angles; catapulting; and cockpit suitability, including visibility for various operational functions and effectiveness of gun and bomb sights. Testing of seaplane boat hulls and floats and amphibious aircraft included all water-handling characteristics. As time passed, aircraft crashes, strafing, and dive-bombing runs disturbed Washington, D.C., residents to the point that testing was moved from Anacostia to a remote area at NAS Patuxent River, Maryland.[10]

Lieutenant Stone participated in many Navy formal airplane trials for seaplanes from June 1918 to January 1923.[11] Descriptions included here are derived from excerpts of official test reports of that time. Where interesting comments were reported, that portion of the actual test report is included. Where available, photographs of aircraft described in the tests are provided.[12]

Airplane trial test reports were made out on a standardized, multiple-page form. The first few pages were a detailed inventory of the aircraft's equipment, as well as aircraft weight-and-balance calculations. The inventory was detailed, cataloging such items as navigation instruments, engineering plant instrumentation, type and size of oil and fuel tanks, type and capacity of generators, propeller and engine description, and much more. The cover page, which is shown below, and the following pages instructed test pilots as to what tests were to be made and how they would be conducted.[13]

Pilots flying formal Navy airplane trials developed a close bond, based upon mutual respect for dangerous work and professional performance. When a particularly demanding test flight was scheduled, if possible, they preferred to fly with each other. The Navy recognized their unusual capabilities, including the ability to solve unique and hazardous problems while experiencing them. Many were eventually assigned to aircrews on the world's first transatlantic flight.

The remainder of this chapter describes aircraft trials and excerpts from those flown by Stone.

Curtiss HS-1 Upgraded to HS-2

The first successful flight test of a twelve-cylinder Liberty engine was conducted on a Curtiss HS-1 flying boat at Buffalo, New York, on October 21, 1917. The results led to the adoption of both the Liberty engine and HS-1 aircraft as standard Navy service-type equipment. In 1918, engineering design changes upgraded the HS-1 to a new aircraft, the HS-2. Both performance and safety were enhanced. Navy prototype tests were conducted from June 4 to July 5, 1918, at the Naval Aircraft Factory in Philadelphia prior to the manufacturer's production run implementing the change.[14] The test crew comprised LCDR A. C. Read, USN; LT W. E. Doherty, USNRFC; LT Graham M. Brush, USNRFC; and Third Lieutenant Stone. In 1919, as we have seen, Lieutenant Commander Read would become Stone's commanding officer for the NC-4 first transatlantic flight. Stone would be the NC-4's pilot.

Following the prototype HS-2 test, Third Lieutenant Stone recommended additional changes that would further improve flight performance for the pilot and the operational performance of the aircraft. Stone's recommendations are shown, following the aircraft's test report.

Oper. "Av"   July 18, 1919

N1 — A4242

AIRPLANE TRIALS

PRELIMINARY INSTRUCTIONS

The officer conducting the trials, immediately upon completion of each test, shall forward one copy of the data to the office of the CHIEF OF NAVAL OPERATIONS (AVIATION), one copy to the BUREAU OF CONSTRUCTION AND REPAIR, and one copy to the BUREAU OF STEAM ENGINEERING. The pilot and crew shall sign the original test sheet.

WEATHER:

    1. Tests of airplanes should be made under favorable weather conditions.

    2. Any change in the weather during the test shall be noted.

WEIGHT OF AIRPLANES:

    1. The weight of the machine is to be determined in such a manner that the center of gravity can be located. The following is an approved method:

    A platform scale is placed under each corner of the handling truck and the machine and truck jacked up on these scales clear of the ground. With the plane of the engine beds horizontal (this horizontal condition is to be determined by a special level provided for the purpose, and at the same time the zero reading of the inclinometer installed on the instrument board is to be checked) readings are taken at each scale simultaneously and recorded on diagram (page 3). The same process is repeated with the truck after the launching of the machine, care being taken to have the truck reasonably dry. Distances between the centers of the jacks are also to be recorded as indicated in both cases.

    2. Before and after tests, hull or floats shall be examined to see that they are free from water.

FUEL:

    1. The fuel shall be weighed before and after tests and the difference of these weights shall be taken as fuel consumed during run. The following procedure is suggested:

    (a) That the tanks be filled to a known mark before the test and that the amount necessary to refill the tanks after the run has been made be taken as the quantity of fuel used during the run.

READING OF INSTRUMENTS:

    1. Instruments shall be read in the order of the respective headings on the data sheet—from left to right. The readings shall be allotted among the pilot and crew in such fashion that the data may be recorded as nearly simultaneously as possible. Each member is to have a separate data sheet with the columns conspicuously marked in which he is to set down data.

    The air speed meter reading is in every case to be recorded in the column marked "air speed."

ANEROID:

    The aneroid is to be at least 6 months old and is to be calibrated at time intervals frequent enough to insure accurate readings, preferably at least once a month.

3/08—3

Cover page of test report of airplane trials

HS–1 flying boat beached

HS–2 flying boat getaway

The test report and Stone's recommended changes, together, provide an excellent view of the HS-2 operating characteristics.

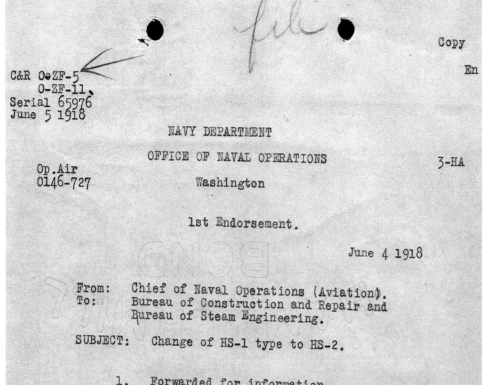

C&R OeZF-5
O-ZF-11,
Serial 65976
June 5 1918

NAVY DEPARTMENT

OFFICE OF NAVAL OPERATIONS   3-HA

Op.Air   Washington
0146-727

1st Endorsement.

June 4 1918

From: Chief of Naval Operations (Aviation).
To: Bureau of Construction and Repair and
        Bureau of Steam Engineering.

SUBJECT: Change of HS-1 type to HS-2.

1.   Forwarded for information.

2.   It is requested that the present HS-1 type
seaplane be changed to the HS-2 type as soon as practicable not to interfere with production.

3.   Comment by the Bureaus concerned is requested on the recommendations of paragraph 13.

4.   Return of papers is requested.

/s/ W. S. Benson.

Copy to
     Bureau of Ordnance
     Bureau of Navigation

HS-1 to HS-2 modification letter

```
                                          COPY      En
C&R  Oe ZF-5
     O- ZF-11
Serial 65976
June 5 1918

                                    May 25th, 1918.


From:  Test Board.
To:    Chief of Naval Operations(Aviation).

Subject:  Test of HS-2 A-1599.

     1.    The Board tested HS-2 A-1599 on May 23 and May 24th.

     2.    The following weights had been obtained previously and
were furnished by Naval Constructor H. C. Richardson:

          Dead weight plus scarf ring, and excepting
              items below- - - - - - - - - - - - - - - 3802 lbs.
          Radiator, starting crank and bracket--- - - -  108  "
          Propeller - - - - - - - - - - - - - - - - - -   55  "
          Water in radiator and engine - - - - - - - -   106  "

          Total dead weight and scarf ring - - - - - - 4071 lbs.

          Two bombs and fittings - - - - -  360 lbs.
          Batteries for intercommunication
                       sets- - - - - -  10   "
              Additional weights:
          Gasoline, 141 gals at 6-3/4 lbs.  952   "
          Oil, 11-1/2 gals at 7-3/4 lbs.     89   "
          Pilot (Lt.McCulloch) - - - - - -  165   "
          Asst. pilot (Lt.Comdr.Read)- - -  112   "
          Observer for'd (Lt.Brush)- - - -  150   "
              Total useful load (minus scarf
                            ring)            1838 lbs.

          Full load - - - - - - - - - - - - - - - - - -5909 lbs.

          Lifting surface - - - - - - - - - 800 sq.ft.
          Loading- - - - - - - - - - - - - -7-3/8 lbs.

The amount of gasoline used in testing motor and in flight just
prior to trials reduced full load to about 5900 lbs.  No allowance
in the foregoing has been made for soakage.  No scales were avail-
able for taking weights.  Radiator, Livingston, type 150.  Propeller,
4 blade, diameter 8'4", pitch 6'8".

     3.    The method for obtaining climb was to level off near the
water under full power maintaining that height for some time, then
starting time when the elevator was pulled back.  The following
were the results obtained:
```

HS-1 to HS-2 test requirements, page 1

Third Lieutenant Stone's engineering design-change recommendations for HS-2 aircraft prior to its production run are contained in the letter on page 138. Pages 135 to 137 include the remaining pages to the change from HS-1 to HS-2 test report.

Curtiss Speed Gnome Scout Airplane Trial

On July 1, 1918, the Navy Bureau of Construction and Repair wrote a letter to the commanding officer of NAS Anacostia authorizing First Lieutenant Stone to fly the Curtiss

-2-   En

End. of min.	Feet.	Speed	R.P.M.	Oil
1st	400	56	1475	.35
2nd	700	57	1475	35
3rd	900	57	----	--

Engine trouble developed before R.P.M. and oil pressure readings were obtained for the third minute.

4. The first indication of trouble was a vibration, then R.P.M. dropped to 1425. The climb was continued a few seconds when the oil pressure started going down rapidly. The seaplane was put into a glide, when just above the water (Oil pressure under 5 lbs.) the throttle was opened partly, when a loud thrump occurred; the motor was cut and landing made.

5. Preliminary examination at the factory showed a broken crank web (on after crank) and cracked crank case.

6. A new engine was installed, also a new rudder, the counter balance of the old rudder having been at the lower part. This rudder was the second modification of the experimental rudder (with 50% greater area). The new rudder was reinforced at bottom of counter balance by a 5/8" tube.

May 24th.
7. On the first attempt the engine developed a bad miss shortly after getting off. The gasoline pump froze and the counter balance of the rudder showed a slight left bend in upper part.

8. The second attempt was successful; weights were as itemized in paragraph 2; following data obtained:

Speed of getaway by speedmeter   39
Slow speed   "   "   37
Landing "   "   "   34

	Altimeter	Climb Speedmeter	RPM	Oil pressure	Temperature gauge
1st minute	395	56	1460	45	
2nd "	642	55	1460	45	
3rd "	837	55	1460	45	
4th "	1050	55	1460	45	
5th "	1250	54	1460	45	
6th "	1450	54	1460	45	
7th "	1637	53	1460	45	
8th "	1850	54	1460	45	1810 1800

HS-1 to HS-2 test requirements, page 2

Speed Gnome Scout A-448, with a French Gnome engine, for experimental purposes.[15] Tests were conducted as authorized, though no written report can be found.

Curtiss Model F Boat Airplane Trial

LT D. H. McCulloch, USN, wrote a letter on July 9, 1918, to the Bureau of Construction and Repair reporting test results on Curtiss Model F Boat A-2314, flown by Lieutenant Stone at Anacostia. The Model F Boat was so successful that the Navy procured forty-seven

```
                                                    COPY
                              -3-                                    En

C&R O-ZF-5
   O-ZF-11      Altimeter   Speedmeter   RPM      Oil      Temperature
Serial 65976    _____   _____   ___    pressure      gauge
June 5 1918                                       _____    _____


9th minute       2037          56        1460      45         1780
10th    "        2212          53        1460      45         1780
```

Speed Run.

Course, 2 miles, wind about 4 M.P.H. port bow and starboard quarter. Speedmeter 62.5, R.P.M. 1525, altitude 20 ft.

```
        Against wind:  Time 1-22.4 - 87.38 m.p.h.
        With    "   :    "  1-16.2 - 94.49   "
        Average                     90.93    "
```

9.   The gasoline pump froze again on this run.

10.   The same weights were used, except the pilots, and other weights added:

```
             Former weights minus pilots- - - - - - 5482 lbs.
             Pilot (Lt.McCulloch)- - - - - - - - - - 165  "
             Asst. Pilot (Lt.Stone)- - - - - - - - - 154  "
             Observer; for'd (Lt.Doherty) - - - - -  142  "
             Sand; for'd - - - - - - - - - - - - -    40  "
             Sand; middle cockpit - - - - - - - - -  205  "
             Sand; tank comp't - - - - - - - - - - - 320  "
                    Total - - - - - - - - - - - - - 6499 lbs.
             Loading, 8-1/8 lbs.
```

No further weights were added as the hull was low in the water. The bombs were covered with spray on getaway; water smooth.

11.   The following results were obtained:

```
Speed of getaway by speedmeter       40
Slow speed          "       "        37
Landing "           "       "        35
```

```
                        Climb.
              Altimeter   Speedmeter    RPM      Oil pressure

1st minute      200          56         1475          45
2nd   "         350          55         1470          46
3rd   "         475          55         1470          46
4th   "         550          55         1470          46
5th   "         700          55         1475          46
6th   "         850          55         1475          46
7th   "         900          55         1475          46
8th   "        1000          54         1480          46
9th   "        1100
10th  "
        Gasoline pump propeller wire broke and climb was dis-
continued.
```

HS-1 to HS-2 test requirements, page 3

advanced versions of the "Modernized F Boat," or the MF Boat. Improvements included sponson projections on each side to improve stability on the water. Its vertical stabilizer was enlarged for aerodynamic stability, and the wingspan and hull design were improved for stability during water work. An aircraft trial was established for contract acceptance of the seaplane. The assigned trial crew was Lieutenant Commander Read, Lieutenant McCulloch, Lieutenant Stone, and LT James L. Breese, USN. Interestingly, in 1919 these same men, with

C&R O-ZF-5
    O-ZF-11
Serial 65976
June 5 1918   -4-   COPY En

Speed Run

Course and wind same; speedmeter 61; R.P.M. 1510; altitude 15 feet:

Against wind:	Time 1-22	- 87.80 m.p.h.	
With "	" 1-16	- 94.73 "	
Average - - - - - - - - - - -		91.27 "	
Against wind:	Time 1-25.2	- 84.51 m.p.h.	
With "	" 1-14.4	- 96.77 "	
Average- - - - - - - - - - -		90.64 "	
Final average- - - - - - - - -		90.95 m.p.h.	

12. In all tests the boat balanced slightly nose heavy under full power; aileron action very responsive and easy to manipulate; rudder action difficult for right turns.

13. In regard to the details of design, the Board recommends the following:

(a) A removable center panel should be designed in order to facilitate the taking out of the engine. The present power plant installation is such that it takes a crew of twenty men ten hours to remove the engine and install a new one.
(b) A wire cage should be put around the gasoline pump to eliminate the danger of the blades of the pump coming off and going into the propeller. It is understood that these pumps are to be discontinued in a short time.
(c) The hatch cover should be redesigned so that it can be opened. As it is now, the wind mill pump interferes.
(d) A radiator bracket should be mounted on the beds so that the radiator shall have a bearing the full width of the bottom tank.
(e) The life belts should be so installed that they do not rest on the control wires. A life belt should be put in the gunner's cockpit. A small stream lined cowling should be designed for the nose of the machine to continue the stream line of the new oil tank which is mounted underneath the engine. The balance fin on the rudder should be redesigned and strengthened.
(f) One more pelon should be put on the elevators. The new oil tank design should be accepted. The new wing type gasoline gravity tank should be accepted. The new gasoline quantity gauges should be accepted.

Signed) A. C. Read   Graham M. Brush
       Lt. Comdr. U.S. Navy   Lieutenant U.S.N.R.F.C.

       W. E. Doherty   E. F. Stone
       Lieutenant U.S.N.R.F.C.   3rd Lieutenant, U.S.C.G.

HS-1 to HS-2 test requirements, page 4

the exception of McCulloch, would crew the NC-4 during the first transatlantic flight. On this occasion their aircraft trial report stated, "The boat lands with no shock whatever, even when 'pancaked' from 8 feet—There is no tendency to porpoise on landings and get-aways." Twenty-two MF Boats were built by Glenn Curtiss before the First World War ended and the contract with Curtiss was canceled. Further production of eighty MF Boats with the hundred-horsepower Curtiss OXX3 engine was conducted at the Naval Aircraft Factory. The

N. C. R. 90.

O-ZF-5

In reply, address not the signer
of this letter but Bureau of Construction and Repair, Navy Department,
Washington, D. C.

NAVY DEPARTMENT,

BUREAU OF CONSTRUCTION AND REPAIR,

Refer to No. *Fileon*
HS-2L Case

WASHINGTON, D. C.

Jn

August 16, 1918.

MEMORANDUM

To: Naval Constructor Burgess.

        I am noting for your information a few points
which Lieutenant Stone raised in our recent discussion
of the HS-2.

        1.   The wingtip float should be raised.   A radical
redesign of the wingtip float appears to be necessary.
It was agreed that the H-16 type float would probably be
of advantage.

        2.   The rudder control is very tiring to the pilot.

The use of a rubber cord has been suggested and Lieutenant
Stone has given Mr. Clark a sketch of the tentative arrangements.   One of the draftsmen ought to work these in better
form and the necessary material for experimental installation
of this type will be ordered down from the Naval Aircraft
Factory for installation on the HS-1 at Anacostia.

        3.   The leads from the gravity tank on the HS-2 should
be so arranged that coupling occurs near the engine.   The
The present arrangement requires a continual bending of
the piping upon removal of the engine from the engine bed,
causing these pipes to break.

        4.   The trap door of the hull is not securely fastened
in the present arrangement.

        5.   A swivel is necessary on the tow cable.   I under-
stand there is difficulty of obtaining a proper size swivel
for this use.   Should a new one be designed?

        6.   The aileron control leads as present installed
wear out very rapidly where they are led out through the hull.

        7.   The present method for securing fabric at the foun-
dation of gravity tank is not satisfactory.

Davis Lum?

H B Luther
R E B.

Stone's recommendation for added changes to HS-1 to HS-2 modification

seaplane would see further engine change, to the Wright-Hispano and Curtiss K-6 engines.
(The MF Boat aircraft trial report of July 30, 1919, at NAS Hampton Roads, Virginia, is
instructive.)[16]

Boeing Seaplane Trial

The commanding officer of NAS Hampton Roads received a letter from the Bureau of
Construction and Repair, dated July 18, 1918, authorizing Lieutenant Stone to conduct

Curtiss Speed Gnome Scout A-448

experimental flights on two assigned Boeing seaplanes.[17] Stone performed the tests, but again, no written report can now be located.

Carolina F Boat A-4343 Airplane Trial

A Bureau of Construction and Repair letter of August 9, 1918, assigned LCDR V. C. Griffin, USN, Lieutenant Stone, and ENS E. B. Koger, USNRF, to conduct airplane trials on Carolina Aircraft Corporation's flying boat. Its designation was "Carolina F Boat A-4343, with Curtiss OXX-6 100 HP [horsepower] engine."[18] This was the first aircraft to be constructed from plywood rather than fabric covering a wood frame. Airplane trials were flown at NAS Morehead City from September 10 through 15. A preliminary airplane trial test report is contained in a test crew's letter. An excerpt from the letter is shown below.

No photograph of the aircraft is available, since the contract process was canceled.

Dirigible DN-1 Test Flight

A September 7, 1918, memorandum between Commander, Third Naval District, and Commander Towers requested that "LT Stone test the first Navy dirigible envelope at

Curtiss Model F Boat

Boeing seaplane

NAS Montauk" on Long Island, New York. Commander Towers would later become commanding officer of Sea Plane Division 1, competing in the first transatlantic flight. Lieutenant Stone would be assigned to this command. The later C-class dirigible would be the Navy's third-generation lighter-than-air ship. A C-class ship would later compete to be the first aircraft across the Atlantic. DN-1, the Navy's first lighter-than-air ship, was a nonrigid dirigible built by the Connecticut Aircraft Company. DN-1 was 175 feet long and had 150,000 cubic feet of hydrogen storage in its lifting sacks. The dirigible was propelled

RECOMMENDATIONS—Continued.

The manufacturer's pilot, Harry Atwood, flew this plane with 15 gallons gasoline and no passengers, total weight about 2600 pounds, at which load the plane took-off after a long run and pilot was unwilling to attempt to climb or turn with this loading.

The experimental features of this type of construction, that is, making all surfaces of ply board, are considered by the Board to have been satisfactorily demonstrated and the failure of the plane to fly should be permitted to cast no reflection on the ply board construction.

It is recommended that if this plane ever becomes the property of the United States, an engine of greater power be installed and further tests carried out. Further, it is thought that the quality of the ply board used in this plane is superior to that generally employed in Naval Aircraft and that its manufacture and use by the Navy should be fully investigated.

SIGNED:

Lieutenant Commander, U.S.N.

1st Lieutenant, U.S.C.G.

In hospital
Ensign, U.S.N.R.F.

Carolina F Boat A-4343 aircraft trial report

by two Sturtevant engines. Its formal aircraft trial was flown at NAS Pensacola on April 20, 1917. Due to its marginal weight and lift capacity, the dirigible had limited endurance and range, and it was not accepted for Navy operations. It was flown only twice more, then permanently grounded.[19]

DN-1 dirigible approaching floating hangar

Gallaudet D-4 Light Bomber Airplane Trial

A Bureau of Construction and Repair letter dated October 25, 1918, assigned a test crew including Lieutenant Stone, CAPT B. L. Smith, USMC, Lieutenant Commander Read and Lieutenant Breese for airplane trials of the Gallaudet D-4 light bomber. Engineering design changes were required, and official testing was delayed until the Gallaudet D-4 light bomber A-2654 was flown at East Greenwich, Rhode Island, on February 15, 1919. Two versions of the aircraft were tested, a landplane and a seaplane. A propeller tip shattered on the landplane. The accident report recommended that "wooden propellers not be painted, since uneven paint application caused the propeller to become unbalanced when rotating. This caused the wooden propeller to shatter at the tip."

The following are excerpts from the seaplane test report: "Sharp turns with power throws solid water in propeller, otherwise sound"; and "Takeoff requires strong force to controls."[20]

Huff-Daland Company HA Fighter 4110 Aircraft Trial

The first airplane trial of this aircraft was not flown by Stone. A second airplane trial was flown January 30, 1919, at NAS Rockaway Beach for the Huff-Daland Company HA Fighter 4110. The HA Fighter had a Curtis two-bladed tractor propeller, two Marlin machine guns mounted over the center of the upper wing, and two Lewis machine

Gallaudet D-4 seaplane light bomber

Gallaudet D-4 landplane light bomber with splintered propeller

guns mounted aft of the cockpit. The landplane version had a Liberty twelve-cylinder high-compression engine, and the seaplane version had a Liberty twelve-cylinder low-compression engine. The flight test crew comprised LCDR R. Ohlf, USN, Lieutenant Stone, and Lieutenant Breese.

> Later, Lieutenant Breese would be assigned as NC-4's seaplane engineering officer when Lieutenant Stone was assigned as pilot during the world's first transatlantic flight.

An extract from Lieutenant Stone's test report:

> Just as the ceiling was reached on one of the climb tests, the motor caught fire. The plane was immediately put in a steep side slip and brought down from 15,000 feet without accident. Upon investigation it was found that the fire was caused by the failure of the circulating pump to function. The blades of this pump had become distorted, and one was broken. Only the oil on the outside of the engine burned. The automatic fire extinguisher was not operated, due to the difficulty of reaching control, and necessity for the pilot to devote most of his attention to maneuvering of the plane.[21]

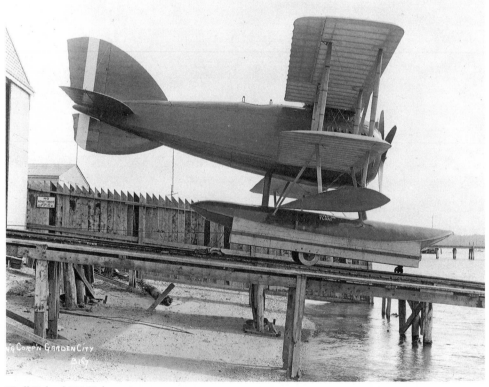

Huff-Daland HA Fighter on ramp

Huff-Daland HA Fighter on beach

On April 21, 1919, First Lieutenant Stone was ordered back to NAS Rockaway as chief test pilot for Seaplane Division 1 in preparation for the NC seaplane's first transatlantic flight. This assignment concluded in June 1919, but Lieutenant Stone's work for the Navy was not over. He continued to test everything from seaplanes to balloons and dirigibles.[22]

N-1 A-4342 Aircraft Trial

Airplane trials were held for N-1 Seaplane A-4342 on July 18, 1919. N-1 was the first experimental aircraft designed and manufactured at the Naval Aircraft Factory. The assigned test crew was First Lieutenant Stone, LTJG E. W. Rounds, USNRF, and Ensign Koger. Ordnance tests were conducted by CDR A. C. Stott, USN, and Lieutenant Commander Griffin. Page 17 and the last page of the N-1 seaplane trial notes are reproduced here to permit examination of the test pilot's recommendations and some of the test findings.[23] Following N-1's aircraft trial, the aircraft was flown from the Naval Aircraft Factory to test the Lewis machine gun, which had been specifically designed for the N-1. The test flight was flown by LT Victor Vernon, and the Lewis machine gun was operated by a Lieutenant Sheppard.

Change in design (and reasons) with gross lead of 5900 lbs. this seaplane was taxied away from beach, (sea smooth, wing 10 knots) before the wind. On half hour was time taken to get from beach to a point far enough to leeward to make a get-away into wind. During this run the engine had to be stopped three times to allow water to cool. An attempt was made to take off into wind under ideal conditions, engine making 1500 r.p.ms. Could not get plaining speed. water boiled. Propeller damaged beyond repair by water beating. This seaplane is entirely useless on water on account of the slow speed of taxying and overheating when using enough power is used to to steer a desired course. It is recommended that this seaplane be stricken from the Navy list.

/s/ E.F. Stone, 1st Lt. USCG
E.W. Rounds, Lt.(jg) USNRF
Esten B. Koger Ens. USNRF

(17)

Esten B. Koger Ensign USNRF

N-1 A-4342 aircraft trial report, front of page 17

July 28, 1919.

With 5400 pounds plane took off easily in 15 knot wind. When landed, soon after the wind dropped to about 5 knots, and after three attempts, it was impossible to get plane off the water. The motor had to be stopped five times in an hour's run to cool off as the slow speed of taxying does not cool as desired. The plane is very slow to respond to controls while on the water. The sea was very smooth and on the last attempts to get off glassy, but in spite of this the propeller tips were badly damaged by water beating. During the trials the motor r.p.m. on the water was 1500.

This plane is of no use as with gas enough for only one and a half hours it was impossible to take it off in a 3-5 knot breeze. Recommended abandoning all tests and surveying the plane.

/s/ E.W. Rounds.

A flight was made with Ordnance representative for purpose of testing 6 pdr. Davis Gun as installed. Six rounds for Davis Gun and one tray for Lewis Gun were carried. Runs were made over target at 1000 ft. altitude course across 6 knot wind as follows:

(a) For practice, Lewis Gun fired.

(b) Lewis Gun and one round Davis Gun at full elevation. Target was hit.

(c) Attempt to fire two rounds with Davis Gun at full elevation. Davis Gun was fired when on, at full elevation target was hit. Gun was reloaded as rapidly as possible with difficulty, - handling loaded and empty shells in the air. A second shot could not be fired, as gun did not bear when reloaded, the target being astern of the plane.

It was found that the gun as installed on this plane can not be fired twice in one run at a target with 1000 ft. altitude.

/s/ Commander A. C. Stott, USN.
Lieut. Comdr. V. C. Griffin,

N-1 A-4342 airplane trial report, reverse of page 17

N–1 seaplane

N–1 seaplane on ramp

Lewis machine gun

R-9 Torpedo Seaplane Trial

Written orders from Bureau of Construction and Repair in July 1919 directed First Lieutenant Stone to conduct torpedo trials for the R-9 torpedo seaplane at Rockaway.[24] No formal test report can be located.

R-9 torpedo seaplane

R-9 torpedo seaplane loading on tug

Aeromarine Model No. 40F Boat with Curtiss OXX-6
Hundred-Horsepower Engine Aircraft A-5041 Trial

An airplane trial was conducted on July 30, 1919, in Willoughby Bay on the Elizabeth River in Hampton Roads, in Virginia. The crew assigned to fly the tests included First Lieutenant Stone, Lieutenant (junior grade) Rounds, and Ensign Koger. An extract from Stone's portion of the airplane trial report states:

- "Weather 15 kts [knots], N.E. [from the northeast], gusts moderate to bad, 3 ft choppy sea."
- "This is not the roughest air in which plane can be flown, but plane is as controllable as any planes of this size and type."
- "Can be taken off in any direction [sea]. Can be landed in any direction under these conditions. Performance satisfactory."[25]

Curtiss MF Boat with Wright–Hispano Suiza
Motors and Pusher Propeller Airplane Trial

As reported in the Curtiss Model F Boat airplane trial of July 9, 1918, the addition of a Lewis machine gun with its gun mount, magazines, and bombs increased the weight enough to require an engine with more horsepower. As mentioned above, the design was changed from the hundred-horsepower Curtiss OXXX3 engine to the Wright-Hispano Suiza 150-horsepower engine. In addition to the Wright-Hispano Suiza engine, the Curtiss K-6 engine was considered. All of these changes were necessary to transform the seaplane into a trainer for gunnery and bombing. Following the trial, a decision was made to cancel use of the MF Boat as a gunnery and bombing trainer, and it was never produced. Although the Curtiss MF Boat had been a Navy standard, modification for a new Wright-Hispano Suiza engine required test verification for performance and airworthiness. The airplane trial was conducted by Lieutenant Stone for this modified seaplane on July 30, 1919, at Hampton Roads.

Aeromarine, Model No. 40, A-5086

Aeromarine, Model No. 40, A-5086

An excerpt from his airplane trial report:

Choppy 3 ft sea and 35 knot wind. No cross swells. Can not be taken off downwind. Can be taken off cross wind and against wind. Can be landed in any direction. Machine handled very slowly on getaway across wind. On getaways, elevators hit water when in neutral position. Performance otherwise satisfactory.[26]

Curtiss MF Boat with Hispano Suiza motors and pusher propeller

Liberty Four-Hundred-Horsepower High-Compression Engine Engineering Test
First Lieutenant Stone conducted engineering tests and aircraft trials on August 8, 1919, at the Army's McCook Air Field, Aviation Engineering and Manufacturing Command, Dayton, Ohio. Stone was ordered to "conduct performance comparisons between high and low compression engines, and strength of materials and critical parts on the high compression engine." Increased horsepower derived from raising engine compression would be critical for NC seaplanes attempting the world's first transatlantic flight.[27] The test aircraft is not identified in surviving records. (NC-4's Liberty engines are on display at the Smithsonian Air and Space Museum Udvar-Hazy Facility in Chantilly, Virginia.)

NC-4 Liberty engines

Carolina F Boat A-4343 Airplane Trial

Carolina Aircraft F Boat A-4343, manufactured by the Carolina Aircraft Corporation of Raleigh, North Carolina, was retested on September 15, 1919. The aircraft trial was flown by Lieutenant Commander Griffin, Lieutenant Stone, and Ensign Koger at NAS Morehead City. Some excerpts from the airplane trial report:

- "UNSAT [Unsatisfactory] Rejected. Maneuvering very difficult except on step at 30 knots. Rudder area and motion insufficient."
- "This plane got on step and gained about 40 knots airspeed very quickly with full load. Speed did not increase above this, and this speed was not sufficient to lift plane into the air. It is recommended that area of vertical rudder be increased, and that an engine of at least 150 HP be installed in any plane of this weight before attempts are made to fly."

The first aircraft trial and its description can be read in the previous September 10 to 15 entry. Since the contract was canceled, no photograph exists.[28]

Sperry Light Bomber and Triplane Seaplane No. 5243 with Liberty 12 Engine Trial

An airplane trial was conducted on Sperry light bomber and triplane seaplane No. 5243 with the Liberty twelve-cylinder engine at Roosevelt Field, Mineola, on Long Island, in New York. This was the first amphibious aircraft with landing gear that could retract into the fuselage, thereby not affecting water landings or takeoffs. Roosevelt Field, scheduled for closure, was kept open solely for this test as a landplane. When it failed due to a crash that severed the landing gear from the fuselage, tests were moved to NAS Rockaway on January 12, 1920, for evaluation as a seaplane. The Roosevelt Field airplane trial was flown by Lieutenant Commander Griffin, Lieutenant (junior grade) Rounds, and LTJG H. W. Roughley, USNRF. Airplane trials conducted at NAS Rockaway were flown by First Lieutenant Stone and Lieutenant Commander Griffin. An excerpt from the January 17, 1920, Rockaway airplane trial report: "Unsuccessful in that plane could not be taken off the water. Aircraft damaged during water takeoff attempt."

A letter dated October 18, 1920, from the president of Board and Survey to Chief, Naval Operations, states, "Plane does not and can not satisfy the contract as it now stands. It does not warrant any further expenditure of funds by the Navy to conduct further trials."[29]

Curtiss 18T Seaplane Number A-3325

Preliminary trials were flown December 5, 1919, at NAS Rockaway by Lieutenant Commander Griffin and Lieutenant Stone. They stated in the official report, "UNSAT 20° nose up and carburetor bowl caused flooding on takeoff."[30]

Loening LS Seaplane A-5606 and A-5243 Test on Performance of Launching Carriage

On August 27 to 30, 1920, Lieutenant Commander Griffin, Lieutenant Stone, and Lieutenant (junior grade) Roughley conducted tests at Fort Washington, on Long Island. They submitted a "Satisfactory" report.[31]

Sperry light bomber and triplane seaplane

Sperry light bomber and triplane seaplane, Roosevelt Field, New York

Curtiss 18T seaplane A–3325

Loening LS seaplane beached

Loening M-81 Seaplanes 5701 and 5642 Airplane Trial

Aircraft trials were flown at NAS Anacostia on January 21 through May 2, 1921. The airplane trials were flown by LCDR Nathan B. Chase, USN, Lieutenant Commander Stone, and Lieutenant Roughley.[32] An excerpt from the airplane trial is shown below:

```
Op-21-48-A


        7.    The tail is too flexible and should be more securely
braced.

        8.    The location of the air speed meter is poor as the
eddy currents from the torpedo affect its readings.

        9.    The vibration in the plane was very bad.  The engines
and radiators have different periods of vibration.  The engine
revolutions were the same in the air as on the water and this may
be due to vibration causing the propellors to flutter.

        10.   During the attempted trials a great deal of taxi-ing
was done in a rather rough sea.  Also landings were made cross
wind and the wind in winds from twenty to twenty-five miles per
hour.  The plane appeared to be very seaworthy under the above
conditions.

        11.   The plane, fully loaded can apparently only get off in
a strong wind and then only after a long run.  When once off it
apparently has very little reserve power and a drop in the engine
power causes the plane to settle to the water.  It appears to be
entirely too heavy for successful flight. Unless the weight of the
plane can be reduced by about 800 pounds, it is not believed it
will be a suitable torpedo plane.

Copy to:  Construction and Repair
          Engineering
          Ordnance
          Superintending Constructor of Aircraft,    /s/ N.B.Chase
             Garden City, Long Island.                   E.F.Stone
                                                         H.W.Roughley
```

Loening M-81 seaplane aircraft trial comments

Loening M-81 seaplane

Loening M–80 landplane

Curtiss CT Seaplane Trial

Airplane trials were held at NAS Rockaway on June 8 to 18, 1921, and were flown by Lieutenant Commander Chase, Lieutenant Stone, and Lieutenant Roughley.[33]

Curtiss CT seaplane

A report to Chief of Naval Operations (CNO) from the President of the Board of Inspection and Survey is shown on page 157.

Naval Aircraft Factory, Philadelphia Seaplane Type P (Patrol) Aircraft A–6040 and Seaplane Type PT (Patrol Torpedo) Aircraft A–6034 Trials

Both aircraft were equipped with the Liberty 1+C engine. Airplane trials were held at the Naval Aircraft Factory from August 4 to 19, 1921. The test crew comprised temporary Lieutenant Commander Stone, Lieutenant Commander Chase, and Lieutenant Roughley.

Op-21-48-A NBC/RP   17 June, 1921.

From: Trial Board
To: Chief of Naval Operations
Via: President, Board of Inspection and Survey

Subject: Trial of the Curtiss C.T. Seaplane.

    1.   The Board met at the U.S. Naval Air Station, Rockaway
Beach, Long Island, N.Y., on 13 June, 1921. Present:

            Lieutenant Commander Nathan B. Chase, U.S.N.,
              Senior Member.
            Lieutenant Commander E.F. Stone, U.S.C.G., Member.
            Lieutenant H.W. Roughley, U.S.N.R.F., Member & Recorder.

    2.   The Board remained in session until 15 June, 1921, at
which time certain repairs and changes being necessary the Board
adjourned until such time as the C.T. Seaplane will again be ready
for trial.

    3.   Several attempts were made to conduct trials but none
were completed owing to the impossibility of keeping the plane in
the air more than five or ten minutes without the engines over
heating. With the top cowling removed the engines still over
heated and with the top and bottom cowling removed it was impossible to get the plane off the water.

    4.   All flights and attempted flights were made in winds
varying from about twenty to twenty-five miles per hour. Even in
the strongest wind the plane was difficult to get off, requiring
a very long run. A great deal of spray was picked up and thrown
over the cock pits. This was somewhat relieved by placing spray
strips on the pontoons. The tail and lower tail booms were subject to punishment by spray and wash from the pontoons and finally
the stabilizer was badly damaged by this wash. This damage occurred, however, in about a four foot seaway. The tail plane
appears to set too low.

    5.   After the first flight the upper fittings on the rear
pontoon struts were found to be cracked and were renewed with
heavier fittings.

    6.   The engine beds are entirely too light and the metal
has cracked in three places. Heavier beds should be installed
before renewing tests.
                                            Et Seq.
                        -1-

CT seaplane test report extract

An excerpt from the A–6040 test report states:

- "The general flying and seaworthy qualities of this seaplane are very good."
- "However, some tweaks were needed to let engine oil temp run cooler; and a long type exhaust manifold replacing current one needed to prevent a fire hazard from

idling aircraft engine flame in exhaust stream along side fuselage. Also suggested was a Gun Ring on the aircraft cockpit and shifting the photographer to the aft cockpit to take photos and be a gunner for aircraft's protection."

An excerpt from the A–6034 test report states:

- "Got off across wind in 55 seconds; wind 15 kts, sea choppy; windward tide. Plane handled satisfactorily except for water beating propeller to get off, elevators must be held well up."
- "Difficult to make turns without skidding probably due to short tail and insufficient fin area aft."
- "Both oil and water ran hot even with top cowling off."[34]

Naval Aircraft Factory Type PT seaplane

Naval Aircraft Factory Tandem FT (Fighter Type) Airplane Trial

On August 4, 1921, an airplane trial was held for the newly designed and manufactured tandem FT fighter-type seaplane at the Naval Aircraft Factory, Philadelphia. Tests were flown by temporary Lieutenant Commander Stone and Lieutenant Roughley. An excerpt from the report states:

The power plant defects in this plane can be overcome, but not those pertaining to its airworthiness and seaworthiness, unless the plane is largely redesigned. In view of its numerous defects and its questionable utility, even though these defects were remedied it is recommended that further experimental work on this plane be discontinued.[35]

No photograph can be found.

Experimental Aircraft Models WE (Amphibian)
and WS (Seaplane) Trial

In the early years of aviation, the Wright brothers lost the confidence of the Navy by rejecting the use of catapults to launch airplanes from ships. Glenn Curtiss had won favor with his early cooperation, and his aircraft met Navy needs. The Wright WE amphibian was an attempt to regain contracting favor. However, the Navy was not impressed. An aircraft trial was flown on January 24, 1923, at the Dayton-Wright Company, Ohio. The trial was flown by LT David Rittenhouse, USN, and Lieutenant Stone. The airplane trial reported failure and warned, "Sufficient tests should be made to demonstrate that these airplanes meet the contractor's guarantee to fulfill the demonstration requirements."[36]

Experimental aircraft Models WE amphibian and WS seaplane

Stone's participation in these official Navy aircraft trials added to his wide-ranging experience, extraordinary capability, and significant impact on aircraft engineering design and implementation. He was greatly respected by his fellow test pilots.

CHAPTER EIGHT

Marine Corps Aviation and Coast Guard Aviation Develop to Support Their Service Missions

1917–1938

*M*any comprehensive books have been written on the history of Marine Corps aviation. However, no comprehensive history of Coast Guard aviation has been published. The author encourages the reading of the History and Museums Division, Headquarters, U.S. Marine Corps, comprehensive publication: Marine Corps Aviation, 1912–1940, by LtCol Edward C. Johnson, USMC, for the history of Marine Corps aviation. A copy can be obtained free on the Internet. Its conclusion is a well researched summary, portions of which are quoted below.[1]

Marine Corps Aviation: 1919–1938

"As aircraft gradually improved in performance and reliability, and as the Marine Corps, like the other services, slowly committed more men and resources to aviation, a rudimentary organization began to take form, and Marine aviators began to see the outlines of a mission: support of Marine expeditionary forces in seizing and holding advance bases."

In the world war, Marine aviators were diverted from their amphibious expeditionary mission and were deployed by the Navy for priority antisubmarine-warfare aerial day patrols and were sent on a smaller scale into a large-scale continental war principally fought in France. Denied the opportunity "to support the Marine brigade, Marine aviators managed to place organized squadrons at the front, and they fought where they were needed."

During the 1920s, Marine aviation "moved toward definition of its role in supporting Marine operations. In the air over Haiti, the Dominican Republic, China, and Nicaragua, Marine aviators actively assisted the ground forces, not only in combat but also in reconnaissance, transportation, and supply. In Nicaragua, by the end of the decade, the Marine air-ground team had become a reality."

"Then in the 1930s, as Marine Corps doctrine crystallized and it began to train for its amphibious warfare mission, Marine aviation achieved full acceptance as part of the Fleet Marine Force, as well as developing a secondary capacity to join naval aviation in carrier operations." From 1913 to 1938, Marine aviators flew 122 different types of aircraft. Until 1920, the first 17 aircraft types were principally Navy and Army models.[2]

Coast Guard Aviation: 1919–1938

To understand the turbulent and budget-deprived times that plagued the Coast Guard and its fledgling aviation community following 1919, it is important to know the events that caused them.

In 1915 the U.S. Revenue Cutter Service was merged with the U.S. Lifesaving Service and became the U.S. Coast Guard. Upon the nation's entering World War I, the Coast Guard was transferred to the Navy Department by executive order. During the war, naval forces grew, and all funding benefit went to the Navy.

From the time of the nation's founding until a constitutional amendment was enacted to pay for the world war, the United States did not have a federal income tax. All federal programs, including national defense, were funded through tariffs and customs duties on foreign countries trading with this country. Since the nation felt secure from invasion behind the barrier of the Atlantic Ocean, the Naval Militia had been disestablished following the Revolutionary War. On August 4, 1790, Secretary of the Treasury, Alexander Hamilton, had established the U.S. Revenue Cutter Service (USRCS) to collect tariffs and customs duties directly from foreign shipping as it entered the nation's territorial seas and to enforce all federal laws on the navigable waters of the United States. The Revenue Cutter Service was also an armed force, responsible for naval defense, should it be needed. As a result, the RCS received adequate resources and men to perform its tasks. The country's Constitution authorized establishment of the Navy. After passage of the constitutional amendment establishing the federal income tax, collecting tariffs and customs duties became less essential, and the service fell on hard times.

The Coast Guard suffered significant ship and personnel casualties during the war, losses that were not replaced. After the war, in August 1919, the Coast Guard was returned to the Treasury Department, where it experienced postwar downsizing, along with the other services. However, the Coast Guard's original peacetime duties were still required; in fact, they were about to expand. There were not enough personnel and equipment to accomplish assigned missions without overworking people and straining the inventory. The Treasury Department and Congress continually offered promises, but no budgetary support appeared. In 1918, for example, Congress authorized ten air stations for the Coast Guard but provided no funding. It is completely understandable that morale in the Coast Guard was very low.

During the war, all Coast Guard aviators had been assigned to Navy functions that were fully funded, manned, and equipped and enjoyed much prestige.[3] When the Coast Guard returned to the Treasury Department, not all its officers were happy. In particular, many Coast Guard aviators enjoyed special relationships with the "movers and shakers" in naval aviation. The Navy, in turn, offered to accept them as regular line officers, many with promotions to more senior grades.[4] The situation erupted into something like a mutiny, with many of the officers requesting interservice transfers to the Navy. The Assistant Secretary of Treasury was assigned the task of writing letters of denial to these officers.[5]

ADM Ellsworth Bertholf, the Coast Guard commandant, had fought the hard political battle in Washington for the Coast Guard Law of 1915, merging the Revenue Cutter Service and Lifesaving Service into the Coast Guard. The last thing he wanted to see was the incorporation of the Coast Guard into the Navy. Worn down, he retired on June 30, 1919.[6]

The Coast Guard fell under the command of temporary Captain Commandant Daniel Foley until RADM William R. Reynolds took the helm as commandant on October 2, 1919.[7] Admiral Reynolds had a major rebuilding job on his hands. The Coast Guard had been reduced to an officer corps of 205, less than 75 percent of authorized strength. The enlisted corps was worse off, with a complement of 3,500 enlisted personnel, or 60 percent of authorized strength.

Insufficient compensation was a major problem. The Pay Act of 1920 helped considerably, but personnel and funding were major issues until enactment of the Eighteenth Amendment to the U.S. Constitution—that is, Prohibition, the cause of the infamous "Rum War"—on January 29, 1919.[8]

The Rum War placed additional requirements on the Coast Guard. The New England and New York offshore waters were particular enforcement problems. Hotels and restaurants in large cities like Boston and New York depended on liquor sales for the profits that permitted them to stay in business.

The war started with normal citizens sneaking drinks, businessmen supplying them by smuggling, and "speakeasy" nightclubs. Early in the war, local and state law enforcement agencies, and federal authorities like U.S. Customs and agents of the Bureau of Internal Revenue, were the primary enforcers of Prohibition.

By 1924, the war had changed drastically. A great deal of alcohol smuggling was carried out on "Rum Row," off the coasts of New York and Boston. Large New England and Canadian schooners, many owned by U.S. citizens, were registered in foreign countries—including England, Canada, and France—to avoid law enforcement. They would sail to Cuba, Canada, Newfoundland, or the West Indies to purchase large quantities of liquor and then sail to just three miles off New York and Boston, remaining in international waters, where they were met by fast small craft and yachts. Smuggling from the sea had grown into an immense and highly coordinated criminal enterprise threatening the peace and stability of the United States.[9]

When the Coast Guard was returned to Treasury, temporary LCDR Stanley Parker was ordered to headquarters as aide for aviation, and the Navy's request for temporary Lieutenant Commander Stone to return to participate in development of the first three aircraft carriers was approved by the commandant. In 1920, Coast Guard commandant Reynolds convinced the Navy to loan the Coast Guard four Curtiss HS-2L seaplanes and two Aeromarine Model 40Fs. These six seaplanes were to operate at the first Coast Guard air station, in Morehead City, North Carolina.

Prior to Lieutenant Commander Stone's reassignment with the Navy, he had brief assignments as executive officer of the cutter *Gossiped* and as temporary commanding officer of Coast Guard Air Station (CGAS) Morehead City, supervising the reconditioning and testing of the six seaplanes and preparing the station for commissioning. LCDR Charles E. Sugden relieved Stone as the air station's temporary commanding officer on November 20, 1919, when Stone was reassigned to Navy duties. CGAS Morehead City was commissioned on March 24, 1920.[10] In turn, Sugden was relieved by the permanent commanding officer, temporary LCDR William P. Wishar, USCG.

At the end of the First World War, Congress limited the Navy to six air stations for seaplanes within the continental United States. Strategic planning led the Navy to transfer to the Coast Guard its air stations at Morehead City and (later) at Cape May, New Jersey. Thus, the Navy would have eight seaplane air stations should the Coast Guard be transferred to the Navy Department during a future war.[11] The six World War I–surplus seaplanes at Morehead City were adequate for Coast Guard operations offshore. The Aeromarine 40F was a two-seat flying boat with a top speed of 180 miles per hour and a forty-eight-foot six-inch wingspan; it was powered by one Curtiss OXX-6, hundred-horsepower engine. Each of the four

Aeromarine, Model No. 40

HS-2L flying boats—serial numbers A-1170, A-1240, A-1474, and A-1735—required a three-man crew and had a top speed of ninety-one miles per hour, a range of 517 statute miles, a wingspan of seventy-four feet, and one Liberty 12 350-horsepower engine.

CGAS Morehead City operated as an experiment, to demonstrate the value of air operations to the Coast Guard. Even though air operations were a total success, the Coast Guard received little attention from the Congress. As a result, the fledgling air station received no funding, and CGAS Morehead City was closed on July 1, 1921, after only fifteen months of operation. That same year, duralumin metal became available, and wood structure in flying boats was to be replaced by metal. The HS-2L structure was of wood; when returned to the Navy, the six seaplanes were declared obsolete and destroyed.[12]

The Coast Guard returned Stone to his temporary rank as lieutenant commander on April 21, 1924. Stone was still assigned to the Navy.

However, Stone was still a Coast Guard officer. The assistant secretary of the Treasury Department, overseeing the Coast Guard, signed a letter dated June 1, 1922, appointing LCDR. E. F. Stone, USCG, to a temporary additional assignment to "represent the Coast Guard to prepare regulations with the Army, Navy and Marine Corps, for consideration of the President relative to pay and allowances of personnel detailed to duty involving flying."

The addition of flight pay to an aviator's salary was to become a continuing source of irritation for nonaviation officers, and Stone's involvement did not make him popular with brother officers who did not fly.[13]

On April 2, 1924, to enforce Prohibition, Congress approved a budget that significantly increased the size of the Coast Guard and transferred to it twenty-five World War I four-stack destroyers from the Navy. Seventy-five-foot and thirty-eight-foot high-speed armed patrol boats were added to the Coast Guard's inventory. (The seventy-five-footers were

Launching HS-2L at CGAS Morehead City, North Carolina

HS-2L about to come up on the step

Curtiss HS-2L in flight

CGAS Morehead City Station crew at station decommissioning, July 27, 1921

nicknamed "six-bitters," because they had six mooring bits.) Many of these Coast Guard destroyers and patrol boats were centrally located in primary enforcement areas near New York and Boston. Their home ports were in New London, Connecticut, and Section Base 7 on the wharf in downtown Gloucester, Massachusetts. Section Base 7 received its first six-bitters on October 21, 1924, and its final boats on July 18, 1925.[14]

With only surface vessels to conduct normal operational duties and additional requirements for the enforcement of federal Prohibition laws, an overwhelming strain fell on men and equipment. Rum-running was so flagrant that the service was not able to cope. Rum-running vessels easily concealed themselves in large areas of ocean, forcing considerable loss of time searching for moving, evasive targets. Once again an opportunity arose to demonstrate the operational advantage of using Coast Guard air assets, this time for Prohibition enforcement.[15]

LCDR Carl Christian von Paulsen, Coast Guard aviator number six and a member of the Stone, Hall, and von Paulsen triumvirate that had initially pursued the formal founding of Coast Guard aviation, was conveniently assigned as commanding officer of Section Base 7.[16]

Seventy-five footer, or "six-bitter"

Section Base 7's seventy-five-foot patrol boats were customarily used to intercept and chase rumrunners.[17] Lieutenant Commander Wishar, Coast Guard aviator number five, wrote the following while serving at headquarters during the Rum War:

But there were so many rum-runners, and the ocean is so big, and the patrol boats had to replenish fuel and supplies, that it was often a heart breaking task. Von Paulsen as a flier knew the value of planes for searching at sea. He interested Lieutenant Commander Stephen S. Yeandle, aide to Rear Admiral Frederick Billard, Commandant of the Coast Guard, in the idea of getting planes for searching the ocean for rum runners. Yeandle in turn discussed the idea with Admiral

Billard who favored it. But there was no money, no appropriation. In spite of this, they planned and "scummed schemes," all on a shoestring. An old O2U-2 single float biplane with a 200 horse-power motor had been stored by the Navy in a hanger at Cape May Section Base. It was surplus. Some enlisted personnel from the first Coast Guard Air Station at Morehead City were at Section Base #7. A small, unused island in Gloucester Bay belonging to U.S. Fisheries near Section Base #7 was acquired for temporary use. It was called Ten Pound Island. A large surplus tent was acquired from the Army for $1.00. It became the hangar. Coast Guard aviation was starting again. Von Paulsen and Melka flew the old crate searching at sea for rum-runners and keeping tabs on patrol boats.[18]

Temporary Coast Guard air operations were established fifty miles from Gloucester at NAS Squantum, Massachusetts, on May 10, 1925, with the surplus Curtiss Marine Trophy racer O2U-2 single-float biplane, in land configuration, from NAS Cape May. The air station was located on the Squantum Peninsula jutting into Boston Harbor off Dorchester Bay. The airfield was a 714-acre site, 30 acres of which were cinder-covered runways in a triangular pattern. The longest runway was east–west and 1,800 feet long. NAS Squantum also operated a seadrome and had a 120-by-120-foot landplane hangar and a 100-by-60-foot seaplane hangar.

NAS Squantum's origin dates to 1910, when its land was leased by the Harvard Boston Aero Association. Later it became home to the Massachusetts Naval Militia.[19] Following entry in World War I, the commandant of the First Naval District was directed, on May 4, 1917, to assume control of the Naval Militia stations at Squantum and Bay Shore, New York, in order to expand Navy flight training capability. Squantum became the nation's first Naval Reserve air station.[20]

In 1922, an OU-1 observation plane, originally a Navy seaplane for Lieutenant Stone's powder-crane catapult installed on battleships and scout cruisers, had become the Navy service standard. Later OU-1 redesign added an interchangeable single main float or landplane landing gear. These redesigned aircraft were designated OU-1C. One OU-1C seaplane at NAS Cape May was further redesigned in 1922 for the Curtiss Marine Trophy race competition, with a modified Aeromarine U-873 engine. The aircraft was further modified into an O2U-2 general utility aircraft, with twin cockpit seats and a Wright Hispano E-3 engine. Before the Navy could enter the O2U-2 in the race, it was damaged during handling by a ground crew sending it to permanent storage in an NAS Cape May hangar. Much later, the Coast Guard would again receive nine landplane-configured O2U-2 Chance-Voughts from the Navy for patrolling the Mexican border.

The first use of an aircraft flying out of Squantum to chase a rumrunner was on June 20, 1925, and the O2U-2 assisted in the first capture of a "rummie" with aviation support on June 24.[21] Permanent Coast Guard air operations were moved approximately one year later to Ten Pound Island. The O2U-2 was reconfigured from landplane to floatplane. Many aircrews thought Ten Pound Island was unsuited for

O2U–2C

floatplane water operations, with its many boulders blocking the shoreline. However, CGAS Ten Pound Island was commissioned June 20, 1926. Concrete was poured for a hangar foundation, and a steel hangar was erected in the summer of 1926. Ten Pound Island would eventually become CGAS Gloucester, later moving to a new facility, CGAS Salem, Massachusetts.[22]

The second attempt to create a permanent Coast Guard air station in 1926 was highly successful, and CDR C. C. von Paulsen became commanding officer of both Base 7 and Ten Pound Island.[23] This time Congress acknowledged Coast Guard aviation's importance in searching for and locating vessels within large ocean areas. The positions of rumrunners, once located, were transmitted to Coast Guard cutters and destroyers for enforcement boardings. This coordinated operation between air and surface forces was exactly what Stone had conceived on board USCGC *Onondaga* eleven years earlier in 1915. Daily scheduled flights from Ten Pound Island accomplished a major reduction of rum-running activity within the O2U-2 operating area.[24]

Air operations against rum-running were not the only activities at Ten Pound Island. A number of radio experiments were held between aircraft and shore, and between aircraft and Coast Guard cutters and destroyers at sea. During these experiments, radio electricians Arthur Descoteaux and Clyde Solt developed the first airborne radio direction finder, using a loop antenna. Transmissions could be heard and navigational bearings taken from

Reserve NAS Squantum shown on Massachusetts Rand-McNally Air Trails Map of the day

as far as 150 miles away.[25] Undoubtedly, these experiments greatly improved the success of surveillance in enforcing Prohibition.

In 1926, in recognition of the importance of Coast Guard aviation in Prohibition-related antismuggling, law-enforcement activities, Congress finally appropriated $152,000 for design and construction of five aircraft specifically for the Coast Guard. The O2U-2 was returned to the Navy on October 27, 1926. The first OL-5 arrived on October 14, 1926—the second on November 3.[26] Three of the five amphibians were modifications of the Navy OL-5, and they were commissioned in December 1926.

The unit price of the modified OL-5 was $32,710. The hull was strongly reinforced for rough-water landings, and the wing-tip floats had special skids. A higher rudder and vertical stabilizer enhanced maneuverability and stability, as did a wingspan of forty-five feet. Fuel tanks were expanded for long law-enforcement patrols, but other limitations restricted operations. The amphibian had room for only a pilot, an observer crewman, and one passenger. In view of its cruising speed of 75 knots, top speed of 120 knots, range of 425 miles, and service ceiling under 13,000 feet, other options were considered. USCG No. 103 crashed in November 1929, No. 101 crashed in June 1930, and No. 102 was decommissioned in April 1935.

Flying the OL-5s, the Coast Guard pioneered a number of techniques to perform assigned missions. Most important was experimentation in heavy-sea landings and in arming the

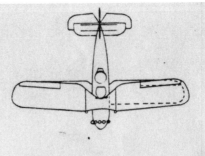

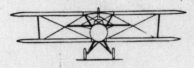

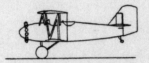

MANUFACTURER:
Chance-Vought
Contract No.: U.S.N.
Span: 36'-0", 34'-6"
Height: 11'-0"
Fuel: 110 gallons
Empty Weight: 2252 lbs.
Top Speed: 147 mph
Cruise Speed: 90 mph
Sea-Level Climb: 1810 fpm
ENGINE: Pratt and Whitney
Take-off Power: 450
Prop. Diameter/Blades: 8'-11½"/2

DESIGNATION: 02U-2

Unit Cost: No Cost
Length: 24'-5¾"
Wing Area: 319 Sq. Ft.
Oil: 8 gallons
Gross Weight: 3703 lbs.
Stall Speed: 58 mph
Range: 450 miles
Service Ceiling: 20,100 ft.

"Wasp" R-1340-B

Places: 2
Std Steel, 3792, fixed pitch

Coast Guard Number	Commissioned	Decommissioned
117	July 1934	August 1934
118	Aug. 1934	Jan. 1940
119	May 1934	April 1937. surveyed
120	Feb. 1935	April 1937, surveyed
121	May 1935	June 1937, surveyed
122	Mar. 1935	June 1937, surveyed

Chance-Vought O2U-2 specifications sheet

OL-5 with machine guns to enforce the law. The two remaining flying boats were given Coast Guard numbers CG-1 and CG-2. While talking with the designer of the OL-5, Commander von Paulsen told him,

> That airplane of yours was a real departure at that time. It was a leader—a good, sound plane with a sound engine that gave no trouble if properly cared for. As for the plane—it flew so easily that I never gave its "deadbeat" flying characteristics much thought. The last one was in use in 1935 and then had been used so much it got worn out. Two had been in crashes—one by clear pilot error and the other by an unavoidable collision with the yacht "Minx" at the New London boat races in June 1930. That one was fully repairable.[27]

CDR C. C. von Paulsen, commanding officer Base 7, and CGAS Ten Pound Island, and ENS L. M. Melka, May 20, 1927

In addition, two Chance-Vought UO-4 amphibians were purchased in December 1926. This aircraft also was an extended Navy design, derived from the UO-1. The UO-4 was a float-style aircraft incorporating the wing design of the new Navy FU aircraft. It carried a crew of two, had a thirty-four-foot three-and-one-half-inch wing span, a top speed of 106 knots, a range of 365 miles, and a service ceiling of 14,900 feet above mean sea level. It was powered by Wright Aero J-50 Whirlwind R-790, 220-horsepower engines.[28] The UO-4s were assigned Coast Guard numbers 4 and 5 and later registered as V104 and V105.

CGAS Ten Pound Island with Loening OL-5 in hangar

CGAS Ten Pound Island photographs

CGAS Ten Pound Island first pilots and hangar crew (commanding officer CDR C. C. von Paulsen rear row, third from left)

Loening OL-5 during maintenance at CGAS Ten Pound Island

Loening OL-5 during maintenance at CGAS Ten Pound Island

Loening OL-5 landing in Gloucester Harbor

Loening OL-5 anchored off CGAS Ten Pound Island ramp

Loening OL-5 resting on beaching gear on CGAS Ten Pound Island ramp

Loening OL-5 resting on beaching gear on CGAS Ten Pound Island ramp preparing for launch

Loening OL-5 machine-gun check on CGAS Ten Pound Island ramp

Vought UO-4

Vought UO-4

Vought UO-4 flown by LT William Foley, USCG, to CGAS Salem from CGAS Cape May via Ten Pound Island

OL-5 on patrol with two six-bitters

OL-5 and six-bitters pursuing rum-runners

In his career, Stone had two interservice transfer assignments for work with the Navy. The first was when the Coast Guard was transferred by a presidential executive order for the duration of the world war. Following the war, Stone was detached from the Navy, on September 11, 1919. The Navy Department, Bureau of Navigation, detachment orders stated:

In parting with Lieutenant Stone, the Bureau desires to express its appreciation of the services he rendered the Bureau during the war. He is not only a skillful pilot, but an officer of excellent judgment and considerable technical attainments in the line of aviation so that he proved himself peculiarly fitted for the duties to which he has been assigned.[29]

During this assignment the Navy offered Stone a promotion to permanent captain, USN, if he transferred to the Navy. He declined and was returned to the Coast Guard as a lieutenant.[30]

As we have seen, Stone was ordered to his second Navy assignment in 1920. With expansion for Prohibition law enforcement, the Coast Guard was particularly short on experienced officers, and the Coast Guard commandant ultimately requested return of Stone from his second special Navy assignment. Temporary Lieutenant Commander Stone was detached from his second assignment with the Navy Department on September 21, 1926, and the Chief of the Navy's Bureau of Aeronautics awarded Stone with a Letter of Commendation, dated November 4, 1926. The bureau chief, Rear Admiral Moffett, commended Stone for "valuable services in the development of catapult and deck arresting gear for aircraft and aircraft carriers, and as a test pilot."

Most Coast Guard aviators, then and now, have believed that Lieutenant Commander Stone was slighted by senior officers in Coast Guard headquarters, Washington, D.C., because his returning assignment to the Coast Guard was only that of executive officer on USCGC (U.S. Coast Guard Cutter) *Modoc*. All who served with him thought he deserved assignment as a commanding officer or another role that would use his demonstrated leadership and technical capabilities. *Modoc's* home port was Wilmington, North Carolina, and it was assigned International Ice Patrol duty off Newfoundland.[31]

USCGC *Modoc*

In 1926, the Navy's Morrow Board recommended a five-year modernization and expansion program that would eliminate the limitations of World War I equipment. The Navy's era of flying-boat domination had come to an end, and the aircraft carrier now would be its most pressing developmental concern. However, this was not true for the Coast Guard. The Coast Guard still required rapid aerial response, rescue capability offshore, and aerial search capability covering large expanses of ocean. The flying boat remained relevant to the Coast Guard until arrival of the helicopter at the end of World War II.

The Coast Guard commissioned CGAS Cape May in 1926, located on part of the old naval air station, and started construction on CGAS Dinner Key, in Miami, Florida.[32] Chief Warrant Officer Charles T. Thrun, Coast Guard aviator three, flew the first Cape May aircraft mission on October 29, 1926, formally activating air station operations.

Additionally, three RD-1 Douglas Dolphin amphibians were procured. Commander von Paulsen was transferred from Section Base 7 to be the new Cape May air station's commanding officer.[33]

Eventually, CGAS Cape May would also be closed. Air station property, however, was retained by the Coast Guard as a section base command. Years later, another CGAS Cape May would be commissioned there, as well as a large "boot camp" to train new enlisted recruits for World War II.

Stone received a permanent commission as lieutenant commander on February 9, 1928, when he was assigned to command the Coast Guard destroyer *Monaghan*, in her home port of New London, Connecticut. *Monaghan*'s primary mission was chasing rumrunners and enforcing Prohibition.[34]

Stone continued to enforce Prohibition and was again assigned command, this time to the Coast Guard destroyer *Cummings*, from June 1929 until June 1931. Throughout this period, he maintained his interest in aviation. During years at sea, he studied swell and sea conditions for the purpose of deriving optimal heavy-sea landing and takeoff procedures for seaplanes.[35]

One of the Prohibition arrests by Stone and the *Cummings* crew describes both the cat-and-mouse play between smugglers and the Coast Guard and the halfhearted support given by the courts.

Cutters, destroyers, and patrol boats attached to the New London Command were assigned grids within New London's area of operations between New York and Boston. On June 14, 1931, during Stone's last patrol on *Cummings*, the destroyer was in its assigned grid when the 165-foot white steamer yacht *Surf*, flying the New York Yacht Club flag, was sighted. *Surf*

CGAS Cape May with old Navy dirigible hangar before its destruction

Coast Guard destroyer *Monaghan*

was on an early-morning course for Shinnecock Light, Long Island, and was riding low in the water, indicating a heavy load. The yacht's crew was enacting a charade, decked out as yachtsmen, smoking cigars, and being served breakfast on deck in grand style. When *Cummings* closed in for a close look, Coast Guard officers noticed dirty working hands smoking the cigars and vertical hull scrape marks from a nested open-sea mooring to another vessel. All her portholes were covered to hide the inside of the yacht. When an armed boarding party was put on board to search, the yacht's owner attempted to bribe the boarding officer. The yacht was seized, approximately four thousand cases of liquor were discovered, and the crew was arrested. Even though the legal case was very strong and the owner was a known smuggler wanted for another bribery attempt, the courts failed to convict anyone.[36]

Truly, enforcing Prohibition was a thankless job!

Coast Guard Aviation Force Growth Begins

Pages thirty-six and thirty-seven of the *Annual Report of the United States Coast Guard for 1928* include an enthusiastic comment by the commandant of the service, RADM F. C. Billard, USCG, stating that the air arm of the Coast Guard should be "enlarged and made permanent because of the 'manifold uses' of aircraft" and that "the direction of saving life and property from the perils of the sea, locating floating derelicts, searching for wrecked seaplanes, assisting in the repair of disabled aircraft, searching for missing vessels and boats and for those reported to be in need of assistance, enforcing the customs and navigation laws and other laws of the United States, extending medical aid in extraordinary emergencies, assisting fishermen, and affording other kindred services where haste and

Coast Guard destroyer *Cummings*

speed are requisite." Rear Admiral Billard's statement was an accurate summary of what the Coast Guard's air forces would become.

In 1928, a Coast Guard aviation section was added to the Washington headquarters staff, under the leadership of LCDR Norman Hall, another triumvirate member. The new section established mission specifications for a new multimission aircraft that "could fly hundreds of miles and land in the open sea for rescues and medical evacuations." This mission could be accomplished only by a large seaplane or amphibian. This, in turn, would lead to procurement of seven Douglas Dolphin RD-2 amphibians and five Viking O-38 seaplanes in 1931.[37] It would also lead to the 1932 concept of a "flying lifeboat."

Hall's aviation section established the nation's first air traffic control system in 1929, at no additional cost to the federal government, and it was a Coast Guard operation. A radio communications network was established, comprising Coast Guard air stations and lifeboat stations along the Atlantic coast. It provided an important service, keeping track of aircraft flying the coastal routes and identifying, locating, and dispatching assistance from the closest Coast Guard units to aircraft in distress. All Coast Guard air stations and lifeboat stations were shown on air navigation charts of the day. The network did not control aircraft but became an efficient communication system. It was a "flight following system," whereby radio reports between coastal flights and the Coast Guard tracked the progress of aircraft. Should an aircraft lose communication for a two-hour period, an emergency response would begin. Many aircraft availed themselves of the service—329 aircraft during the first two months. By 1932, over 1,400 radio communication transit reports had been processed by Atlantic Coast Guard units. Eventually, the system was expanded to include the Gulf of Mexico and Pacific coastlines.

Ultimately the Coast Guard air-traffic-following system was a victim of its own success. The Bureau of Air Commerce developed a nationwide air traffic control system in 1936, and the Civil Aeronautics Authority was established in 1938. The Coast Guard system was no longer needed in this capacity, but it continued to expand to broadcast messages and provide communication between Coast Guard cutters, aircraft, and shore stations and their boats.[38]

CHAPTER NINE

Catapults and Aircraft Carriers

1917–1926

*W*ith the end of World War I, a presidential executive order in August 1919 returned the Coast Guard to the Treasury Department.

The Navy knew Stone from wartime service, as a test pilot with demonstrated experience in advanced physics and engineering disciplines, and as the pilot of NC-4 on the first transatlantic flight. The Navy requested Lieutenant Stone's services again, as a test pilot and to lead development of shipboard and aircraft carrier catapults and arresting gear. While assigned to USS Huntington *during the war, Stone had initiated work on an engineering design for a brake on the cruiser's catapult car. On November 20, 1919, the Coast Guard commandant approved the Navy's request and ordered Stone to report to the Aircraft Division in the Bureau of Construction and Repair at the Washington, D.C., Navy Yard.*[1]

Mr. Lee N. Pearson, historian of the Naval Air Systems Command states, "When I was doing research on catapults, I found a couple of papers that were indicative of Stone's role. His work on flying off land machines from the coal barge and early catapult work have seemed to me to be essential to the development of the carrier *Langley*."

The catapult referred to in the paper was actuated by compressed air, and one of Stone's projects was developing a brake that would keep the car from going over the side on every shot.[2]

The following is a summary of catapult development prior to Lieutenant Stone reporting to the Aircraft Division, Bureau of Construction and Repair:[3]

1917—Ford Instrument Company provided a blueprint to the Navy for a bomb-throwing pneumatic catapult to penetrate armor plate.

1918—Early Navy internal report was issued on catapult launchings.

1919—Washington Navy Yard on April 15 requests conversion of *Jupiter* (Coal Barge 302) to a catapult barge. Washington Navy Yard then requests "return of *Jupiter* to the Washington Navy Yard for purpose of flying off platforms for shipboard airplanes."

1920—*Jupiter* became ready for aircraft catapult launch experimentation.

A great deal of discussion took place from 1920 to 1925 over design and installation of pneumatic aircraft catapults on the top of battleship and cruiser gun turrets.[4] There was concern that aircraft catapults might block vision from naval gun directors, periscopes, and control boards that compute gunfire solutions by inputting ship's course and speed, the target's position relative to the ship, and the target's course and speed.

After reporting for duty, Stone was active as a test pilot flying landplanes from *Jupiter*, anchored in the Potomac River. At the time, torpedo and torpedo-tube pneumatic launching equipment were being removed from battleships and cruisers.[5] Torpedo air compressors would soon be used only for aircraft catapults. Stone again experienced firsthand the common problems experienced by the fleet with pneumatic aircraft catapults. There was difficulty regulating air pressure throughout the aircraft launch and, therefore, in maintaining consistency of the propelling thrust. Pilots were not happy.[6]

Summer 1920—The Navy General Board suggested the use of pneumatic catapults for "starting airplanes from stowage on turret tops."[7]

September 25, 1920—Operations Department approved a General Board recommendation "for carrying and launching airplanes on battleships but not at turret height in battleships forty-five and fifty-five; and must be governed accordingly in design of directors, periscopes and armored ship control board in Battle Station number two for turret height."[8]

1921, USS *Arizona* (BB-39) turret catapult, with Newport 28 aircraft

Atlantic Fleet first catapult test, August 13, 1920, pilot LCDR V. C. Griffin, USN

August 13, 1920, USS *Oklahoma* (BB-37) Vought aircraft on number-two turret

Atlantic Fleet catapult test, August 13, 1920, pilot LT A. C. Wagner, USNRF

Atlantic Fleet catapult test, August 13, 1920. Vought seaplane coming alongside USS *Oklahoma* motor sailer for recovery and hoist to ship's catapult.

On December 14, 1921, Stone invented a gunpowder catapult design that maintained consistency of propelling thrust and eliminated dependence on cumbersome torpedo air compressors, which took valuable ship space.[9] By using naval ordnance three- and five-inch gun cartridges, propelling thrust could be controlled.[10]

Stone worked with Mr. Carl F. Jensen of the Bureau of Ordnance (BUORD), and Jensen produced formal engineering drawings for Stone's test powder catapult. The test gun included Stone's hydraulic brake for the catapult car, eliminating the common problem of the propelled car breaking the mechanical stop at the end of the run, causing the carriage to fly over the side of the ship.

Everyone started jumping on the bandwagon, claiming the idea for a powder catapult as their own. As a result Stone and Jensen submitted a U.S. patent application for the powder catapult. Even though the application gave the U.S. Navy unrestricted and unlimited rights to use the powder catapult, the invention was nonetheless handled as classified. Controversy arose over classification, use, and ownership of the idea. The Navy Judge Advocate General (JAG) settled the matter, agreeing with Stone and Jensen, and he suggested that BUORD provide assistance for patent application. The Navy JAG ruled that Stone "indeed invented the powder catapult."[11]

> **"Subject: Turret Catapult—mfg of,**
> "1. Forwarded, requesting that the work referred to in the attached correspondence be undertaken by the Naval Gun Factory at the earliest date. Special emergency priority should be assigned to this work and every effort made to complete the one catapult for test by August 15."[12]

Controversy aside, the idea of a powder catapult gained strong support from both BUAIR and BUORD. To test the powder-catapult concept, BUORD wrote to the commandant and to the superintendent of the U.S. Naval Gun Factory and provided engineering drawings. The test catapult was manufactured and successfully tested.

1922—The Bureau of Aeronautics requested comments from other bureaus and the fleet concerning a study by BUAIR on the feasibility of using powder as a substitute for compressed air for catapult operations.

1922—The Navy Department approved the director of war plans and the General Board recommendation that "Scout Cruisers of the *Omaha* type each be equipped with two Mark I catapults and two 2-seater airplanes." The Mark I was powered by compressed air.

1922—A memo from Desk E (Delano) of a conference with Admiral Strauss relative to airplanes for battleships reports, "He was undecided whether only a spotting plane or whether a spotting plane and 2 combat planes shall be assigned BB [to a battleship]. Will postpone question of deck and turret catapults until Aero has finished subject of design of turret catapult. Lists Ord. [ordnance] Installations that turret catapults must not interfere with."

```
37716/373
(A3)-O MES                    2nd endorsement
CONFIDENTIAL                                    APR 21 1923

From:        Chief of the Bureau of Ordnance.
To  :        The Judge Advocate General.

Subject:     Patent - Powder as a Source of Power for Catapulting
             Airplanes.

Enclosures:  (A) 4 enclos. Bu.Ord. file 37716/373 of April 19,1923.
(Herewith)   (B) 2   "     "   "   "    37716/365 of Mar.12 and 17,1923.

    1.  Referred.

    2.  The Chief of Bureau, until recently, was not aware of the fact
that the suggestion to use powder as a source of power for a catapult
originated with Lieutenant Stone.  If such is the case, it is not de-
sired in any way to deprive him of such credit as may be found due him.

    3.  Lieutenant Stone is on duty in the Bureau of Aeronautics and
Mr. Jeansen is employed in the Bureau of Ordnance.  No matter who sug-
gested this form of catapult, the fact remains that it was developed in
Government time and at Government expense, namely, in the Bureau of
Ordnance Drafting Room and at the Naval Gun Factory under the approval
of the Chief of the Bureau of Ordnance.

    4.  Under the conditions, it is believed that the idea, (and any
patent), becomes the property of the Government.  It is further believed
that any patent taken out should be kept secret in order that the de-
velopment should not become a matter of public knowledge.

    5.  It is not believed that either Lieutenant Stone or Mr.Jeansen
have any claim to any rights under any patent issued and that, even
should so-called "commercial rights" exist, they would remain the proper-
ty of the Government by reason of the status of Lieutenant Stone and Mr.
Jeansen.

    6.  The Chief of Bureau of Ordnance, having formed an opinion re-
garding the case, does not desire to judge the matter.  In any event,
it comes within the cognizance of the Judge Advocate General's Office
and is therefore forwarded for decision.

                                    Chas B McVay Jr
                              Chas. B. McVay, Jr.,
                              Chief of Bureau.

DECLASSIFIED
Authority NND745071
By        NARA  Date 2/3/05
```

BUORD 2nd endorsement letter to Navy Judge Advocate General acknowledging Stone invented the powder catapult

1923—Pay and Supply, New York, stated: "Air plants for propulsion of catapults are under cognizance of Construction and Repair and charges for future installations on battleships and similar vessels should be made to accounts under C&R and Eng, and cost for modifying torpedo air compressor system is likewise chargeable to C&R; but will allow the charge to stand as at present chargeable to O&OS for modifying on *Omaha*."

June 12, 1923—An interdivision memorandum from BUAIR Plans Division to Material Division, Aer-P-BB 900-1, 203-O, asked:

1. Please furnish this division with the present status of the following projects:

Installation of catapults on battleships.

Installation of catapults on light cruisers.

Installation of catapults on destroyers.

Installation of catapults on training ships.

Airplane stowage on submarines.

Pulitzer racing planes.

Schneider Cup racing planes.

June 18, 1923—A memorandum from Material Division responded, "MK [Mark] I catapults on BB and LC [light cruiser] in process, installation on destroyers, [has] not been approved."

1924—NAS San Diego forwarded drawings and photograph of installation of the Mark I catapult for training purposes. It further requested that a five-hundred-ton steel coal barge be assigned for the installation.

1924—Commander in Chief (CINC) Battle Fleet, concurred with "installation of aircraft catapults on battleships and requested early installation for tests."

1925—The Washington Navy Yard contemplated using the five-inch/.51-caliber cartridge as ammunition for the catapult gun.

1925—BUAERO submitted proposal to the Navy Department "for catapult development, construction and installation for the next few years." The department approved the plan, and it became "Naval Aeronautical policy."[13]

The final result for Stone's Mark V P-type turntable powder catapult is described by a naval communication message from CINC Battle Fleet: "All ships having catapults launched their planes and maintained good communication during force practice, especially good work was done by powder catapult and MO [USS *Missouri* (BB-63)] plane."[14]

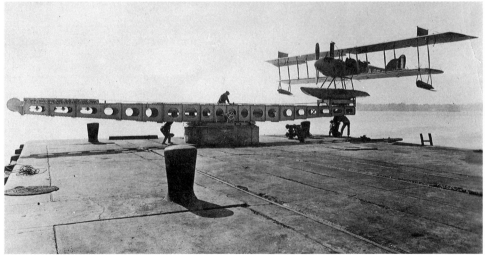

Earlier pneumatic turntable catapult tested at Navy Aircraft Factory. Later was converted to Stone's Mark V P-type powder turntable catapult

BUAERO (later BUAER) then submitted a proposal, approved by Secretary of the Navy, for catapult development, construction, and installation.[15] A conference was held between BUAERO and BUORD to discuss design of the Mark V P-type turntable catapult, with a view toward fixing the design limitations affecting the technical bureaus so that enough information would be available to proceed with formal design.[16] Project Order 640 was written for BUORD to manufacture four powder catapult guns.[17]

Stone's powder catapults were soon installed on battleships and cruisers. His work on shipboard catapults was complete when the test of the prototype powder catapult was successful. His new assignment was to lead development and installation of catapults and arresting gear for aircraft carriers.

Stone's experience and education were perfect for this task. He had a firm grasp on physics and engineering principles for aircraft catapults, as well as experience landing on and taking off from the recently remodeled coal barge *Jupiter.*

U.S. Navy planners had envisioned four 35,000-ton aircraft carriers with thirty-five knot speeds. This speed, headed into the wind, was needed for early propeller aircraft takeoffs and landings, and thirty-five knots was also needed to operate with the new *Lexington*-class battle cruiser class under construction. Postwar budget battles for fiscal years 1920 and 1921, in a disarmament atmosphere, encouraged Congress to veto proposed aircraft-carrier funding.[18] Congress's frugality actually hastened development of catapults and arresting gear by denying funding to the four thirty-five-knot aircraft carriers.

The compromise was to convert *Jupiter* into the experimental aircraft carrier USS *Langley* (CV-1). Instead of four large, fast carriers, the 11,000-ton, fifteen-knot *Langley* was commissioned on March 20, 1922. She was the crown jewel of the fleet until 1927, when *Saratoga* (CV-3) and *Lexington* (CV-2) joined the fleet. Due to the slow speed at which she launched and retrieved aircraft, *Jupiter* would be converted again, to a seaplane tender, in 1937.[19]

As early as 1910 and 1911, the United States proved that aircraft could fly on and off a ship's deck, but little had been done since Eugene Ely's demonstration with the Curtiss Pusher aircraft. Both the British and the Japanese governments started development of aircraft carriers in 1918. HMS *Hermes* and Japan's *Hosho* were, realistically, cruisers with flight decks. Ironically, both *Saratoga* and *Lexington* were originally battle cruisers, their hulls converted during construction to aircraft carriers in 1922.[20] 1922 was also the year when, on July 3, the first class of aviation student pilots at NAS Pensacola was trained in landplanes in preparation for aircraft carrier operations.

Soon after Rear Admiral Moffett took the helm at BUAERO, he was appointed technical adviser to the 1921 U.S. delegation to the Washington Naval Conference. As it turned out, this was a grand opportunity to make the case for U.S. Navy fast fleet carriers. Battle cruisers *Saratoga* and *Lexington,* under construction, were prohibited by the treaty. Moffett handled negotiations during this conference and solved the treaty problem by converting both cruisers to aircraft carriers. Although pleased with the results, Moffett was amused by the lack of interest in aviation by the other negotiators; in fact, it made his negotiation to convert the cruisers easier.[21]

Both *Langley's* slow speed and the need to use her as a test bed for the conversions of *Saratoga* and *Lexington* hastened development of aircraft arresting gear for landings. As aircraft weight, weight of ordnance, power, and takeoff and landing speeds increased, the need for both catapults and arresting gear became increasingly important.

Langley originally had two pneumatic catapults, but one was removed. Landplane propeller aircraft of the time did not require catapults for takeoff, but seaplanes did. Seaplanes were stored on a catapult carriage. The carriage was connected to the carrier's catapult for takeoffs. For landplanes, arresting cables were laid out athwart ship (from side to side), with weights on either end. The weights were made of greased, slotted boilerplate, greased so they would slide easily across each other. When the aircraft's arresting hooks engaged the cable, the cable's bitter end would drag the first weight. As additional cable played out, the second weight was engaged, then the next, and so on. This brought the aircraft to a sudden stop that broke the tail section off, since aircraft were not originally built for this stress on their airframes.[22]

USS *Jupiter,* Coal Barge 302

USS *Langley* (CV-1)

First *Langley* landing

Escorts making smoke to hide USS *Langley*

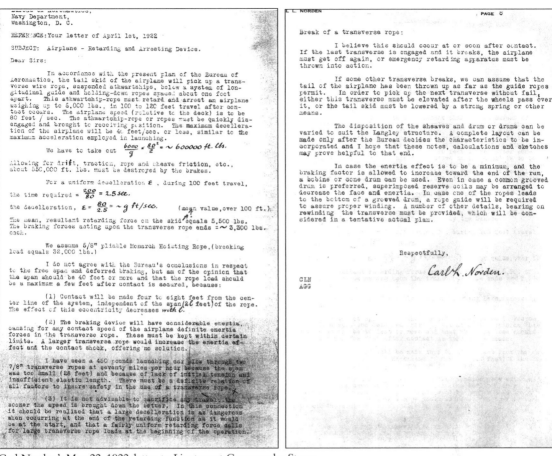

Carl Norden's May 22, 1922, letter to Lieutenant Commander Stone

When *Saratoga* and *Lexington* construction was changed from battle cruisers to a new class of aircraft carrier, a pneumatic catapult and arresting gear were included in the modification requirements. The pneumatic catapult was still used to assist with some takeoffs.

Saratoga and *Lexington* conversion was a slow process, due to inadequate funding and cost overruns.[23] To kick off development of aircraft-carrier arresting gear, Lieutenant Stone sent a BUAERO letter dated April 1, 1922, to Carl L. Norden and to Warren Noble Engineering Corporation of North Carolina, giving requirements for Mark I experimental arresting gear for USS *Langley* and inviting a contract proposal. The arresting-gear design requirement was "to stop a 6,000 pound aircraft traveling 80 feet/second by uniform deceleration in a run of approximately 150 feet."[24]

Warren Nobel Engineering Corporation responded with a May 16, 1922, letter, a proposed design, and drawings. Carl Norden responded with a May 22 letter and engineering design, with complete formulas and calculations. (See pages 1 and 8 of Carl Norden's proposal letter above as a sample.)[25] Norden not only responded to Stone's request

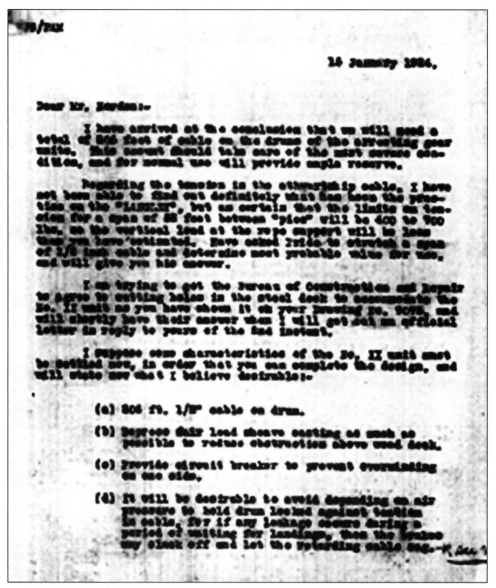

Lieutenant Commander Stone's acceptance letter to Norden, page 1

for a proposal but also offered changes that would improve performance. Stone accepted Norden's proposal.

In addition to Lieutenant Stone's work on the carrier arresting gear, BUORD reserved, in its letter S7716/367(T3-G5-O, VBJ to BUENG, via BUAIR) of May 7, 1923, four Mark VII, Mod. (Modification) 6 torpedo air compressors, intended for installation on Battleship No. 50 and Battle Cruiser No. 6, to go instead to *Lexington* and *Saratoga* for aircraft catapults.[26]

Many technical letters, design changes, and engineering drawings went between Stone and Norden, and Norden traveled often to meet with Stone in Washington, D.C. Information

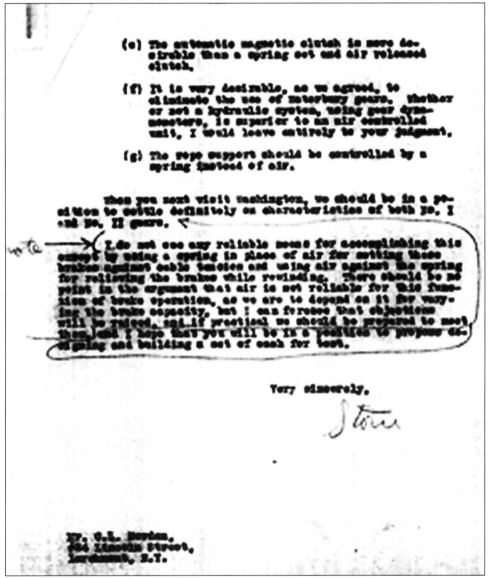

Lieutenant Commander Stone's acceptance letter, page 2

concerning the operational capability of Navy warships was normally classified. When Norden was cleared for classified information, Stone sent him a letter dated December 24, 1923, that included "confidential deck-plan drawings for aeroplane carriers numbered two and three, *Saratoga* and *Lexington*." This prompted more design-change discussion from Norden, including moving the cable drum below deck, and a controversy arose concerning holes cut in the steel deck to accommodate the second arresting-gear unit. Stone's reply of January 15, 1924, supplied the needed design decisions.[27]

By 1924, engineering drawings and details described in letters had advanced to the point that prototype equipment was being manufactured. NAS/NOB (Naval Air Station/Naval

Operating Base) Hampton Roads, Virginia, had been selected as the shoreside test site for both aircraft carrier catapult and arresting gear. A. M. Pride, assigned to NAS Hampton Roads, was therefore included in distribution of engineering drawings and design descriptions. He communicated directly with Lieutenant Stone, stating that the design appeared practical. He suggested an appropriate arresting-gear height above the deck and suggested that an accelerometer be adapted for the test aircraft rather than for the catapult car. This would make it useful for testing both catapult and arresting gear. Stone requested Pride to rig a test arresting-gear wire. Since no tension meter was provided, Pride, by adapting other materials, provided a scale arm with spring balance to measure line tension. He provided test results and notified Stone that the catapult had been installed and that the trestle was two-thirds complete.[28]

Stone received formal contractual engineering designs for Mark I and Mark II arresting gear from Norden in a March 29, 1924, letter. The design was impressive, since it weighed less than half his original proposal and was superior in many other respects. BUAERO replied with a formal letter approving the preliminary design, assigning specific shipboard spaces for the equipment, and requiring a "$3^{1}/_{2}$ safety factor for arresting gear."[29]

Stone was promoted to temporary lieutenant commander on April 21, 1924.

Several interesting observations can be made from Norden's handwritten letter to Stone below. First, both Stone and Norden were involved in the physics and engineering formulas chosen. Also, Norden had complete trust in Stone as the Navy's leader for this task. This can be seen on page 2, following his signature, where Norden suggests he send correspondence to Stone's home to avoid a meddling BUAERO bureaucracy.[30]

On August 9, Stone received the formal final design for testing from Norden and convened an engineering conference to reach agreement on what steps would be taken to obtain the first test unit of the Norden arresting gear for aircraft carriers. Present were Carl Norden, Commander Webster, USN, LCDR E. F. Stone, USCG, and Lieutenant Pennoyer, USN. The conferees agreed to a contract with Norden for final detailed production drawings, and divided the manufacture of component parts of the arresting gear to be tested between Norden and the Washington Navy Yard. BUORD was asked to agree with delivery in mid-October. The conferees agreed that the Washington Navy Yard would assemble the parts and ship the entire unit to the Norfolk Navy Yard for functional performance testing. The Mark II catapult and test gear were already at the Norfolk yard.[31]

Lieutenant Commander Stone received Norden correspondence dated August 19, 1924, giving Norden's account of the conference and reporting assignment responsibilities and contract initiation. This letter also advised Stone that Norden had booked passage to Cherbourg for a September vacation. Norden had assigned his senior engineer, Theodore H. Barth, to be his representative. From this point on, Barth was fully involved with arresting-gear development and testing. Stone received four letters from Barth during June,

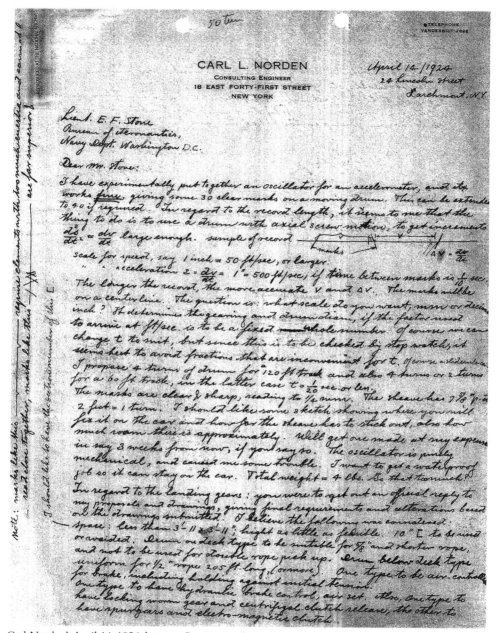

Carl Norden's April 14, 1924, letter to Stone, page 1

July, and August. These letters dealt with a request by a Commander Whiting, USN, for an arresting-gear specification requirement of ten- or fifteen-second rewind time; a report on results from twenty-six shots into a Norden arresting-gear test bed; a request for data from the NAS/NOB Hampton Roads tests conducted by Pride; a request concerning contract payment; and a statement that he was ready for Navy tests. He made many coordinating trips to NAS/NOB Hampton Roads.[32]

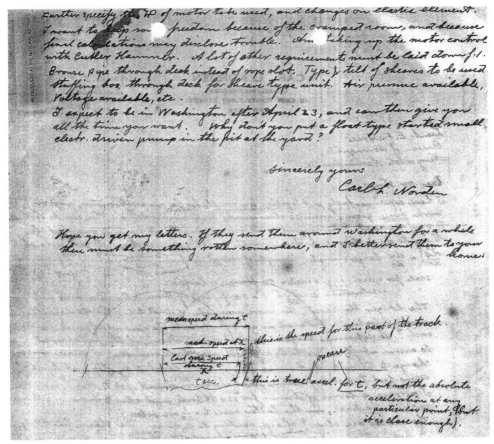

Carl Norden's April 14 letter, page 2

When the Coast Guard had returned to the Treasury Department in 1919 and the Navy first requested Stone to participate in the development of catapults and the first three aircraft carriers, demand for experienced shipboard officers had not been critical. However, as we have seen, times dramatically changed when the Coast Guard acquired Navy destroyers later in the Prohibition era to fight the Rum War. With the addition of these ships, the Coast Guard found itself short of experienced midgrade officers to command them. The Coast Guard commandant, RADM F. C. Billard, needed Lieutenant Commander Stone's return to the Coast Guard from temporary assignment to the Navy in order to command a destroyer. Admiral Billard received telephone calls from a Captain Land and Commander Whiting of the Navy's Bureau of Aeronautics explaining the importance of Stone's work. The Navy bureau chief, Rear Admiral Moffett, made a personal request to continue Stone's services.[33]

Recognizing the importance of Stone's work for the Navy, Rear Admiral Billard wrote the following January 6, 1925, letter to Moffett: "I will permit Lieut. Commander Stone to continue on duty with your bureau until the work upon which he is now engaged is so far progressed that you can spare his services without detriment to the interests of your bureau."[34]

Admiral Moffett replied on January 8, 1925:

> My dear Admiral Billard, I wish to thank you for your letter of January 6, in which you grant permission to Lieutenant Commander Stone to continue duty in the Bureau of Aeronautics until the work on which he is now engaged is so far progressed that his services can be spared without detriment to the best interest of this bureau.
>
> I can not commend too highly the work which Lieutenant Commander Stone has done in this Bureau. It is owing to his technical ability, attention to duty and perseverance that the development of the powder catapult has been perfected, made ready for production and issued to the service. Lieutenant Commander Stone is still employed upon catapult work and also on the installation of arresting devices for the new aircraft carriers *Lexington* and *Saratoga*. This work is of the highest priority at present in the Bureau, and because of its great importance and Stone's familiarity with it, it is necessary that he should continue in this Bureau.
>
> However, I fully realize the need of the Coast Guard for Lieut. Commander Stone's services, and appreciate all the more your cooperation in permitting him to stay on here. In view of the shortage of commissioned officers in the Coast Guard and your urgent need for Lieutenant Commander Stone's services, as soon as practical the Bureau of Aeronautics will detail one of its own officers to understudy Lieutenant Commander Stone with the object of relieving him when this officer becomes indoctrinated in this work and proves himself capable of taking over the responsibilities of this task.
>
> Sincerely yours
>
> (s) W. A. Moffett
>
> Rear Admiral, USN.[35]

F. W. Pennoyer, USN, was Stone's appointed understudy.

Adding to the relevance of the aircraft carrier, LT John D. Price, USN, made the first night aircraft carrier landing on board *Langley* on April 8, 1922.

In 1925 there was a flurry of activity between Lieutenant Commander Stone, Norden/ Barth, A. Ward of NAS/NOB Hampton Roads, and the Washington and Norfolk Navy Yards. A September 2 letter from Ward provided Stone with an installation status for catapult and arresting-gear testing. All the pneumatic compressor parts were currently at the Norfolk Navy Yard, and installation at NAS Hampton Roads would occur around 20–25 October. The Navy Yard was doing a good job of it, Ward reported, and approximately two thousand pounds per square inch would be available for the tests. The posts and wire for the second arresting-gear wire were installed, and Ward wanted to know if Stone wanted a rail or guide on each side of the track to carry the aircraft's hook and first wire in line with the second wire. Ward had ordered machine milling equipment and other material that would be needed. He closed with an urgent plea for additional manpower. Postwar budgets had left naval aviation short of manpower in most areas.[36]

Lieutenant Commander Stone's leadership and patience were about to be tested. The Norfolk Navy Yard was responsible for arresting-gear delivery to NAS/NOB Hampton Roads by December 1, contingent upon receiving Norden's parts. The yard was to pay Norden for the parts, but Norden had not received payment, and the yard had not received payment for its own work. Payments had been tied up between the assistant supply officer, the contracting officer, the Norfolk Navy Yard, and the rest of the bureaucracy. Mr. Barth stated he sent a "piping hot letter" to the commandant of the Navy Yard, followed by a "nice lady-like letter to the Assistant Supply Officer."

The commandant of the Norfolk Navy Yard jumped into the debacle with a conference and sent a stern letter to the Bureau of Supplies and Accounts asking it to straighten things out. He sent a letter dated 19 October to Stone with this information and voiced concern as to whether parts be received from a "temperamental" Norden on time. Stone smoothed the waters, and things got back on track.[37]

The Barth letter, shown below, illustrates several interesting points. First, Barth respected Stone's suggested design change for a spring-loaded release for the catapult car to reduce time between aircraft retrievals. The second paragraph is a humorous end to the contract payment debacle described in the above paragraphs. Third, Norden and Barth were starting to show concern for how late hours and stress were weighing on Stone.

In spite of delays, Barth shipped the equipment assigned to Norden during December. As is normal with a new product design, many small adjustments took place as the arresting-gear test equipment was slowly being assembled at the Norfolk Navy Yard. NAS/NOB Hampton Roads sent Stone good news on January 21, 1926: "The new set of Arresting Gear will come from the Navy Yard Monday afternoon. Most probably we can operate next Thursday." Following arresting-gear installation at Hampton Roads and during preparation for installation on *Saratoga* and *Lexington,* use of the new equipment naturally led to quite a few minor design changes. These changes all had to be executed through contract changes.[38]

Everything came together in early 1926, and formal test plans were in place for catapult and arresting-gear installation on *Saratoga* and *Lexington.*

Stone's next task was to oversee the outfitting of *Saratoga* and *Lexington* with catapults and arresting gear. Following installation, the commanding officer of *Saratoga* requested that BUAERO have Lieutenant Commander Stone on board during the new aircraft carrier's sea trials, a high compliment from a fellow naval aviator.[39]

The design of arresting gear for aircraft carriers today is essentially the same, with changes to accommodate the weight, mass, and speed of jet aircraft. The major changes from Stone's work have involved the launching catapult. Early on, the pneumatic catapult was replaced with a hydraulic design.

On September 21, 1926, Lieutenant Commander Stone was detached from the Navy Department and returned to Coast Guard duty. Mark I and Mark II arresting-gear development was essentially complete, and he had been relieved by LCDR F. W. Pennoyer,

THEODORE H. BARTH

SUITE 2182
HOTEL McALPIN
NEW YORK

112 East 22nd Street,
New York,
October 26, 1925.

Lieutenant Commander E. F. Stone,
3800 14th Street, N. W.,
Washington, D. C.

Dear Mr. Stone:

I think the spring loaded release for the
catapult car mentioned in your letter and described by
you when I was in Washington last might be a good thing.
If you will send me your layout I will gladly submit my
comments on it.

I have received numerous letters from
various departments endeavoring to explain away the
recent mix-up. These letters are full of "regrets and
assurances". I have buried the tomahawk for the time
being and sincerely hope that I will not have to take it
up again.

I am slowly but surely becoming accustomed
to my new surroundings. I wish you could arrange to visit
me here in New York. I am sure we could get a great many
things squared away. The change would do you good. You
could overnight it in my new quarters, provided you do
not mind breaking in new sheets and pillow cases.

My kindest regards to you and Mrs. Stone,

Sincerely yours,

THB:H

Theodore H. Barth's October 26, 1925, letter

NAS Hampton Roads

TEST MEMORANDUM.

AERONAUTICS TEST NO. 1,   ARRESTING GEAR   "SARATOGA"
                        FORE & AFT CABLES AND TENSION CONTROL.

	Date Tested	Result of Test.
(A) TIGHTNESS-		
1. Tank, cylinders, and all piping shall be tested for tightness under a pressure of 300# sq.in. after the system is filled with oil. No leakage should occur.		
REPORT:-		
1. Pressure drop in fifteen minutes.		
(B) OPERATION-		
1. With all fore and aft wires in place, fiddle bridges up and hydraulic pistons at upper limit of travel, adjust tension rod nuts until wires are under 800# tension. Tension in wires is to be determined by strain gauges inserted in each of the two outboard wires and sighting in other wires until sag of all wires is the same. Gradually admit air to tank until hydraulic pistons take up against lower stops. Release air. Lower fiddle bridges. Admit air as before.		
REPORT:-		
1. Air pressure in tank when hydraulic pistons begin to move.		
2. Air pressure for each 10# increase in cable tension.		
3. Air pressure and cable tension at which relief valve on tank opens.		
4. Is lead of all cables thru deck casting and over sheaves fair?		
5. Do tension rods show tendency to bear against any part of cylinders?		
6. Are all working parts properly lubricated and all exposed parts protected against corrosion?		
7. Are cover plates for trough at forward end of wires easily removable? 1-1-(2)		

Aeronautic Test No. 1, arresting gear, USS *Saratoga,* page 1

USN. In spite of the importance of his work with battleship and cruiser catapults, and with catapult and arresting-gear for aircraft carriers, neither the Navy nor the Coast Guard rewarded him with suitable recognition.[40]

As was the case with the gunpowder catapult, others were quick to claim leadership for arresting-gear development after Stone returned to the Coast Guard. There are some who claim that Lieutenant Commander Stone worked for Lieutenant Commander Pennoyer,

TEST MEMORANDUM.

AERONAUTICS TEST NO. 1. ARRESTING GEAR "SARATOGA"
FORE & AFT CABLES AND TENSION CONTROL

	Date Tested	Re of T

(C) OPERATION-

1. With every other fore and aft wire in place, i.e. with only one wire on each cylinder, repeat test B.

REPORT:-

1. Air pressure in tank when hydraulic pistons begin to move.

2. Air pressure for each 10# increase in cable tension.

3. Do tension rods show a tendency to bear against any part of cylinders?

4. Do cylinders tend to bind due to eccentric loading? If serious, special report is to be made to Bureau of Aeronautics.

Note: Wires should be tested up to 1600# tension. If this tension is not reached in above additional tests shall be made after necessary adjustment of tension rod nuts.

References:-
(a) Detail Specs., Par. U-26-b.
(b) Plan 199-824-41 & 42 - Tightening Cylinders.
       199-824-NCD   - Fore, end cables.
(c) Bu. Aero. 1st. CV2&3;S83-3/CV2&3, 18 Aug. 1925, to Bu. C&R, S83-3/CV2&3
(d) Bu. Aero. 3rd end. Aer-M-111-AAM C-64448 of February 7, 1927.

1-2-(2)

Aeronautic Test No. 1, arresting gear, USS *Saratoga,* page 2

because when Stone departed his assignment in the Navy, they both were lieutenant commanders. In the original personnel assignment, Lieutenant Pennoyer was clearly junior to Lieutenant Commander Stone. A review of the original files clearly shows that Stone was in charge of arresting-gear development and that Pennoyer relieved him after the task was essentially complete. This account is based upon original source documents in the National Archives, not references to other historians' accounts.

TEST MEMORANDUM.

AERONAUTICS TEST NO. 2.　　ARRESTING GEAR, ATHWARTSHIPS　　　"SARATOGA"
　　　　　　　　　　　　　　CABLES AND BRAKES.

LOCATION:			Date Tested	Resul of Tes
Set No. 1	25" aft	Frame 148		
3	27" ford	" 155		
5	22-1/2" ford	" 167		
7	27" aft	" 177		
8	25" "	" 187		
10	27" ford	" 195		
12	27" "	" 205		

(A) TIGHTNESS-

1. Air piping shall be tested to 250# sq.in. air pressure.

(B) OPERATION-

　　Each set shall be tested as follows:

1. Loosen the friction clutch and turn the drum by hand until it reaches its limit of travel toward the side stand. Measure and record the clearance between drum and side stand at three points nearly equidistant on drum circumference. Alignment should be correct within .004 inch.

2. Check bearing surfaces of gearing between drum and oil pumps. Record percentage. Minimum should be 90%.

3. Check bearing surface of gearing between drum and clutch. Should be 90%.

4. With clutch and brake band loose pull out wire until drum takes up on wood chocks on bulkhead. Record distance fore and aft on flying deck, which wire may be pulled out. Drum should clear nearest point on bulkhead by 1/4".

5. Tighten clutch and retrieve wire using electric motor.

6. Check brake shaft for alignment and freedom of motion with all bracket bolts drawn tight.

7. Check brake arm for alignment with cylinder and connecting rod.

2-1-(2)

Aeronautic Test No. 1, arresting gear, USS *Saratoga*, page 3

　　The complete government and Carl L. Norden/Theodore H. Barth correspondence files on arresting-gear development were transferred from BUAERO and BUORD to the National Archives in Washington, D.C. These files are very comprehensive. A review of these files reveals that Pennoyer did not receive any correspondence addressed to him

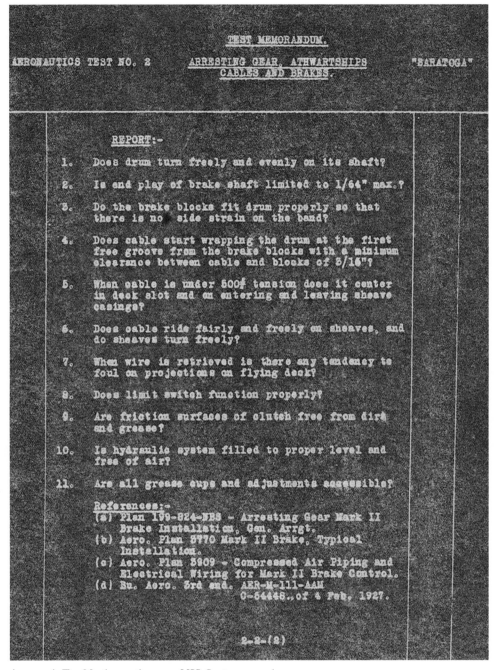

TEST MEMORANDUM.

AERONAUTICS TEST NO. 2   ARRESTING GEAR, ATHWARTSHIPS   "SARATOGA"
                                        CABLES AND BRAKES.

REPORT:-

1.   Does drum turn freely and evenly on its shaft?

2.   Is end play of brake shaft limited to 1/64" max.?

3.   Do the brake blocks fit drum properly so that
     there is no side strain on the band?

4.   Does cable start wrapping the drum at the first
     free groove from the brake blocks with a minimum
     clearance between cable and blocks of 5/16"?

5.   When cable is under 500# tension does it center
     in deck slot and on entering and leaving sheave
     casings?

6.   Does cable ride fairly and freely on sheaves, and
     do sheaves turn freely?

7.   When wire is retrieved is there any tendency to
     foul on projections on flying deck?

8.   Does limit switch function properly?

9.   Are friction surfaces of clutch free from dirt
     and grease?

10. Is hydraulic system filled to proper level and
     free of air?

11. Are all grease cups and adjustments accessible?

References:-
(a) Plan 199-824-NBS - Arresting Gear Mark II
    Brake Installation, Gen. Arrgt.
(b) Aero. Plan 5770 Mark II Brake, Typical
    Installation.
(c) Aero. Plan 5909 - Compressed Air Piping and
    Electrical Wiring for Mark II Brake Control.
(d) Bu. Aero. 3rd end. AER-M-111-AAM
                        C-64468., of 4 Feb, 1927.

2-2-(2)

Aeronautic Test No. 1, arresting gear, USS *Saratoga,* page 4

by contractor developers or manufacturers as Stone did. Pennoyer received only three information copies of correspondence that had been addressed to Stone at BUAERO or other senior officers. One was received just prior to Stone's departure, two after his departure. Furthermore, after Stone's departure, senior BUAERO officers maintained tight

USS *Saratoga* hangar deck

USS *Saratoga* and O2U aircraft takeoff

1926, USS *Saratoga* anchored, with Jenny aircraft on deck

1930, USS *Lexington*

oversight of the arresting-gear program; all letters answering arresting-gear correspondence received by BURAERO were answered by senior officers, such as CAPT V. C. Griffin, of NC transatlantic flight fame.

Except for one personal letter sent directly to Norden's senior engineer, Mr. Barth, Lieutenant Commander Pennoyer signed no official correspondence relative to arresting-gear development. Mr. Barth sent a copy of Pennoyer's personal letter to Stone in correspondence dated December 7, 1925. He did not use Pennoyer's recommendations and wanted "to discuss it with Stone and Pennoyer on his next trip to Washington." The dates on these letters correspond with the period Rear Admiral Moffett promised to start training a replacement for Lieutenant Commander Stone prior to his return to Coast Guard duty.[41]

Throughout his assignments with the Navy, Stone energetically supported attempts to initiate aviation in the Coast Guard.[42]

In the late 1940s, the growing relevance of the aircraft carrier in modern warfare depended upon a capability to launch, arrest, and operate heavy, high-speed aircraft without restricting aircraft design. Performance characteristics of later-arriving jet aircraft were far beyond the limits of a hydraulic design. Correcting this problem was very important. The aircraft carrier battle group is a powerful intimidator, just by being visible to potential adversaries. Deterring others from attacking the United States is as important a part of the aircraft carrier's mission as deploying the actual power of the ship.

Based upon the physics formula $V2 = 2as$, where V is the end launch speed, a is mean acceleration, and s is length of the power run of the catapult, peak acceleration during the launch determines the needed strength of the aircraft to withstand the launching itself.

It is, therefore, important to keep the peak acceleration close to the mean acceleration, in order to get as much energy as possible into the launch without adding a lot of extra strength and weight to the airplane. Doing this enables the shortest catapult run length possible.

These requirements eventually led the Chief of Naval Operations, on June 1, 1954, to initiate Project Steam, a joint program between NAVAIRPAC and BUAER that led to installation of the steam catapult on U.S. aircraft carriers.

CHAPTER TEN

Years of Technical Advancement and Growth

1930–1935

*I*n *the ensuing years after its tentative inception, Coast Guard aviation proliferated rapidly and dramatically, with many different aircraft types at air stations, following the models established at Morehead City and Ten Pound Island.*

Sikorsky S-39

The Sikorsky S-39 was in Coast Guard service from 1930 to 1935. It was one of fifteen miscellaneous aircraft confiscated by the U.S. Customs Division of the Treasury Department. Some were used by the Border Patrol, and some were turned over to the Coast Guard. With a wingspan of fifty-two feet, a top speed of 119 miles per hour, and a range of four hundred miles, the S-39 had a crew of two and was powered by one Pratt & Whitney R-985 Wasp Jr. three-hundred-horsepower engine. On September 13, 1930, Sikorsky lent the S-39 seaplane shown below to the Coast Guard to conduct aerial patrols of the International Yacht Race off Newport, Rhode Island.[1]

Shreck O-38

In 1931, the Coast Guard acquired a Shreck O-38 seaplane to conduct experimental landings in heavy offshore seas. The seaplane handled excellently in rough water. Coast Guard number CG-8 was assigned, later changed to V-107. Originally a French FBA-Shreck design, it had a maximum speed of ninety knots; its cruise speed was seventy-five knots, and its stall speed was forty-one knots. The range was 390 miles. Each seaplane cost $6,500. After the Viking Flying Boat Company in New Haven, Connecticut, purchased manufacturing rights to the Shreck O-38, five more of these seaplanes were purchased by the Coast Guard for CGAS Cape May and new air stations at Dinner Key in Miami,

Sikorsky S-39 off Newport, Rhode Island

Florida; St. Petersburg, Florida; Biloxi, Mississippi; and Charleston, South Carolina.[2] The seaplanes were decommissioned shortly before World War II.

Shreck Boat Company O-38, Number OO-1, later V-2, purchased October 1936

Viking Boat Company Shreck O-38

Viking Boat Company Shreck O-38

Viking Boat Company Shreck O-38

Douglas OS-38

In 1931, the War Department ordered a single Douglas OS-38C, tail number 32-394, for the Coast Guard. When commissioned in December 1931, it was assigned Coast Guard number CG-9, later changed to V-108. The airplane was decommissioned in April 1934.[3]

Fokker PJ-1 Flying Lifeboat

In 1932, it became obvious that the Constitution's Eighteenth Amendment would be repealed, and steam began to run out of Prohibition law-enforcement efforts. From December 5, 1933, onward the Twenty-First Amendment was the law of the land, and Prohibition was dead. Although law enforcement was still an important mission in other areas, Coast Guard aviation mission emphasis changed to search and rescue (SAR) and medical evacuations, often directed toward open-sea landings far offshore to rescue stricken mariners in need of urgent shoreside medical care.

Departing from Coast Guard destroyer *Cummings*, Lieutenant Commander Stone returned to aviation and served as the senior member of the aircraft-trial board for the new Coast Guard PJ-1 flying lifeboat seaplanes, being built from June 1931 to early March 1932.[4]

Conceived in 1928 at LCDR Norman Hall's aviation section at headquarters, the Fokker-design PJ-1 "flying lifeboat" was developed in conjunction with the Coast Guard by the

Douglas OS-38C

General Aviation Company, Baltimore, Maryland, and was delivered in 1932. It enjoyed the distinction of being the first aircraft specifically designed for Coast Guard use on the open sea. The Coast Guard purchased four PJ-1 seaplanes.

The Fokker PJ was often referred to as a marine ambulance, and the type was named for stars: No. 112 was *Altair,* 113 was *Acrux,* 114 was *Acamar,* and 115 was *Arcturus.* The seaplane had a seventy-four-foot, two-inch wingspan, a top speed of 120 miles per hour, and a seven-man crew. It was powered by two Pratt & Whitney Wasp C-1, R-1340 engines. It had a pusher-type propeller and engine.[5]

The photo on page 215, bottom, is PJ-1 *Antares,* offshore, evacuating two severely burned seamen from the tanker SS *Samuel Q. Brown.* The evacuees needed immediate hospitalization. After landing in the open sea, *Antares* sent a small boat with a specially designed litter (stretcher) to transfer the burned seamen to the aircraft. *Antares* delivered the two burned seamen to land within an hour and a half, thereby saving their lives.

A daring offshore rescue was made on January 1, 1933, by LCDR Carl Christian von Paulsen in PJ-1 *Arcturus.* A boy in a small skiff had drifted offshore from Cape Canaveral, Florida, the previous night and had become lost at sea in a winter storm. The nearest Coast Guard cutter was eighty-five miles away from the search area. CGAS Miami was notified the following morning, and *Arcturus* was launched to conduct a search. After searching most of the day, it located the skiff and boy as darkness approached. The sea was running fifteen feet, or thirty feet from trough to crest, and the skiff was drifting farther offshore in the Gulf Stream. No surface craft were in the vicinity, temperatures

PJ-1 on ramp resting on beaching gear

were low, and the boy was in a very weakened condition—it was most probable he would not survive another night.

Unable to remain on scene and keep the skiff in sight during the night, *Arcturus* would have to soon depart the scene. *Arcturus*'s crew decided to accept making a risky offshore landing to rescue the boy. The seaplane was designed for six-foot seas, or twelve feet from trough to crest; landing in seas twice that height, the crew would experience violent forces as the seaplane decelerated unevenly, like a skipping rock on water. Upon landing, impacting swells caused the port wing-tip float to collapse, leaving the float hanging and jeopardizing the wing. The float had to be cleared away.

The radioman volunteered for the task and dove overboard with a line around his waist. Clearing the float, he was hauled back on board just before a twelve-foot shark broke the ocean surface. Three crewmen stationed on the starboard wing to weigh it down and keep the seaplane from capsizing hauled the boy on board *Arcturus*, and preparations were made for takeoff. Departure was imperative, without the port wing float.

In spite of the rough sea, a successful takeoff was made, but not without wing fabric being torn, forcing another landing. Drifting overnight with makeshift sea anchors, the seaplane found itself shooting breakers and washing up onto the beach. The boy was saved, but *Arcturus* was lost.[6]

Fokker PJ-2 flying lifeboat

The PJ-1 was later modified to a PJ-2, with a tractor engine and propeller configuration. Some early aviators thought it was the best seaplane the Coast Guard ever had. Further PJ development was halted when the General Aviation Company went out of business. Overall Coast Guard development changed to concentrate on speed and landplane design.[7]

PJ-1 water landing

PJ-1 embarking medical evacuation patient

Consolidated N4Y-1

Consolidated N4Y-1 two-seat trainers, also known as PT-11Ds, were purchased in 1932 from the Army Air Corps for pilot training at CGAS Cape May, New Jersey.[8] The first was initially given Coast Guard number CG-10, later V-110. The N4Y-1 had a thirty-one foot, six-inch wingspan, a top speed of 118 miles per hour, and one Lycoming R-690-A two-hundred-horsepower engine.

PJ-2 in flight over harbor

PJ-2 water takeoff

Douglas RD-1 thru RD-3 Flying Boats

Cape May air station operations were so successful that thirteen RD flying boats were purchased from 1931 to 1933. The Douglas RD series of flying boats began with a smaller, lighter version aircraft called Sinbad. The RD-1 was not just an amphibian, it was a flying boat. During the 1930s Coast Guard flying boats were named after stars in the universe. The Coast Guard received its first production RD-2 amphibian, the *Procyon* (CG-27), from the Douglas factory in New York in February 1931. Later, its official number was changed

Consolidated N4Y training planes

Consolidated N4Y training plane

to V-108. The 1933 Coast Guard aircraft register has the *Procyon* stationed at CGAS Cape May, with the international registered radio call sign NUMRG and the Coast Guard call sign 24G. NUMRG was the first international call sign registered to a U.S. military aircraft.[9]

Advancements in design led to differing RD model numbers, from RD-1 to RD-3. In 1932, RD-3 *Adhara* (V-111) was accepted by the Coast Guard and assigned the international radio call sign NUMRJ and Coast Guard call sign 24J. It was assigned to the new CGAS Gloucester, Massachusetts, when operations were moved there from Ten Pound Island. On

August 5, 1932, RD-3 *Sirus* (V-109) was accepted and assigned to CGAS Miami, Florida. Its international and Coast Guard radio call signs were NUMRH and 24H.

When Stone returned to aviation, his old commanding officer on *Onondaga,* CAPT Benjamin M. Chiswell, USCG, who had shared the imaginations of Third Lieutenants Stone and Hall in 1916 and birthed Coast Guard aviation, retired from service. Captain Chiswell had earned the Navy Cross during World War I, had been the first Coast Guard vice commandant, and had been considered for commandant in 1932 before he retired.[10]

On March 8, 1932, Lieutenant Commander Stone reported to CGAS Cape May as its commanding officer. On April 4, 1933, while serving at Cape May, Stone flew to NAS Anacostia in Washington, D.C., for a meeting at Coast Guard headquarters. Earlier that morning, the Navy's airship *Akron,* J-3, had been destroyed in a storm off Barnegat, New Jersey. Heavy seas and foul weather prevented rescue craft from reaching the crash scene. When Stone received word the *Akron* had crashed, he immediately departed NAS Anacostia in his RD-4 amphibian for CGAS Cape May.

After refueling at Cape May, he departed before daylight into the same storm to attempt the rescue of Admiral Moffett and his other Navy friends on board *Akron.*[11] All he could find were two bodies. In spite of forty-knot winds and heavy seas, he landed and recovered both, one that of Lieutenant Commander Curmine, executive officer of *Akron.*[12]

Upon returning to NAS Anacostia, he was asked by a *Washington Times* news reporter why he had flown such a dangerous rescue mission.

Stone's response was: "It was the least I could do."[13]

CGAS Cape May, 1932

Following his command at CGAS Cape May, Lieutenant Commander Stone received orders to be inspector of naval aircraft at the Douglas Aircraft plant in Santa Monica, California. At the same time, he was also responsible for the test and acceptance programs for Grumman JF-2 amphibians and for the Treasury secretary's first aircraft, the RT-1, at the Northrop plant.

Douglas RD-4 Flying Boat

The Coast Guard accepted the first amphibious RD-4 flying boats on February 20, 1935. The four models of RD flying boats had different fuselage, tail, and engine configurations.

RD-4

USS *Akron*, J-3, tethered to USS *Patoka* (AO-9)

RADM William A. Moffet, USN, and Lieutenant Commander Ros, USN, on *Akron's* bridge

In all, ten RD-4s were delivered to the Coast Guard by April 1935: *Spica* (V-125), *Mizar* (V-126), *Alloth* (V-127), *Vega* (V-128), *Deneb* (V-129), *Aldebaran* (V-130), *Rigel* (V-131), *Capella* (V-132), *Bellatriz* (V-133), and *Canopus* (V-134). The RD-4 had a three-man crew, a wingspan of sixty feet, a top speed of 147 miles per hour, a range of 660 miles, and two Pratt & Whitney R-1340-C1 Wasp 454 horse-power engines.[14]

In spite of many heroic flights by earlier aviation crews, the first Distinguished Flying Cross (DFC) medals were awarded to Coast Guard pilots who flew the RD-4 amphibian. The first of the DFC medals was awarded by the Secretary of the Army to LT Carl B. Olsen, USCG. The narrative from his citation is shown below:[15]

CITATION TO ACCOMPANY THE AWARD OF
THE DISTINGUISHED FLYING CROSS
To
LIEUTENANT CARL B. OLSEN
UNITED STATES COAST GUARD

The Distinguished Flying Cross is awarded to Lieutenant Carl B. Olsen, USCG, in recognition of outstanding heroic action in flying an airplane of the Coast Guard approximately 300 miles to sea under the difficulties of darkness, storms and rough seas for the purpose of removing and transporting to a hospital on shore an officer of the Army, on board the United States Army Transport Republic, who was critically ill, saving his life.

Douglas RD-4 Dolphin

The second DFC was awarded by the Secretary of Treasury to LT Frank Leamy, USCG, for the evacuation of a seaman with a severed right arm from the fishing vessel *White Cap*. The landing and takeoff was made at night in heavy seas. Lieutenant Leamy's citation narrative is shown below:[16]

CITATION TO ACCOMPANY THE AWARD OF THE
DISTINGUISHED FLYING CROSS

To

LIEUTENANT COMMANDER FRANK A. LEAMY
UNITED STATES COAST GUARD

The Secretary of the Treasury, acting for the President, has awarded you the Distinguished Flying Cross, in recognition of your outstanding performance, on May 21, 1937, in flying an airplane of the Coast Guard a distance of approximately sixty miles from the Salem Air Station, to contact the trawler WHITE CAP, in the open sea, and removing from that trawler an officer whose left arm had been severed. The patient was then safely transported to Salem, Massachusetts, for emergency treatment and further hospitalization. The flight was made under adverse conditions and rough seas which made landing and take-off hazardous. The Department takes great pleasure in commending you for the distinguished service rendered which saved a life.

RD-3

The third DFC was awarded by the Secretary of Treasury to LT Richard Burke, USCG. His citation narrative is shown below:[17]

CITATION TO ACCOMPANY THE AWARD OF THE
DISTINGUISHED FLYING CROSS
TO
LIEUTENANT RICHARD L. BURKE
UNITED STATES COAST GUARD

The Distinguished Flying Cross is awarded to Lieutenant Richard L. Burke, USCG, in recognition of outstanding heroic action in flying an airplane of the Coast Guard from Air Station Cape May to a point 130 miles south off Cape Ann Massachusetts to remove a critically ill seaman from the trawler Shawmut. *Lieutenant Burke flew through a series of squall lines and fog for a period of two and one half hours locating the* Shawmut *by means of his radio direction finder. Letting down through the fog he made visual contact with the trawler and landed alongside in a heavy swell. The semiconscious patient was transferred by boat and with the aid of an oil slick laid out by* Shawmut *a successful take-off was made. After a one and one half hour flight through the squall lines Lieutenant Burke landed at the Boston Airport and the patient was transported to the Marine Hospital. The successful removal of the critically injured seaman to medical attention in a timely manner saved his life.*

RD–1

RD series radio rack suite

CHAPTER ELEVEN

A New Treasury Secretary Expands Aviation Missions

1934–1938

*H*enry Morgenthau became Treasury secretary in 1933. Morgenthau and Franklin D. Roosevelt *(FDR) had been college classmates and were close friends. They called each other by their first names. Morgenthau's letters and memoranda to FDR addressed him as "Franklin." Even though FDR was president of the United States, Morgenthau's relationship was strong enough for him to overrule budget and policy that he did not agree with, even though it originated with FDR's cabinet, the White House staff, or the Congress.*

During the Great Depression, FDR had to raise people's enthusiasm and morale. He ordered scientific expeditions to the ends of the earth, and world records provided fodder for the Movietone newsreels that ran every week in the theaters and gave people morale boosts at a cheap price. Morgenthau saw his Coast Guard as a "smaller Navy" under the Treasury, in much the same way as FDR had been Assistant Secretary of the Navy years before. Both were aviation enthusiasts.

Morgenthau was an aggressive supporter of Coast Guard aviation's growth. In 1934, one of his actions was to transfer Customs Service air detachments, with their conglomeration of fifteen aircraft of various types, to the Coast Guard, including the Coast Guard's second Sikorsky S-39 seaplane, which had been confiscated from smugglers. However, the benefit to the Coast Guard from the new aircraft was very small, and the transfer created problems with spare parts, aircraft maintenance, and pilot qualifications.[1]

Along with Customs Service aircraft came a new emphasis on law-enforcement missions. From Texas to California, the Coast Guard cooperated with a number of law-enforcement agencies along the U.S.-Canadian and U.S.-Mexican borders to detect illegal activity. Coast Guard aircraft and personnel assisted the U.S. Customs and Border Patrol Services, the Secret Service, the Bureau of Narcotics, the Alcohol Tax Unit, the Department of Agriculture's Bureau of Biological Survey, and the Texas Rangers.

A Coast Guard air detachment (CGAD), a small version of a Coast Guard air station (CGAS) and supported by the larger parent unit, was commissioned at Del Rio, Texas, and was then moved to Biggs Field in El Paso. Air detachments for aerial patrol were also commissioned at San Diego, California, and Buffalo, New York. Enlisted gunner's mates were assigned to the detachments to instruct in the use of firearms. Detachment personnel participated in undercover law-enforcement operations supporting the Bureau of Narcotics and the Customs Service for interdiction of narcotics smuggling. The secretary obtained Public Works Administration (PWA) funding for additional air stations and new aircraft. The Coast Guard increased the number of personnel assigned to flight training at NAS Pensacola, Florida, to support this effort.

By 1936 there were six air stations, three air detachments, and forty-two aircraft in the Coast Guard inventory.[2]

New Standard Aircraft Company NT-2

Two NT-2 aircraft were confiscated from smugglers by the Alcohol Tax Division of the Treasury Department and transferred to the Coast Guard in 1934. They were given Coast Guard numbers V-123 and V-124. Built by New Standard from an earlier original Belgian Stampe-Vertongen D-29-A design, they were not upgraded NT-1s. The two-seat NT-2 had a thirty-foot wingspan, a top speed of eighty-five knots, a stall speed of forty-one knots, and one Wright J-6-7 Whirlwind 225-horsepower engine. Both aircraft were destroyed in crashes in 1935.[3]

New Standard NT-2

New Standard NT-2

Chance-Vought O2U-2

The Navy transferred six Chance-Vought two-seat O2U-2 aircraft to the Coast Guard in 1934 and three more in 1935. Several were stationed at CGAD El Paso to patrol the U.S.-Mexican border for use in the suppression of smuggling and illegal border crossings. Others patrolled the U.S.-Canadian border. They were given Coast Guard numbers starting with V-117. They were fabric covered and had a wingspan of thirty-six feet, a top speed of 147 miles per hour, a range of 450 miles, and one Pratt & Whitney R-1340-B Wasp 450-horsepower engine that turned a two-blade, eight-foot, eleven-and-one-half-inch-diameter, standard steel 3792 fixed-pitch propeller. In the photo on page 227, top, standing next to the O2U-2 A-1 is Secretary of the Treasury Morgenthau and the commandant of the Coast Guard, RADM Harry Hamlet. The aircraft's Lewis machine-gun configuration has the same mounting ring as the OL-5s purchased by the Coast Guard in 1926. The identifier "A-1" was used by the overhaul facility preparing the aircraft for service. After receipt by the Coast Guard, it was changed to CG-301 and later to V-117. The photo on page 228 is an El Paso O2U-2 received from the Navy in 1935 with fabric in such bad shape that the aircraft was stripped and re-covered by detachment personnel and their wives at a "sewing bee."[4]

Stone received orders April 23, 1934, as inspector of naval aircraft for the Douglas Aircraft Company in Santa Monica, California. At this time he also was responsible for the test and acceptance programs for Grumman JF-2 amphibians and for the Secretary of the Treasury's RT-1 aircraft at the Northrop plant.[5]

Chance-Vought O2U-2 received in 1934

Chance-Vought O2U-2 received in 1934

Chance-Vought O2U-2 received in 1935

Grumman JF-2 Duck

Under a Navy contract, the Coast Guard procured two JF-2 Duck amphibians, and the Navy gave ten more to the Coast Guard in 1934. The Coast Guard eventually operated fourteen of these amphibians.

In addition to normal stateside operations, these rugged amphibians and their pilots deployed with Coast Guard cutters and Navy ships in both the Arctic and the Antarctic Oceans. A Coast Guard pilot and JF-2 supported the U.S. Navy's Byrd polar expedition; another made the first flight in Antarctica with the U.S. Coast Guard icebreaker *Northwind,* on Operation High Jump; and from 1938 flew against the Germans infiltrating Newfoundland, Greenland, and Iceland as part of the Greenland Patrol. Just prior to Germany defeating Denmark, a treaty with the United States was signed tasking the United States to defend Greenland and Iceland from German aggression. Canada also requested U.S. assistance in defending Newfoundland. The objective was to prevent Germany from gaining a foothold in the western Atlantic. Thus the Greenland Patrol was formed. Since the United States was neutral in 1938, any use of force against Germany to defend the three countries by the U.S. Department of the Navy or War Department would have been considered an act of war. Since one of the Coast Guard missions is enforcement of laws and treaties, protecting against Axis forces operating in Greenland or Iceland would be treaty enforcement. The Coast Guard captured German and Norwegian German-sympathizer communications and weather-reporting personnel long before the United States entered World War II.[6]

Coast Guard Grumman JF-2 in the Arctic as part of the U.S. Navy's Byrd expedition

Grumman JF-2 makes first flight in Antarctica with USCGC *Northwind* on Operation High Jump

Painting of CGC *Northstar* on Greenland Patrol, returning JF-2-5 Duck scout, by Gus Swensen

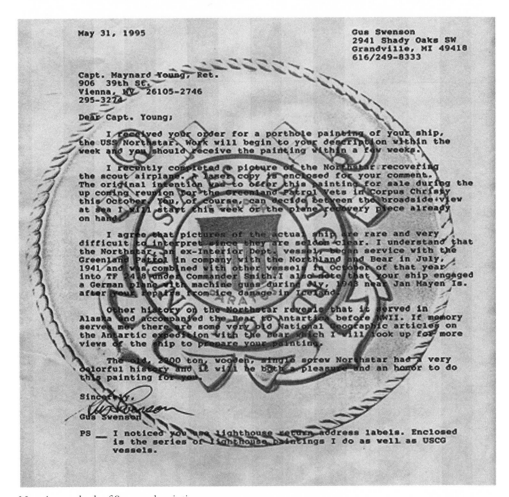

May 31, 1995

Gus Swenson
2941 Shady Oaks SW
Grandville, MI 49418
616/249-8333

Capt. Maynard Young, Ret.
906 39th St.
Vienna, WV 26105-2746
295-3274

Dear Capt. Young;

    I received your order for a porthole painting of your ship, the USS Northstar. Work will begin to your description within the week and you should receive the painting within a few weeks.

    I recently completed a picture of the Northstar recovering the scout airplane. A laser copy is enclosed for your comment. The original intention was to offer this painting for sale during the up coming reunion for the Greenland Patrol vets in Corpus Christy this October. You, of course, can decide between the broadside view at sea I will start this week or the plane recovery piece already on hand.

    I agree that pictures of the actual ship are rare and very difficult to interpret since they are seldom clear. I understand that the Northstar, an ex-Interior Dept. vessel, began service with the Greenland Patrol in company with the Northland and Bear in July, 1941 and was combined with other vessels in October of that year into TF 24.8 under Commander Smith. I also note that your ship engaged a German plane with machine guns during July, 1943 near Jan Mayen Is. after your repairs from ice damage in Iceland.

    Other history on the Northstar reveals that it served in Alaska and accompanied the Bear to Antartica before WWII. If memory serves me there are some very old National Geographic articles on the Antartic expedition with the Bear which I will look up for more views of the ship to prepare your painting.

    The old, 2600 ton, wooden, single screw Northstar had a very colorful history and it will be both a pleasure and an honor to do this painting for you.

Sincerly,

Gus Swenson
Gus Swensen

PS __ I noticed you use lighthouse return address labels. Enclosed is the series of lighthouse paintings I do as well as USCG vessels.

Notation on back of Swensen's painting

Grumman JF-2 on launching ramp at CGAS Port Angeles, Washington

Grumman JF-2 preparing for the U.S. Navy's Byrd Arctic polar expedition

JF-2

Stone believed exchanging the existing JF-2 engine for a Wright Cyclone engine, with larger frontal area and cowling, would improve frontal streamlining and increase the JF-2's performance and speed.[7] One of these amphibians was traded with the Navy for the Douglas XR30-1, which was transferred to Stone at the Douglas Aircraft plant. The XR30-1 would become the Treasury secretary's airplane.[8] On December 14, 1934, a memorandum from the Coast Guard commandant to the Secretary of Treasury advised:

> The Coast Guard in cooperation with the Grumman Aircraft Engineering Corporation and the Wright Aeronautical Corporation is investigating the possibilities of taking the following world records with the JF-2 amphibian. These records will all be attested by the National Aeronautical Association to the Federation Aeronautique Internationale:
>
> 1. Maximum speed (straight away—3 kilometer course),
> 2. Altitude,
> 3. Speed for 100 kilometers (62.137 miles) without pay load.
>
> Lieutenant Commander E. F. Stone is requested to pilot the plane during the above as he has had more experience in flights of this nature than any other in the U.S. Coast Guard.

Flying his modified JF-2 aircraft, Stone established the world speed record for a single-engine amphibian aircraft: 191 miles per hour over a three-kilometer test course at Buckroe Beach, Virginia, on December 20, 1934. The Secretary of the Treasury commended Stone for this feat, and Stone received a Certificate of Record from the National Aeronautic Association. On May 1, 1935, he was promoted to the rank of commander.[9]

Certificate of record, National Aeronautic Association, World Seaplane Record, December 20, 1934

LCDR Elmer F. Stone, December 20, 1934, breaks world speed record for seaplanes

Instrument Flight Rules (IFR), for flying in conditions of low or no visibility, were being implemented nationwide in 1935. Special training programs were being initiated for military pilots to certify them for IFR-cleared flights. A memorandum from the commandant to the Treasury secretary dated February 23, 1935, advised that all Coast Guard aviators, except three in final completion phase, "had completed the course in instruction in blind flying" and were now certified.[10]

In July 1935, LCDR Frank A. Erickson, a Coast Guard aviation pioneer, received his naval aviator Wings of Gold at NAS Pensacola. He had great foresight and developed the first naval helicopter and its employment in support of law enforcement, search and rescue (SAR), and antisubmarine warfare. He conducted the first shipboard landings with LT Stewart Graham and made the first lifesaving mission with a helicopter.

The Secretary-class cutter was designed to embark an amphibian aircraft. In 1937, aircraft and Coast Guard cutters were "married," with each 327-foot Secretary-class cutter embarking a Grumman JF-2 amphibian. These cutters were assigned patrol missions against smuggling off the West Coast and fisheries violations off Alaska. They also served on ocean-station duty, protecting the newly emerging commercial transoceanic air routes. Later, in the Second World War, they would be important in convoying merchant ships, deployed with destroyers in the Battle of the Atlantic.

JF-2 lifted on board USCGC *Spencer*

JF–2 preparing for lowering to water for takeoff

JF–2 on board USCGC *Storis*

Stinson RQ-1

One RQ-1 was purchased from Stinson in 1934 for electronics testing. It was assigned to CGAS Brooklyn, New York, located on Floyd Bennett Field. The Coast Guard assigned it serial number 149. The RQ-1 had a four-person crew, a forty-one-foot wingspan, a 133-miles-per-hour top speed, a 350 mile range, and one Lycoming R-680-6 225-horsepower engine with a Smith controllable-pitch propeller.[11]

RQ-1

RQ-1

Northrop RT-1 Delta Golden Goose

Nineteen thirty-five was the year the Treasury secretary received his own aircraft, flown by the Coast Guard, the Northrop RT-1 Delta Golden Goose. It was the only Delta ever purchased by the military, at a cost of $45,000. For its day it was a slick executive aircraft.[12] Up to that time, Hamilton Standard, Inc., had not sold any of their constant-speed propeller hubs, and the RT-1 was the first operational aircraft with Hamilton Standard controllable-pitch propellers.

Only three aircraft had test versions of the Hamilton Standard controllable propeller:

- Boeing 247 twin engine Wasp Model H
- A Stearman single-engine Wasp Junior direct-drive aircraft
- An Army Douglas observation aircraft with a single-engine, twin-row, radial Junior Wasp geared engine.[13]

This RT-1 had a two-blade, direct-drive propeller with a ten-foot diameter. In October 1936 the Coast Guard changed its serial number from 382 to V-150. It had a crew of two, a wingspan of forty-seven feet nine inches, a top speed of 219 miles per hour, a cruise speed of eighty-five knots, a 1,650-mile range, a service ceiling of twenty thousand feet, and one Wright Cyclone SR 1820-F3 735-horsepower engine.

Following positive results with RT-1, an engine upgrade was recommended for use in the RD-4 to include two Wasp C 450-horsepower engines with Hamilton Standard controllable propellers.

The RT-1 aircraft was decommissioned in 1940.[14]

RT-1 Delta

RT-1 Delta at CGAS Arlington, National Airport, Virginia

Northrop RT-1 Delta

Lockheed R30-1 Electra

On April 19, 1936, the Coast Guard purchased one Model 10-B Electra for the commandant's flagship and redesignated it XR30-1.[15] Amelia Earhart would fly the same model aircraft on her around-the-world flight when she disappeared in 1937. The XR30-1 had a crew of two and could carry twelve passengers. It was originally registered by the Coast Guard as number 383, later V-151. It was also made available to the Treasury secretary and assistant secretary. The aircraft had a fifty-five-foot wingspan, a 210-mile-per-hour top speed, an 850-mile range, and two Pratt & Whitney Wasp R-985-48 engines with two-blade Hamilton Standard controllable-pitch propellers.

Lockheed R30-1 Electra

R30-1

Waco J2W

In 1937, three Waco J2W cabin-model EQC-6 observation biplanes for the newly commissioned Secretary-class cutters were purchased. These aircraft could be operated with conventional land wheels, skis, or floats. All three were later transferred to CGAD El Paso, Texas. They were two-seat aircraft with a thirty-five-foot wingspan, a 150-miles-per-hour top speed, a 600-mile range, and one Jacobs L-4R R-755 225-horsepower engine with a two-bladed Hamilton Standard propeller.[16]

J2W

J2W on skis at the Waco Aircraft Company hangar in Troy, Ohio

Fairchild J2K-1

Two Fairchild J2K-1 and two J2K-2 aircraft were purchased as search aircraft in 1936, two for CGAS St. Petersburg (V-160 and V-161) and two for CGAS Charleston (V-162 and V-163).[17] The Wacos had a crew of four, a thirty-six-foot four-inch wingspan, a 138-miles-per-hour top speed, a cruise speed of 127 miles per hour, a 560-mile range, and Cirrus Hi-Drive engine with a two-blade Sensevich wood propeller.

Fairchild J2K-1

Fairchild J2K-2

Hall Aluminum PH-2

LCDR William J. Kossler, USCG, received orders to be the aircraft inspector at the Hall Aircraft Company at Bristol, Pennsylvania, in 1934. The PH-2 was scheduled to replace the PJ-1 and PJ-2 flying lifeboats, which had proved very successful in offshore landings in heavy seas. Kossler's PH-2 findings, however, were negative in the extreme concerning ability to perform in rough seas offshore, despite the fact that the aluminum PH-2 was a proven seaplane patrol bomber for the Navy. Quite in contrast to the Coast Guard, the Navy operated the seaplane from sheltered water seadromes at naval air stations, sending them on long patrol missions. Rough seas were seldom encountered. Politics overruled engineering findings, and instead of holding aircraft trials for the PH-2 Kossler was transferred to the position of chief of aviation engineering at headquarters. The trial board consisted of CAPT L. T. Chalker, CDR C. C. von Paulsen, LT C. B. Olsen, LT W. A. Burton, and Mr. H. S. Cocklin.

Seven PH-2s (V-164 to V-170) were purchased by the Coast Guard for SAR.[17] The PH-2 was the same as the PH-1, except for more powerful engines and specialized SAR equipment and capability. At the time, they were the largest aircraft acquired by the Coast Guard and had a very long range of 2,242 miles. They had a crew of five, a seventy-two-foot two-inch wingspan, a top speed of 155 miles per hour, four .30-caliber machine guns, and two Wright Cyclone F51 R-1820-51 875-horsepower engines with three-bladed Curtiss CS32D constant-speed propellers. PH-2s were assigned to Coast Guard air stations in Elizabeth City, North Carolina; Miami, Florida; Brooklyn, New York; Biloxi, Mississippi; San Diego, California; and San Francisco, California.

Operations in the field proved Kossler correct in his findings; the aircraft did not perform well in heavy seas offshore, and several crashed on landing.[18]

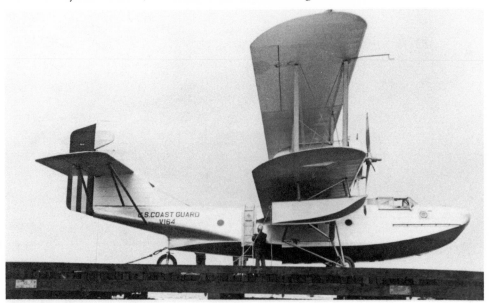

Hall Aluminum PH-2 on ramp with beaching gear

PH-2 removing beaching gear on CGAS Cape May launching ramp

PH-2 on CGAS Brooklyn tarmac

PH-2 parked, resting on beaching gear

PH-2 taking off, CGAS Brooklyn seadrome

CGAS Elizabeth City PH-2 with NAS Norfolk,Virginia, beaching crew offloading litter basket patient

Curtiss SOC-4

The Coast Guard acquired three Curtiss SOC-4 Seagull aircraft (V-171 to V-173) from the Navy in 1938. This Curtiss biplane was the last in operational service with the Navy, as a scout aircraft for battleships and cruisers. These aircraft had been built for catapult takeoffs and water landings. They served with Coast Guard cutters *Bibb*, *Taney*, and *Spencer*. Since these cutters did not have catapults, the SOC-4 was hoisted over the side for takeoffs and hoisted back on board after water landings. The SOC-4 had a crew of two, a thirty-six-foot wingspan, a 165-miles-per-hour top speed, a 675-mile range and one Pratt & Whitney R-1340-18 engine.[19]

With promotion came a new assignment. On May 21, 1935, Commander Stone reported on board Air Detachment, San Diego, California, as the commanding officer. CGAD San Diego was one of several detachments built to cooperate with a number of law-enforcement agencies along the U.S. and Mexican border to detect illegal activity. CGAD San Diego later became CGAS San Diego, with search and rescue as its prime mission.[20]

SOC–4 being lowered from USCGC *Bibb*

SOC-4 moored with anchor

SOC-4 on wheel carriage

SOC-4 on wheel carriage on ramp

SOC-4 on wheel carriage on tarmac

Coast Guard Air Station San Diego, California, 1936

Construction of the air station was undertaken by contractor M. H. Golden Co. in 1936, with funds provided by the Federal Public Works Administration. The site had to be dredged from the bay and filled to elevate it to grade level. Long piles were driven into the soil at the building sites for stabilization. The contract called for one hangar with a lean-to, a mess hall, a barracks building, two aprons, a taxiway to runways on Lindbergh Field, and a small wooden seaplane ramp. During the construction period, the Coast Guard air detachment was located in half of a commercial hangar on Lindbergh Field.[21]

Coast Guard Air Station San Diego, California, 1937

Coast Guard Air Station San Diego, California, 1961

Prelude to Another World War—an Aviation Icon Passes

It was expected by his aviation peers that Commander Stone would be an admiral, holding positions of influence at Coast Guard headquarters in Washington, D.C. It was anticipated Stone would bring long-withheld prestige to aviation in the Coast Guard within the flag community. But the Coast Guard had long been a seagoing service, with its admirals advancing from seagoing assignments on board cutters. Many admirals viewed aviation as a threat, encroaching on budgets for traditional surface craft and personnel. What his peers did not know was that Stone was under enormous emotional strain from the jealousy of senior officers at headquarters.

2

        I am the last of the small group who went through the starve-to-
-death days of founding CG aviation. Olie and the others came later,
after we began to get some money for new planes. Before that we existed
by begging, borrowing and stealing.

        Several of the early birds dropped out, like Stanley Parker, "
"Jiggs" Donahue, Gene Coffin and Bill Wishar. The real heros were the
old Triumvirate of Norman Hall, "Dutch" von Paulsen and "Archie" Stone.
They hung on like grim death until we got the show on the road.

        Finest of these was Archie. He was the first man to fly the Atlantic.
He was pilot and navigator of the NC-4 in 1919. "Puttee" Read was the
plane commander, but Puttee gott cold feet and would have aborted the
flight if Archie had not treatened to bend a fire extinguisher over his
head. As it was, after flying all night in mist and rain, they picked
up the peaks behind Punta del Gada dead ahead at daybreak.

        In 1920 the Navy turned the Coast Guard back to Treasury -- less
Archie Stone. They offered him a boost of one grade in rank to stay
in the Navy. But the Old Skipper wanted to get back home, and he finally
managed it about 1925. Billard and other top CG officers were jealous
of Stone, so they sent him first on ice patrol and then as CO of the
destroyer Cummings. He didnt get back in aviation until about 1931.

        During these years he got us first some Navy cast-offs -- some UO-4s
and OL-5s. Then through Eddie Rickover he got us money for new planes.

        I think the jealousy of other CG people hurt him badly. He and I
were on a board to observe the acceptance tests on the dog ship of the
PBYs in San Diego. The evening before his death we were sitting in his
house comparing notes and sipping a little refreshment. The Skipper
suddenly sat back and said "Deacon, I find that I ain'T got no classmates
no more, 'ceptin' ol' Harry Coyle". His own classmates had been cutting
his throat. Next day he droppeddead with a heart attack.

        He had married Myrtice Pace, eldest child of Mr. John Pace who owned
most of Pensacola and about half of Escambia County. "Mama" liked to
talk the Cracker talk she grew up with, and Archie adopted it. Their
daughter "Didi" married a bright Navy file named "Jeeves" Folsom. He
is retired and they live in Washington.

Commander Edge's letter, page 2. "Archie" was the nickname given to Stone at the Revenue Service School of Instruction, predecessor of the Coast Guard Academy. *Note: Edge took some liberty here in crediting Stone with "navigator" of NC-4, although he was the acknowledged pilot—and Edge probably intended to write "Eddie Rickenbacker" instead of "Eddie Rickover."*

Stone knew that some who he had thought were classmates and friends were perpetrating political assassination, Washington style. Some actually placed false negative items in his official officer service record and magnified gossip about him.

On May 19, 1936, CDR C. F. "Deacon" Edge, Coast Guard aviator fourteen, was the Stone family's dinner guest. Edge was well known within the Coast Guard for his aerial mapping of Alaska to locate sites for air stations to support missions there. He was a well-respected man and a close friend of Stone's, who often confided in him. Page two of a letter written by Commander Edge appears on the preceding page. In it, he describes early Coast Guard aviation behind the scenes and Stone as a man of vision who was shunned by those who feared service culture, budget, and operational changes.[22]

The next day, May 20, 1936, while inspecting a new patrol aircraft, Stone walked to a concrete hangar abutment and sat down. Then he fell over—stricken by a coronary thrombosis.

Commander Stone died unexpectedly before fulfilling expectations. He was buried on Coast Guard Hill in Arlington National Cemetery, a site reserved for admirals and Coast Guard personnel who had been outstanding in their performance of duty.[23]

In the late 1940s, at headquarters, another Coast Guard aviation pioneer, CAPT Frank Erickson, developer of the naval helicopter, fed up with and disappointed at what had happened at Coast Guard headquarters, traveled to the National Archives National Military Records Center in St. Louis. He retrieved Stone's officer service record, removed false negative documents, and gave Stone's record to the Coast Guard historian to file with other historical documents.

This story ends where the first chapter began. Events leading to the First World War and then to the Second World War inspired a few visionary men from each of the armed services and civil aviation. Among many, the list includes aircraft designers Glenn Curtiss; Anthony Fokker; Eddie Stinson; Igor Sikorsky; Norden bombsight inventor and businessman Carl Norden; famous World War I leading ace CAPT Eddie Rickenbacker; soon-to-become-famous World War II aviator "Jimmy" Doolittle; RADM William A. Moffett, USN; RADM John H. Towers, USN; LCDR E. W Rounds, USNRF; LTJG Marc A. Mitscher, USN, later to become admiral and commander of a fast carrier task force in the World War II Pacific theater; and enthusiasts like Britain's Prince of Wales.

Perhaps the most outstanding of them all in the years between the world wars was Elmer F. Stone, the first Coast Guard aviator. His vision of seaplanes supporting Coast Guard missions has grown into a modern Coast Guard air force comprising versatile airplanes and helicopters supporting missions worldwide, in peace and in war.

In only twenty-five years, Stone served as commanding officer for Coast Guard cutters and destroyers, both Navy and Coast Guard air stations, was the pilot for the first transatlantic flight, a test pilot for early Navy seaplanes, a test pilot for development of the first aircraft carrier *Langley* (CVS-1), inventor of the standard battleship and cruiser aircraft powder catapult, the leader in the development of the modern aircraft carrier landplane arresting gear, and the outfitter and tester of aviation support components of the newly launched second and third aircraft carriers *Lexington* and *Saratoga*.

Many senior Coast Guard officers viewed Stone as a true visionary. While living, however, he was recognized by his Coast Guard in only two letters of commendation. Significant recognition was received from Presidents Wilson, Coolidge, and Hoover, from Navy and Army officers, from the U. S. Senate, and the Secretary of the Navy. Sadly, significant Coast Guard appreciation and recognition for his many achievements came only after his death.

His posthumous accolades are impressive. He is enshrined by his naval aviation peers in the National Museum of Naval Aviation Hall of Honor at Naval Air Station Pensacola, Florida, and he is honored by his peers in the Coast Guard Aviation Hall of Fame at the Coast Guard Aviation Training Center in Mobile, Alabama.

Stone's death in 1936 was a mere year before Amelia Earhart's disappearance. Three years later, another world war began in Europe and became like its predecessor a "mother of invention," advancing global navigation and long-range flight. In another three years the United States would enter the war and multiengine bombers would be routinely ferried across the Atlantic and Pacific. The years following Stone's death witnessed a period of accelerated technological development. Stone was an icon to early aviation engineers. Had Stone lived, he probably would have surmounted the professional jealousy and would have been appointed to a prestigious position within a combined Navy–Coast Guard wartime organization. Possible assignments might have involved continued aircraft carrier development or the development and equipping of a Navy–Coast Guard combat air-sea rescue system for both Atlantic and Pacific theaters. Whatever the assignment might have been, the peer pressure that ultimately led to his untimely death would have been swept aside by the exigencies of war.

APPENDIX A

Time Line of Events (1776–1938)

Year	Date	Remarks
1775	April 19	Lexington Alarm fought, American Revolutionary War begins.
1775	October 13	Continental Congress funded a naval force of two frigates and directed it to search out and destroy English munitions ships that were providing powder and guns to English forces fighting the Americans. Ultimately, the Continental Naval Militia numbered some fifty ships. At war's end this naval force was disbanded, the ships sold, and the crews sent home.
1783		New federal government funded by customs and tariff duties.
1790	August 4	Revenue Marine Cutter Service established by Secretary of Treasury Alexander Hamilton to collect customs and tariff duties from foreign shipping. At the time, it was the new federal government's sole naval armed force.
1794		Congress ordered construction and manning for the new navy's first ships, six frigates. The Constitution of the United States, ratified in 1789, had empowered Congress "to provide and maintain a navy."
1800s		U.S. coastal schooner sail-ship commerce grows with Caribbean and South American countries.

1812		War of 1812 fought by both Navy and Revenue Cutter Service.
1850		Second Industrial Revolution started around 1850, when technological and economic progress gained momentum with the development of steam-powered ships and railways.
1861		Civil War begins, Navy and Revenue Cutter Service start conversion from wood sail-ships to steel hulls, steamships, and naval guns with rifled naval.
1865		Civil War ends, funding for naval modernization ends.
1901		ENS Holden C. Richardson, USN, and ENS George C. Westervelt, USN, graduate from Naval Academy.
1903	December 17	Wright Brothers successfully fly first airplane at Kitty Hawk, North Carolina.
1905		ENS T. G. Ellyson, USN, graduates from Naval Academy.
1906		ENS John H. Towers, USN, graduates from Naval Academy.
1908		ENS Jerome C. Hunsaker, USN, graduates from Naval Academy.
1910		CAPT Washington Irving Chambers, USN, initiates Navy interest in air power supporting the fleet.
1910	April 30	Stone appointed cadet in Revenue Cutter Service School of Instruction, predecessor of the U.S. Coast Guard Academy.
1910	November 14	Mr. Eugene Ely, a Curtiss pilot, makes the first shipboard aircraft takeoff.
1911	January 18	Ely makes first shipboard landing.
1911	January	Original Curtiss Flight Class at Coronado, California: Army lieutenants G. E. Kelly and John Walker and CAPT Paul W. Beck; LT T. G. Ellyson, USN, becomes naval aviator number one.
1911	March 17	LT John Rogers, USN, reports to Wright brothers training camp for flight instruction, becomes naval aviator number two.
1911	May 8	Captain Chambers requisitions the Navy's first two aircraft, A-1 and A-2.
1911	June 27	LT John H. Towers reports to Curtiss Training School for flight instruction, becomes naval aviator number three.
1911	July 6	Greenbury Point, Navy's first flying camp is established at Annapolis, Maryland.

1911	August 23	New aviators and TRIADs are ordered to Greenbury Point.
1911	October 10	LT Holden Richardson, USN, is ordered to the Bureau of Construction and Repair and becomes Navy's first engineering maintenance officer.
1911	November 12	Lieutenant Ellyson in A-3 is successfully launched by catapult at Washington Navy Yard.
1911	November 14	B-1 is modified with a float system at Greenbury Point.
1911	December 20	ENS Charles H. Maddox experiments with wireless communications in A-1 flown by LT John H. Towers, USN.
1911	December 29	TRIAD pilots and aircraft transferred from Greenbury Point to Glenn Curtiss facility in Coronado, California.
1911	Fiscal Year	Approved Chambers board recommendations funded: air training command Pensacola, Florida, aviation office under the Secretary of the Navy, training ship for aviation operations at sea, aircraft assigned to each major combat ship; establishes a 150-officer and 350–enlisted man Naval Flying Corps and establishes a Naval Reserve Flying force.
1912	May 22	Marine Corps enters naval aviation when 1stLt Alfred A. Cunningham, USMC, reports for flight instruction. He becomes naval aviator number five and Marine Corps aviator number one.
1912	October 3	Airborne antisubmarine recoilless rifle, designed by CDR Cleland Davis, USN, tested at Indian Head, Maryland, Proving Ground.
1912	October 8	Bureau of Medicine and Surgery Circular Letter 125221 promulgates first medical standards for prospective naval aviators.
1912	October 26	LT John H. Towers conducts tests to locate submarines from airborne flying boat. From eight hundred feet locates submarines thirty to forty feet below Chesapeake Bay's surface.
1912	November 20	Aircraft trial for Navy's first flying boat C-1 completed by LT Theodore G. Ellyson.
1912	December	Lieutenant Ellyson is successfully launched from pneumatic catapult in C-1 at the Washington Navy Yard.
1912	December	LT Alfred A. Cunningham, USMC, crashes from pneumatic catapult shot from warship under way. Pressure corrections are made and the flying boat becomes operational on board warships at sea.

1912	December	Captain Chambers relieved by CAPT Mark L. Bristol, USN, as Assistant Aide for Materiel, Secretary of the Navy. Secretary of the Navy appoints Captain Chambers to chair board developing plan for "organization of a Naval Aeronautic Service."
1913	March 31	New flying boat D-1 is equipped with improved instruments: airspeed indicator, altimeter, chart board, compass, and inclinometer.
1913		Navy establishes organization to manage aviation resources and programmed growth. The Aircraft Division in Bureau of Construction and Repair located at the Washington, D.C., Navy Yard composed of one experienced aviator engineer, LCDR Holden C. Richardson, USN.
1913	Spring	Secretary of the Navy establishes designation "Air Pilot." Denotes higher level of skill than needed for land machines.
1913	June 7	Stone and classmate Hall graduated from Revenue Cutter Service School of Instruction, completing engineering curriculum, receiving a commission as third lieutenants, U.S. Revenue Cutter Service (USRCS).
1913	June 12	LT Jerome C. Hunsaker, USN, is ordered to Massachusetts Institute of Technology (MIT) to establish aeronautical engineering courses within the Department of Naval Architecture.
1913	August 30	Lieutenant Bellinger successfully tests Sperry gyroscope stabilizer in C-2. It is forerunner of autopilot.
1913	October 5	Lieutenant Richardson successfully conducts aircraft trial for Navy's first amphibian flying boat E-1, named OWL.
1914		Curtiss-Wanamaker Transatlantic Project.
1914	January 30	Aviation training established in Pensacola, Florida, when USS *Mississippi* (BB-23) and USS *Orion* (AC-11) arrive in Pensacola with Lieutenant Towers and aviation unit from Greenbury Point. Greenbury Point, and other flight instruction schools are closed.
1914	March	Increasing number and types of aircraft bring new aircraft alpha-numeric designation protocol.
1914	April 1	Naval aviation goes to war in the Mexican crisis.

1914	July 1	Office of Naval Aeronautics is established under Division of Operations, Secretary of the Navy. It is the first formal recognition of naval aviation.
1914	November 16	Naval Aeronautic Station (NAS) Pensacola is established when command is transferred from the station ship.
1914	November 23	Director of Naval Aeronautics is established, with CAPT Mark L. Bristol, USN, as the new director.
1914	August	Hostilities break out in Europe.
1915	January 28	Revenue Cutter Service and Life Saving Service merged into U.S. Coast Guard.
1915		Congress establishes National Advisory Committee for Aeronautics (NACA) in 1915.
1915	March 22	Naval Aviator designation replaces Naval Air Pilot designation.
1915	April 16	LT Patrick N. L. Bellinger, USN, is successfully launched in flying boat AB-2 from a catapult mounted on a barge anchored in Pensacola Bay.
1915	June 1	Navy awards contract for first lighter-than-air ship, D-1, from Connecticut Aircraft Company in New Haven.
1915	November 5	LCDR Henry C. Mustin is successfully catapulted in flying boat AB-2 from USS *North Carolina* (ACR-12) under way in Pensacola Bay.
1916	January 11	Compass modified from the British Creigh-Osborn design sent to NAS Pensacola for testing. This compass was the standard throughout World War I.
1916		Glenn Curtiss opens the Atlantic Coast Aeronautical Station on Boat Harbor Point, Newport News, Virginia, for Curtiss's MF-Boat seaplane instruction.
1916	January/February	After observing Curtiss aviation school on Boat Harbor, CAPT Benjamin M. Chiswell, USRCS, Commanding Officer, U.S. Revenue Cutter *Onondaga,* 3rd LTs Norman B. Hall, USRCS, and Elmer F. Stone, USRCS, envision aircraft assisting vessels in distress, searching for disabled vessels and obstructions to navigation, and for law enforcement.
1916	March 21	USRCS Commandant issues orders for Third Lieutenant Stone to test air search operational concept for distressed vessels, obstructions to navigation and for smugglers. Glenn Curtiss supports test, loans Curtiss MF flying boat. Test is successful.

1916	April 1	Stone ordered to U.S. Navy Aeronautic Station, Pensacola Florida for flight training.
1916	April	Captain Chiswell, on USRC *Onondaga* at Washington, D.C., Navy Yard, lobbied during wardroom lunch with Assistant Secretary of the Treasury Byron R. Newton and Glenn H. Curtiss for flying surfboat when on water converted to ordinary motor surfboat. In response, Curtiss designed and constructed the B–T1 "Lifeboat" seaplane.
1916	May 30	Chief of Naval Operations requests bureaus to develop gyroscope-based instruments for the compass, bombsight, and baselines (or turn-and-bank, or slip) indicators.
1916	July 12	LT Godfrey deC. Chevalier in flying boat AB-3 is successfully catapulted from USS *North Carolina* (AC-12) while under way in Pensacola Bay.
1916	July 22	RADM David W. Taylor requests Aluminum Company of America (ALCOA) to develop a lightweight alloy for fabrication of zeppelin girders.
1916	August 29	Captain McAllister, USRCS, assigned to new Coast Guard Headquarters position as Chief Engineer, Aviation Section, drafts Senate legislation to provide $1,500,000 to establish an "Aerial Coast Patrol." Legislation revamped into the Navy Deficiency Act of August 29, 1916. Funding was delayed until 1924.
1916	October 24	Bureau of Steam Engineering requests Naval Aircraft Factory to develop a radio direction finder for aircraft.
1916	October 28	Second LT Norman B. Hall ordered to the Curtiss Aeroplane and Motor Company's factory at Hammondsport, New York, to study aircraft engineering.
1917		Congress denies Navy's 35–45-knot aircraft carrier request. Navy diverts to seaplanes.
1917	April 6	United States enters World War I. Navy freezes officer orders for flight training. Enlisted and warrant officers only trained. Navy had nine Academy officer aviators. Coast Guard had eight Academy officer aviators. Navy in sad shape.
1917	April 7	U.S. Coast Guard transferred to the Navy Department by Executive Order for World War I.

1917	April 10	Stone completes flight school, becomes naval aviator number thirty-eight and Coast Guard aviator number one.
1917	April 26	Armored cruiser *Huntington* conducts first catapult dead load test at Mare Island Navy Yard.
1917	May 28	*Huntington* takes on board a seaplane and kite balloons in Pensacola for experimental deck operations.
1917	July 2–October 13	Third Lieutenants Stone and Robert "Jiggs" Donahue, USRCS, assigned to armored cruiser USS *Huntington* as Curtiss R-6 aircraft pilots. Stone conducts engineering study on Navy catapult problem.
1917	July 4	First Liberty aircraft engine arrives at the U.S. Bureau of Standards for test.
1917	July 17	Navy builds Naval Aircraft Factory at Philadelphia Navy Yard.
1917		Navy expands aviation engineering support organization in Bureau of Construction and Repair with testing support established in Board of Inspection and Survey in Bureau of Steam Engineering and scientific support established at Naval Research Laboratory (NRL).
1917		Commander Towers writes proposal recommending NC aircraft be the first to cross the Atlantic by air. He pointedly states that he has the background to lead such a flight and requests command of the flight.
1917	August	Rear Admiral Taylor, USN, Chief, Bureau of Construction and Repair documents need for long-range seaplane to neutralize German submarine threat to shipping (ASW).
1917	September 12	Glenn Curtiss proposed two option designs, based upon his BT-1 seaplane design for the Coast Guard flying lifeboat, to Rear Admiral Taylor.
1917	October	Catapults removed from Navy ships due to carriage engineering design problem.
1917	October 13	Second Lieutenant Stone assigned to Navy's Bureau of Construction and as Seaplane Test Pilot, and one of test pilots in development of the first aircraft carrier, USS *Langley* (CVS-1).
1917		Army Signal Corps establishes aviation engineering and manufacturing command at McCook Field in Dayton, Ohio.

1917	October 21	First successful flight-test of a twelve-cylinder Liberty engine conducted on a Curtiss HS-1 Flying Boat.
1917	November	The Navy concludes a combined Navy/Curtiss effort production contract with the Curtiss Company in Buffalo for engineering services for design and manufacturing drawings for a thousand-horsepower flying boat. Contract design is based on enlarged three engine B-T1 flying lifeboat.
1917	December	Admiral Taylor and Commander Griffin of the Bureau of Steam Engineering jointly recommended to Navy secretary Josephus Daniels that Navy aircraft be the first to fly the Atlantic prior to the target date of summer 1919.
1917	December 21	Secretary of the Navy Josephus Daniels approves construction of four seaplanes of the NC-1 type.
1917	December	Admiral Taylor and Commander Griffin recommend to Navy secretary Daniels a target departure from Newfoundland for NC seaplanes not later than May 14, 1919.
1918		British and the Japanese governments start developing aircraft carriers. Resulting carriers HMS *Hermes* of the Royal Navy and *Hosho* of the Imperial Japanese Navy are actually cruisers with flight decks.
1918	February	Secretary Daniels approves Taylor and Griffin December NC seaplane operation recommendation and gives it "AA" priority. He assigns Commander Towers to lead the NC design and production effort.
1918	June 7	Stone promoted to second lieutenant.
1918	July	Stone promoted to first lieutenant.
1918	Summer	William H. Workman, representing the British Handley-Page 0/400 twin-engine bomber, first to rally interest in transatlantic flight. The Aero Club of America assists publicity campaign.
1918	August to July 1919	NAS Rockaway Beach, New York City, prior to picking transatlantic flight seaplane crews, responsible for support, maintenance, and line crew aircraft handling of the NC-1-type seaplanes, CDR Stanley V. Parker, USCG, commanding officer.
1918	September 1	NC-1 fully assembled at NAS Rockaway.
1918	October 4	NC-1's preflight tests, with three low-compression three-hundred-horsepower engines, completes with a gross weight of 16,930 pounds.

1918	November 7–9	First NC-1 long flight, a round-robin flight from NAS Rockaway Beach to NAS Anacostia, Washington, D.C., to NAS Hampton Roads, Virginia, and return to NAS Rockaway Beach.
1918	November 11	World War I ends. Rear Admiral Taylor's long-range ASW flying boat vision shifts to first transatlantic flight and NC seaplane development.
1918		NC-1 record-breaking flight for most people carried, 51 total. The 22,028 pound aircraft takes off with forty-eight passengers and one stowaway. NC-1 flew a thousand yards at an altitude of fifty feet.
1919	January 29	Eighteenth Constitutional Amendment passes, Prohibition enacted, Rum War begins.
1919	February 16	NC power plant decision made for Liberty engines with direct drive and high compression with twin tandem installation tested on NC-2 consisting of tandem engines in each wing.
1919	March	Heavy squall line passes NAS Rockaway, destroying anchored NC-1's port wing tip and float, aileron, control column, and one elevator control horn.
1919	April 5	Towers memorandum decision to replace NC-1 damaged wing with NC-2's wing.
1919	April 15	Navy Yard requested overhaul of *Jupiter* (Coal Barge 302) to a catapult barge for aircraft catapult tests from ships.
1919	April 21	CDR John H. Towers, USN, ordered to NAS Rockaway to command Seaplane Division I for first transatlantic flight; transfer of NC-1-type seaplane oversight activity ordered from the Bureau of Construction and Repair and the Bureau of Steam Engineering to NAS Rockaway.
1919	April 21	First Lieutenant Stone ordered to NC Seaplane Division One for duty in connection with transatlantic flight.
1919	May 3	NC Division 1 commissioned, NC-1, NC-3, and NC-4 operational.
1919	May 4	NAS Rockaway hangar fire damages NC-1 and NC-4. NC-2 parts cannibalized to repair NC-1 and NC-4.
1919	May 6	NC seaplane radios installed and functioning.
1919	May 8	NC-1, NC-3, and NC-4 depart NAS Rockaway Beach for Trepassey Bay, first departure point for first transatlantic flight. Navy aircrews would com-

pete with four teams of British pilots flying from St. Johns, Newfoundland; one British team flying westward from Ireland and U.S. Navy dirigible C-5.

1919	May 16	NC-1, NC-3, and NC-4, depart Trepassey Bay for Lisbon, Portugal, on first transatlantic flight.
1919	May 17	NC-1 and NC-3 land in heavy seas to use RDF to fix navigational positions. Both flying boats damaged, preventing takeoff.
1919	May 27	Lone NC-4 arrives in Lisbon, first successful transatlantic flight.
1919	May 30	NC-4 departs Lisbon for Portsmouth, England.
1919	May 30	NC-4 lands on river at Ferrol, Spain, with engine cooling leak.
1919	May 31	NC-4 departs Ferrol, Spain, for Plymouth, England.
1919	May 31	NC-4 arrives Plymouth, England.
1919	June 5	NC crews meet President Wilson in Paris, France for congratulations. French government awards silver memorial art.
1919	June 9	Commander Towers and the NC-4 crew report to the British Air Ministry. Officers are decorated with the Royal Air Force (RAF) Cross, and Rhodes is decorated with British Air Force Medal for noncommissioned personnel.
1919	Mid-June	NC crews board USS *Zeppelin* for a return voyage to New York, are treated to a ticker-tape parade.
1919	August	Coast Guard returns by Executive Order to Treasury Department. Service in sad shape from World War I and postwar cutbacks, officer corps 75% authorized strength, enlisted corps 60%.
1919	August	Coast Guard Commandant, RADM William R. Reynolds, USCG, convinces Navy to loan Coast Guard four Curtiss HS-2L seaplanes, and two Aeromarine Model 40s to operate at the first Coast Guard Air Station in Morehead City, North Carolina.
1919	September 11	Navy returns Lieutenant Stone to the Coast Guard. Lieutenant Stone assigned as temporary commanding officer of CGAS Morehead City.
1919	September 25	Revenue Cutter Service converts from RCS to Navy rank structure. Stone now a temporary lieutenant commander.
1919	September 25	CNO, Operations Department, approves General Board recommendation for aircraft stowage on

		battleship turret tops and launching airplanes using pneumatic catapults.
1919	November	Navy requests Lieutenant Commander Stone's return to participate in development of the first three aircraft carriers.
1919	November 20	Lieutenant Commander Stone reports to the Aircraft Division in the Bureau of Construction and Repair at the Washington, D.C., Navy Yard. Assignment is for one of the test pilots flying off *Jupiter* (Coal Barge 302).
1920		First wind tunnel built at NACA Langley Memorial Laboratory, Hampton (Virginia) for Army, Navy, and industry.
1920		Coast Guard Aviation involvement in Rum War commences.
1920	March 24	First Coast Guard air station commissioned (on closed Navy air station property), CGAS Morehead City, North Carolina.
1920	November 11	FDR decorates NC crews with Navy Cross.
1921	July 1	CGAS Morehead City closes due to lack of congressional funding.
1921	July 12	Aviation Division in the Bureau of Construction and Repair and the Board of Inspection and Survey in the Bureau of Steam Engineering reorganized into new Bureau of Aeronautics (BUAERO or BUAER). Engineering flight tests conducted at NAS Anacostia and Navy Aircraft Factory. Research now supported by new Naval Research Laboratory (NRL), and Aviation Operations is placed under the Chief of Naval Operations (CNO).
1921		Rear Admiral Moffett is appointed technical adviser to U.S. delegation to Washington Naval Conference. Moffett trades two battle-cruiser hulls for U.S. fast fleet aircraft carriers. Makes the case for U.S. Navy fast fleet carriers.
1921	September 2	Stone reverts to permanent rank, lieutenant.
1921	December 14	Lieutenant Stone invents a gunpowder catapult for aircraft that maintains consistency of propelling thrust and has a hydraulic car brake.
1922	March 20	*Langley* (CV-1) is commissioned.
1922	April 1	Lieutenant Stone leads development of *Langley* catapults and aircraft arresting gear. *Langley* used

		as test bed for catapult and arresting gear development for *Saratoga* and *Lexington*. Stone issues request for procurement letter to engineering firms for design of arresting gear.
1922	May 22	Lieutenant Stone accepts Carl Norden engineering firm's arresting gear proposal.
1924	March 29	Lieutenant Stone receives formal contractual engineering design from Norden for Mark I and Mark II arresting gear.
1924	April 2	Congress significantly increases budget and size of the Coast Guard. Transfers twenty-five World War I four-stack destroyers to enforce Prohibition from Navy to Coast Guard.
1924	April 21	Stone is promoted to temporary lieutenant commander.
1925	January 1–6	Coast Guard Commandant requests return of Lieutenant Commander Stone due to shortage of experienced officers for destroyers. Rear Admiral Moffett requests that Stone stay until important work is concluded.
1925	January 6	Coast Guard commandant letter to Rear Admiral Moffett permits Lieutenant Commander Stone to continue with BUAERO until assigned work has progressed so Stone's return is not detrimental to BUAERO.
1925	January 8	Admiral Moffett's reply to Coast Guard Commandant states he will assign understudy and will return Stone when most important work is done.
1925		Lieutenant Commander Stone's Mark V P-type (powder) turntable catapult testes are approved as the standard for battleships and cruisers.
1925		Following Powder Catapult work, Lieutenant Commander Stone continued as leader for aircraft carrier catapult and arresting gear development and final design, manufacture, and installation on aircraft carriers *Saratoga* and *Lexington*.
1925	May 10	Temporary Coast Guard air operations established at Reserve NAS Squantum, Massachusetts, off Dorchester Bay with O2U-2, in landplane configuration. Shortly thereafter, O2U-2 converted to seaplane configuration.

1925	June 20	First Coast Guard use of an aircraft (O2U-2) to chase a rumrunner.
1925	June 24	Coast Guard O2U-2 assists in first capture of "rummie" with aviation support.
1926	January/February	*Saratoga* and *Lexington* arresting gear acceptance test at NAS Hampton Roads.
1926	Spring	Lieutenant Commander Stone oversees installation of catapults and arresting gear on *Saratoga* and *Lexington*.
1926	May 20	First permanent Coast Guard air station is established, CGAS Ten Pound Island, in Gloucester Harbor, Massachusetts. O2U-2, in seaplane configuration, moved from NAS Squantum. Concrete poured for hangar foundation and steel hangar erected in summer.
1926		Coast Guard Air Station Cape May, New Jersey, is commissioned.
1926		Congress appropriates $152,000 for design and construction of five aircraft specifically for the Coast Guard. Three OL-5s and two UO-2 amphibians.
1926	September 21	Installation of *Saratoga* and *Lexington* catapults and arresting gear essentially complete. Navy returns Lieutenant Commander Stone to the Coast Guard. Stone is assigned executive officer USCGC Modoc.
1926	October 14	First Coast Guard OL-5 arrives, the second on November 3.
1926	October 27	O2U-2 returned to the Navy.
1926		Coast Guard Radio Electricians Arthur Descoteaux and Clyde Solt develop first airborne radio direction finder using a loop antenna.
1926		Navy's Morrow Board modernizes Navy. Aircraft carrier replaces seaplanes as dominant aviation resource. Seaplanes remain dominant for Coast Guard operations.
1927		*Saratoga* (CV-2) and *Lexington* (CV-3) join fleet.
1928		Coast Guard Head Quarters, Aviation Division, establishes mission requirements for long-range flying lifeboat.
1929	June 13	Coast Guard Head Quarters, Aviation Division, establishes nation's first Air Traffic Following Service.

1930	May 23	President Hoover awards NC crews with Special Congressional Gold Medal.
1930–35		Sikorsky S-39 seaplane transferred to Coast Guard.
1931		Coast Guard purchased Viking Boat Company Shreck O-38.
1931		War Department orders one Douglas OS-38 for the Coast Guard.
1931–33		Coast Guard purchases Douglas RD-1, RD-2 and RD-3 amphibians.
1932	June 1	First seaplane designed and built for Coast Guard, PJ-1/PJ-2.
1932		Coast Guard purchases Consolidated N4Y-1 two-seat trainers, also known as the PT-11D, from the Army Air Corps.
1932	June 1	Coast Guard Air Station Miami, Florida, commissioned.
1933		Henry Morgenthau becomes Treasury Secretary. Transfers all Customs Division and Immigration Division air detachments and aircraft to Coast Guard.
1934	March 9	Coast Guard commences aerial border patrol operations on Canadian and Mexican borders.
1934		New Standard NT-2 aircraft confiscated from smugglers by the Alcohol Tax Division of the Treasury Department, and transferred to the Coast Guard.
1934		Navy transfers Chance-Vought two-seat O2U-2 to Coast Guard.
1934	October 27	Navy transfers JF-2 Ducks to Coast Guard, and Coast Guard purchased additional Grumman JF-2 Ducks on Navy contract.
1934	December 6	Coast Guard Air Station Biloxi, Mississippi, commissioned.
1934		Coast Guard purchases Stinson RQ-1.
1935	January 10	Lieutenant Commander Stone, flying his modified JF-2 aircraft, establishes world speed record for single engine amphibian aircraft.
1935		Stone promoted to commander.
1935	February	Coast Guard aviators certified for IFR flight.
1935	February 15	Coast Guard Air Station Salem, Massachusetts, commissioned.

1935	February 20	Coast Guard purchases Douglas RD-4.
1935	February 20	Coast Guard purchases a Northrop RT-1 VIP aircraft for Secretary of the Treasury.
1935	March 1	Coast Guard Air Station St. Petersburg, Florida, commissioned.
1935	June 1	Coast Guard Air Station Port Angles, Washington, commissioned.
1935		Coast Guard Patrol Detachment San Diego, California, commissioned.
1936	April 19	Coast Guard purchases an R30-1 Lockheed Electra for the Commandant's flagship.
1936	May 20	While inspecting a new patrol aircraft, Stone is stricken by a coronary thrombosis. Commander Stone abruptly dies.
1936	June 3	Secretary-class cutters are designed and built to carry and operate float planes.
1936	October	Coast Guard purchases Viking Flying Boat OO-1.
1936		Coast Guard purchases J2K-1 and two J2K-2 aircraft as search aircraft.
1937		*Langley*'s speed for launching and retrieving aircraft proclaimed too slow, ship converts to seaplane tender.
1937	March	Coast Guard Patrol Detachment Charleston, South Carolina, is commissioned.
1937	April	Coast Guard Air Station San Diego, California, is commissioned.
1937		Coast Guard purchases Waco J2W cabin model EQC-6 observation biplanes.
1938	April	Coast Guard purchases Hall PH-2/3 Flying Boat.
1938	April 23	Coast Guard Air Station Brooklyn, New York, is commissioned.
1938		Coast Guard acquires Curtiss SOC-4 Seagull from Navy.

APPENDIX B

Technology Inspired by the First Transatlantic Flight

1919–1938

After the Armistice, the Navy built a second set of NC seaplanes, NC-5, NC-6, NC-7, NC-8, NC-9, and NC-10. These were built initially as trimotors, but four were later converted to the NC-4 four-engine configuration. These six NC-type flying boats served from 1920 through 1922, divided between the Navy's East and West Coast Squadrons before being retired.

It often happens that when there are heroes at the completion of successful military operations that draw considerable public attention, its leaders are sent on programmed travel itineraries to recruit new volunteers for their military service. Thus was the case for the Navy members of the NC-4 crew, who were sent on a recruiting mission around the country. They would fly and display the NC-4 as part of that effort.[1]

The Navy's successful attempt by NC seaplanes to cross the Atlantic in 1919 was more than a first crossing. It was a very dangerous undertaking that highlighted the need for advancement in four major areas of science and engineering before aviation could advance further: climatic weather measurement and reporting; electronic navigation and associated instrumentation; radio communication; and electronic in-flight instruments for blind flying—or in today's terminology, Instrument Flight Rules, or IFR flight.

Eight years later, when Lindbergh made the first nonstop civil-aviation crossing of the Atlantic, he had fair weather en route and better weather reporting, and he was greatly assisted by his new electrically stabilized earth inductor compass. The earth inductor compass isolates the magnetic element that *seeks* direction for the visual indicator that *tells* the pilot his direction. The magnetic element is an electric generator, or common electric dynamo, that uses the earth's magnetic lines of flux in place of an artificial electric field.

NC-4 on recruiting assignment, December 30, 1919

The generator's output is determined by the angular relation between its brushes and the earth's flux. Rotation of the generator shaft actually acts as a gyroscope, thereby resisting any motion tending to disturb stability.

Shipboard magnetic compasses mounted on gimbals were the only directional instruments available to the NC seaplanes. They had no stabilization, were inaccurate while flying in rough air or while making a turn, and bounced off their gimbals during rough-water takeoffs.

Weather observations in 1919 were limited to what an isolated observer could actually see and locally measure when a helium-filled balloon was launched, tracked, and used to determine surface and upper wind direction and velocity. Pilot weather briefings based upon many scientific weather observations communicated over a large network and plotted on weather observation maps that included intended flight path would not come until many years later.[2]

One development that was derived from the Navy's attempt at the first transatlantic flight was the bubble sextant, developed by LCDR Richard E. Byrd, USN. It was important to aviation because it did not depend upon a visual horizon, as ship navigators did, to measure the elevation of celestial bodies. On a ship, the line from a handheld sextant to the horizon represents a horizontal line. The angle between a line from the sextant to a celestial body and the horizontal line represents the vertical angle of the body relative to the horizontal.

Celestial navigation is based upon solid geometry and solid trigonometry. It is a graphic presentation of mathematical solutions as a "plot" on a navigation chart.

The earth is a sphere inside a larger celestial universe sphere of stars and planets, where longitude is both an angle and a time measurement from a fixed point—in this case Greenwich, England. Fifteen degrees of longitude is equal to one hour's distance from Greenwich. We can therefore measure the sun's and all celestial bodies' travel relative to the earth. These two solid geometrical spheres, one inside the other, also allow a navigator to measure and compute a location's latitude and longitude. The navigator uses Greenwich mean time (GMT), the height of two or more celestial bodies measured from the horizon, and mathematical tables calculated by the U.S. Hydrographic Office and the Naval Observatory. The navigator's observation represents a solid trigonometric triangle from the celestial body's angular height, which determines a line of position (LOP) on the earth's surface. Two, or preferably three or more, lines of position determine a navigational fix, or position, on the earth's surface.[3]

For celestial navigation to be applied to aircraft flying above the horizon, it is necessary to replace the visual horizon when measuring the height of a celestial body above the horizon. As preparation for the world's first transatlantic flight, Commander Towers assigned Lieutenant Commander Byrd the task of devising navigation equipment and methods. Byrd and his coequal on the other side of the ocean, L. B. Booth of the British Royal Aircraft Establishment, developed the bubble sextant, where a level bubble for reference is an artificial earth's horizon, and the angular measurement of a celestial body is observed with reference to the bubble.

Byrd also worked with the U.S. Hydrographic Office to develop for selected celestial bodies navigation tables that were simpler to use than the *Nautical Almanac* used on board surface ships. The remaining tools for celestial navigation are the same as those on board ships. Later, Byrd's tables would become the Hydrographic Office publication *Air Nautical Almanac*.[4] This innovation allowed celestial measurement from aircraft at any altitude; an accurate plot of navigational fixes is kept, and when visual sight of the horizon or the stars and planets is lost, one can continue with dead-reckoning (DR) computations. DR starts from a known point. By using the formula *distance equals velocity, or speed, multiplied by time* and using compass-rose degrees that represent an aircraft's track, a plot can be made. An aircraft's course is corrected to a specific track by adding corrections for wind drift, the earth's magnetic deviation, and variation from geographic true north at the North Pole. A drift indicator is used to measure the angle of wind drift by sighting vertically to the ocean's surface and aligning a magnetic compass track of visual points on the surface. This is compared with the aircraft's compass heading, and the difference is drift angle.[5] Had NC-1 and NC-3 maintained current celestial and DR plots, they would not have become lost and would not have had to land to determine their positions. Landing in heavy seas ended their quests.

While CDR Norman Hall, USCG, was not a naval aviator, he had flown Curtiss aircraft during his instruction by Glenn Curtiss to become the Coast Guard's first aviation engineering officer at the Curtiss Atlantic Coast Flying Station. At Curtiss's invitation, Hall continued to fly the H-10 as a test bed for aviation navigation systems.[6]

Curtiss H-10 flying boat flown by CDR Norman Hall, USCG

Three in-flight instruments based upon gyroscopic stability were developed after the first transatlantic flight: the fluxgate compass, an artificial horizon (or attitude gyro), and a turn–and–bank, or slip, indicator. In very basic terms, the gyroscope prevents an aircraft's magnetic float compass (ship's wet compass) from bouncing in rough air. The fluxgate compass operates as an electrically driven gyrostabilized magnetic compass, providing stable compass headings.[7]

During the first transatlantic flight the crews determined when the aircraft was in a bank, dive, or climb by two floating bubbles in sealed arched-glass tubes representing pitch and roll. One instrument was installed fore and aft to measure pitch angle, and the other was installed athwartships to measure roll angle. This was not reliable in rough air, since the bubbles would bounce around giving false readings. The artificial horizon is an electrically driven gyroscope-stabilized ball around which the aircraft banks, dives, and climbs.

A turn-and-bank, or slip, indicator uses an electrically driven gyroscope to indicate that the aircraft is turning and how fast it is turning.[8] It also indicates when the rudder and ailerons are not coordinated.

During the first transatlantic flight, NC-1 and NC-3 radio-direction-finder (RDF) antennas were located directly below the center tandem pusher and tractor engines. At that time, suppression of noise from sparkplugs had not been invented. Just as sparkplugs without noise suppression can cause staticlike interference in a car radio, they interrupted

NC-1 and NC-3 RDF patterns. ENS Herbert C. Rodd, USNRF, had moved the NC-4's RDF antenna to a location outboard of the center tandem engines, thereby minimizing electronic spark noise. In addition, Ensign Rodd was a very experienced radio operator who knew how to tune a radio to get the most from it. As a result, Rodd was able to work around any sparkplug-noise problem. This was not the proper engineering solution. That would come later with electronic noise suppression.[9]

Evolution of naval aircraft instrument panels

The preceding photographs of Navy aircraft cockpit instrument panels from 1920 to 1936 are examples of increasingly complex aircraft design and improved flight instrumentation.

In addition to instrumentation advancement, improvements were made in fuel-line joint gasket materials, aluminum construction, and metal (as opposed to wood) hulls and fuselages.[10] In the summer of 1921, when duralumin metal became available, the Naval Aircraft Factory in Philadelphia began designing and testing the first metal hulls for flying boats. The F5-L was the first flying boat modified to metal construction.[11] As important to flight personnel as metal aircraft were parachutes, which were not issued until 1922.[12]

Two deck watch officers on board two of the destroyers on station along the first transatlantic flight plan became aviation pioneers after completing their naval service. One, Leroy Grumman, became a design engineer for Loening Aircraft Company and later founded the Grumman Aircraft Engineering Corporation, in Bethpage, New York. Grumman was one of the most important builders of U.S. Navy aircraft from 1930 to the end of World War II. In 1942, RADM John S. McCain, USN, stated, "The name Grumman on a plane . . . had the same meaning to the Navy that 'sterling' had to silver."[13]

The other deck watch officer, Juan T. Trippe, went on to found Pan American Airways, the world's first airline, on March 14, 1927. Pan American Airways first operated from a seaplane terminal in Miami, Florida, at Dinner Key. It was the hub for U.S. Mail delivery and passenger air travel from the United States throughout the Caribbean and Central and South America during the 1930s and 1940s. After Pan American abandoned the seaplane, Coast Guard Air Station Miami was commissioned on the expanded Dinner Key facility.[14]

Nineteen twenty-six brought war-fighting requirements much different from those imposed by the limitations of World War I equipment. The era of flying-boat domination came to an end, and the aircraft carrier would now dominate strategy.[15] From 1920 to 1928 the Navy responded to peacetime budgets. One of the Navy strategies was to expand and extend long-distance flight capability. After the first transatlantic flight, the F5-L was fitted with high-compression, geared-down Liberty engines, giving it long-range capability equal to that of the NC transatlantic flying boats. On December 30, 1920, twelve F5-L and two NC flying boats from the Pacific Seaplane Squadron departed NAS North Island in San Diego, California, and flew nonstop to Balboa, Panama. In 1926, a squadron of F5-L flying boats commanded by LCDR Bruce G. Leighton accompanied a 12,371-mile fleet cruise and maneuver to the West Indies. They were supported by the seaplane tenders USS *Shawmut* and USS *Sandpiper*. These flying boats withstood weather and seas just as well as the ships did. They operated effectively in thirty-five to forty-knot winds, and they rode out gales of eighty knots at sea anchors.[16]

Engineering advancements continued to improve naval aircraft operational capability. Examples include the first practical air-cooled radial engines, the Sperry gyrostabilized automatic pilot, a reversible-pitch propeller, improved radio-direction-finder performance, metallurgy advancements for aircraft structure and fittings, aircraft testing to prove the practicability of bombing and sinking large naval vessels and submarines, development of Carl L. Norden's high-altitude bombsight, and the development of catapults and of the aircraft carrier.

APPENDIX C

List of Acronyms, Abbreviations, and Rank Structures

Navy and Coast Guard Rank Structure

Equivalent Revenue Cutter Service Rank Structure

ENS	Ensign	Third Lieutenant (3rd LT)
LTJG	Lieutenant (junior grade)	Second Lieutenant (2nd LT)
LT	Lieutenant	First Lieutenant (1st LT)
LCDR	Lieutenant Commander	Captain
CDR	Commander	Senior Captain
CAPT	Captain	Captain-Commandant
RADM	Rear Admiral	Rear Admiral
VADM	Vice Admiral	

Other Services Ranks:

LtCol	Lieutenant Colonel (USMC)
Col	Colonel (USMC)
BG	Brigadier General (Army)
MajGen	Major General (USMC)

Navy Technical Bureaus:

BUAERO	Bureau of Aeronautics, later ...
BUAIR	Bureau of Aviation
BUNAV	Bureau of Navigation
BUORD	Bureau of Ordnance
CC	Member of Constructor Corps within the Bureau of Construction and Repair
JAG	Judge Advocate General

Operational Commanders:

CNO	Chief of Naval Operations
CINC	Commander in Chief
CINCLANT	Commander in Chief, Atlantic Fleet
CINCPAC	Commander in Chief, Pacific Fleet
CO	commanding officer
XO	executive officer
OPS	operations officer
OIC	officer in charge (usually an enlisted person)

Units:

NAS	Naval Air Station
NAF	Naval Air Facility
NOB	Naval Operations Base
CGAS	Coast Guard Air Station
CGAD	Coast Guard Air Detachment
USS	U.S. Ship
USRSC	U.S. Revenue Service Cutter
USCGC	U.S. Coast Guard Cutter

Service Branches:

RAF	Royal Air Force
USCG	U.S. Coast Guard
USCGR	U.S. Coast Guard Reserve
USMC	U.S. Marine Corps
USMCR	U.S. Marine Corps Reserve
USN	U.S. Navy
USNR	U.S. Navy Reserve

| USNRF | U.S. Navy Reserve Fleet |
| USRCS | U.S. Revenue Cutter Service |

Other:

ASW	antisubmarine warfare
DR	dead reckoning
GMT	Greenwich mean time
HP	horsepower
IFR	Instrument Flight Rules
LOP	line of position
RDF	radio direction finder
SAR	search and rescue
U.S.A.T.	U.S. Army Transport

APPENDIX D

Photograph and Document Credits

Page	Title	Reference Source
vi	CDR E. F. Stone, USCG official portrait, Washington, D.C.	Official Military Personnel Service Record, Coast Guard Historian files
4	Hall of Honor plaque, VADM Patrick N. L. Bellinger, USN	Hall of Honor National Naval Aviation Museum, NAS Pensacola, Florida
4	Hall of Honor plaque, RADM Richard E. Byrd Jr. USN	Ibid.
4	Hall of Honor plaque, LCDR Godfrey deC. Chevalier, USN	Ibid.
4	Hall of Honor plaque, Mr. Glenn H. Curtiss, Civilian	Ibid.
5	Hall of Honor plaque, CDR Theodore G. Ellyson, USN	Ibid.
5	Hall of Honor plaque, Mr. Eugene Ely, civilian	Ibid.
5	Hall of Honor plaque, RADM William A. Moffett, USN	Ibid.
5	Hall of Honor plaque, RADM Albert C. Read, USN	Ibid.
6	Hall of Honor plaque, CAPT Holden C. Richardson, USN	Ibid.

6	Hall of Honor plaque, ADM John H. Towers, USN	Ibid.
6	Hall of Honor plaque, ADM Marc A. Mitscher, USN	Ibid.
6	Hall of Honor plaque, CDR Elmer F. Stone, USCG	Ibid.
7	Hall of Honor plaque, CAPT Washington I. Chambers, USN	Ibid.
7	Hall of Honor plaque, Dr. Jerome C. Hunsaker, Civlian	Ibid.
9	Curtiss 40HP Pusher on first shipboard takeoff, USS *Birmingham* (CL-2)	National Archives Reference Group (RG) 80G, ID 460956. Cagle, "The Wings Unfold," Association of Naval Aviators *Wings of Gold* (Summer 1986), 43.
10	Curtiss 50HP Pusher on first USS *Pennsylvania* (ACR-4)	National Archives RG 80G, shipboard landing, ID 460956. Cagle, "The Wings Unfold," *Wings of Gold* (Summer 1986), 44.
10	First shipboard landing, USS *Pennsylvania* (ACR-4)	National Archives RG 80G, Cagle, "The Wings Unfold," *Wings of Gold* (Summer 1986), 44.
11	Curtiss Pusher amphibian close up	National Archives RG 80G, ID 460956.
12	Curtiss hydro-floatplane hoisted on board, then lowered to water for getaway and landing by beach	National Archives RG 80G, ID 460956. *Wings of Gold* (Fall 1977), 14. San Diego, Dauntless
12	Glenn Curtiss in water along beach with hydro-float-plane at North Island, 1911	*Wings of Gold* (Fall 1977), 16. San Diego, Dauntless
13	A-1 in flight over Coronado, California near Curtiss Airfield, 1912, Del Coronado Hotel in background	*Wings of Gold* (Summer 1986), 45.
14	Curtiss instructing LT Ellyson at San Diego Aero Club Meet, January 29, 1911	*Wings of Gold* (Fall 1977), 17. San Diego, Dauntless
14	Original Curtiss Flight Class, January 1911. Left to right:	U.S. Naval Institute photo archive.

Army lieutenants G. E. Kelly,
John Walker, Navy lieutenant
T. G. Ellyson; Army captain
Paul W. Beck

16	Navy's first aircraft, A-1, LTJG Ellison and passenger Captain Chambers	Cagle, "The Wings Unfold," *Wings of Gold* (Summer 1986), 45.
16	Curtiss and Chambers A-2	National Archives, RG 80G, ID 43C6C.
17	LT Holden C. Richardson, USN	U.S. Naval Institute photo archive.
17	Wright B-1 after pontoon installation	U.S. Naval Institute photo archive.
19	A-1 on first catapult attempt at Greenbury Point	U.S. Naval Institute photo archive.
19	Davis recoilless ASW gun	National Archives, RG 80G, ID 43C6C.
20	C-1 catapulted at Washington Navy Yard	Ibid.
22	Wind tunnel model of first aircraft designed and manufactured using wind-tunnel tests	Ibid.
24	*Thomas W. Lawson*	National Archives, RG 72G, ID 424473.
25	*Wyoming*	Ibid.
27	Class of 1913, U.S. Revenue Cutter Service School of Instruction (Stone sitting far left)	Coast Guard photograph, Historian files.
28	USRCS *Onondaga*	Ibid.
28	Curtiss Atlantic Coast Aeronautical Station	National Archives, RG 80G.
29	Curtiss and Baldwin in 1934	National Archives, RG 80G.
30	1916 Curtiss F Boat	National Archives, RG 80G, ID 426941.
32	First successful catapult launch from underway ship	National Archives, RG 80G.
35	Chiswell letter to Hunniwell, Navy Construction Corps, April 18, 1916	Coast Guard Historian files.
36	Curtiss triplane lifeboat	National Archives, RG 72G, ID 424489.
36	Curtiss lifeboat without wings	Coast Guard Historian files.
37	October 15, 1936, Coast Guard Aviation Instruction, Article 101, Navy Deficiency Act of August 29, 1916	Ibid.

38	First Coast Guard Aviation Group, NAS Pensacola	Coast Guard photograph, Historian files.
39	Commandant NAS Pensacola letter designating Stone naval aviator number thirty-eight	Stone Military Personnel Record, Coast Guard Headquarters, Washington, D.C.
41	Naval Aviator Wings of Gold	Navy Uniform Regulations
42	*Jersey Journal,* Black Tom Island explosion	Front Page, Sunday, July 30, 1916.
43	HS-1 bomb drop off New England coast	National Archives, RG 80G, ID 424491.
45	U.S. Army Signal Corps McCook Field, 1917 (total Army air assets)	Roger E. Bilstein, *Orders of Magnitude: A History of the NACA and NASA, 1915–1990* (Washington D.C., 1989), 6.
45	McCook Field Propeller unit (all early wooden propellers were made here)	Ibid.
46	USS *Huntington* (ACR-5) recovering R-6 torpedo float plane	National Archives, RG 80G, ID 4556.
47	USS *Huntington* at anchor in Pensacola Bay, 1917 (note aircraft on stern catapult rails)	National Archives, RG 80G, ID 43D51.
47	Enlarged view of kite balloon and observers, 1917(note the personnel ladder and telephone line running to the ship)	National Archives, RG 8072G, ID 460952.
48	Kite Balloon lashed to deck	National Archives, RG 80G, ID 460952.
48	WWI, USS *Huntington* Curtiss R-6	National Archives, RG 80G.
49	*Huntington* aircraft on catapult	National Archives, RG 802G, ID 4556E.
49	*Huntington* aircraft on catapult	National Archives RG, 80G, ID 4556.
50	*Huntington* aircraft departing catapult	National Archives RG, 80G, ID 45567.
50	*Huntington* aircraft departing catapult	National Archives RG, 80G, ID 45571.
51	Page from USS *Huntington's* log book, December 1, 1916	National Archives, RG, 86.

55	Stone's World War I Victory medal	U.S. Naval Institute photo archive.
65	Secretary of Navy approves three-engine seaplane	National Archives, RG 72, Correspondence of the Secretary's Office, Relating to Aviation, 1917–1921, 3068-12.
72	Engineering drawing of NC seaplane final design	National Archives, RG 80G.

Chapter 5, unless indicated otherwise, aircraft photographs were obtained from National Archives, College Park, Maryland, Reference Group 80G (BUAERO Photo Files). Not all photographs were marked with identification numbers (ID). Document images were obtained from National Archives, Washington, D.C., Reference Groups E50, 72G, CNO/SECNAV, "General correspondence relative to aircraft types, 1917–1925 and 1926–1934," box 374–408.

76	NC-4 on cross-country flight from NAS Rockaway to NAS Anacostia to NAS Hampton Roads and return to Rockaway	National Archives, RG 80G.
77	NC-1 with 50 passengers and crew, which set a world record	Ibid.
80	NAS Rockaway seaplane ramp blocked with washed-up sand	National Archives, RG 80G.
80	NC-1 after the storm at low tide showing the port lower wing panel destroyed and upper wing tip damaged	Ibid.
82	NC fuel consumption data obtained from NC-2	National Archives, RG 80G.
84	Commander Towers' orders to command NC Division 1	National Archives, RG 72, Correspondence of the Secretary's Office, Relating to Aviation, 1917–1921, 3068-12.
86	NC-4 at NAS Rockaway Beach ready for depature	National Archives, RG 80G.

Chapter 6, unless indicated otherwise, aircraft photographs were obtained from National Archives, College Park, Maryland, Reference Group 80G (BUAERO Photo Files). Not all photographs were marked with identification numbers (ID). Document images were obtained from National Archives, Washington, D.C., Reference Groups E50, 72G, CNO/SECNAV, "General correspondence relative to aircraft types, 1917–1925 and 1926–1934," box 374–408.

| 89 | C-5 departing NAS Cape May, New Jersey | National Archives, RG 80G. |

90	NC crews at NAS Rockaway during NC Division 1's commissioning muster	Ibid.
91	CDR John H. Towers, USN	National Naval Aviation Museum, Research Library, NAS Pensacola, Florida.
91	CDR A. C. Read, USN	Ibid.
92	LCDR Patrick N. L. Bellinger, USN	Ibid.
92	Marc A. Mitscher, as a captain, USN, in later years	Ibid.
93	ENS Rodd's NC-4 radio position	National Archives, RG 80G.
93	NC-4 moored at NAS Rockaway	National Archives, RG 80G.
94	NC-4 moored at NAS Rockaway	Ibid.
95	NC-1, NC-3, and NC-4 taxi for takeoff on first transatlantic flight	U.S. Naval Institute photo archive.
97	1919 NAS Chatham, Massachusetts	Coast Guard Aviation Association files, photograph taken by LT P. B. Eaton, USCG, 1919 Commanding Officer, NAS Chatham.
97	1919 approach from seaward to NAS Chatham	Ibid.
101	NC-4 with Olmsted propeller	National Archives, RG 80G.
102	NC-4 departing Trepassey Bay	Ibid.
102	First transatlantic flight plan	Curtiss Aeroplane and Motor Corporation, *The Flight across the Atlantic* (New York City 1919), 6, author(s) not listed.
106	NC-1 in tow by pulling boat from USS *Fairfax*	National Archives, RG 80G.
108	NC-3 off port side of USS *Harding*	National Archives, RG 80G.
109	Damaged NC-3 moored in Ponta Delgada Harbor	National Archives, RG 80G.
113	NC-4 landing on the Tagus River, Lisbon Portugal	National Archives, RG 80G.
113	NC-4 moored behind mother ship	National Archives, RG 80G.
114	Stone's Portuguese Order of the Tower and Sword	2005 photograph of Stone's medal on display at Coast Guard Academy Museum.
114	The crew of the NC-4, in Lisbon	National Archives, RG 80G.
116	National Archives photograph of famous painting of NC-4 in full color	Ibid.

117	Lord Mayor Brown's welcome at Plymouth, England	Ibid.
118	Admiral Plunkett and NC crews en route to Grand Hotel	Ibid.
119	French NC-4 commemorative medal by Morian	2005 photograph of Stone's silver piece on display at Coast Guard Academy Museum.
120	Lieutenant Novell and Bernt Balchen on New York's Broadway for New York's reception of the first transatlantic flight aviators	Ibid.
121	Franklin D. Roosevelt, on the Navy Department steps, decorating NC crews with the Navy Cross	Ibid.
121	Stone's U.S. Navy Cross	2005 photograph of Stone's medal on display at Coast Guard Academy Museum.
121	Stone's British Royal Air Force Cross awarded June 9, 1919, by the Prince of Wales	2005 photograph of Stone's medal on display at Coast Guard Academy Museum.
121	Navy Intelligence letter of September 25, 1919	Stone Military Personnel Record in Coast Guard Headquarters, Historian files.
122	President Hoover presenting Congressional Gold Medal to individuals of NC-4 crew	National Archives, RG-80G, Historian files.
122	Special Congressional NC-4 Medal and Ribbon	2005 photograph of Stone's medal on display at Coast Guard Academy Museum.
123	Assistant Secretary of the Navy letter to LT E. F. Stone, USCG, dated August 23, 1919	Stone Military Personnel Record in Coast Guard Headquarters, Historian files.
123	Personnel of NC-4. Left to right: copilot LTJG Walter Hinton, USNRF; commanding officer LCDR A. C. Read, USN; pilot LT Elmer F. Stone, USCG	Historian files.

Chapter 7, unless indicated otherwise, aircraft photographs were obtained from National Archives, College Park, Maryland, Reference Group 80G (BUAERO Photo Files). Not all photographs were marked with identification numbers (ID). Document images were obtained from National Archives, Washington, D.C., Reference Groups E50, 72G, CNO/SECNAV, "General correspondence relative to aircraft types, 1917–1925 and 1926–1934," box 374–408.

124	RADM William A. Moffett, first Chief of BUAERO, in cockpit	National Archives, RG 80G,
125	1922 naval aviation observer wings (breast pin)	Navy Uniform Regulations.
126	NAS Anacostia, 1918	National Archives, RG 80G, ID 424789.
127	McLoughlin's *Aces of the Air*	Historian files.
128	April 7, 1921, memorandum on naval aviation growth	National Archives, RG 86.
129	NAS Anacostia, 1932	*Wings of Gold* (Winter 1983), 36.
131	Cover page of test report of airplane trials	National Archives, RG 86.
132	HS-1 flying boat beached	National Archives, RG 80G, ID 462297.
132	HS-2 flying boat getaway	National Archives, RG 80G, ID-44494.
133	HS-1 to HS-2 modification letter	National Archives, RG E50/72, ID 25-25B.
134	HS-1 to HS-2 test requirements, p. 1	Ibid.
135	HS-1 to HS-2 test requirements, p. 2	Ibid.
136	HS-1 to HS-2 test requirements, p. 3	Ibid.
137	HS-1 to HS-2 test requirements, p. 4	Ibid.
138	Stone's recommendation for added changes to HS-1 to HS-2 modification	Ibid.
139	Curtiss Speed Gnome Scout A-448	National Archives, RG 80G.
140	Curtis Model F Boat	National Archives, RG 80G, ID 651114-651557.
140	Boeing seaplane	National Archives, RG 80G, ID 452751.
141	Carolina F Boat A-4343 aircraft trial report	National Archives, RG 72.
142	DN-1 dirigible approaching floating hangar	National Archives, RG 80G, ID 45553.
143	Gallaudet D-4 seaplane light bomber	National Archives, RG 80G.
143	Gallaudet D-4 landplane light bomber with splintered propeller	Ibid.
144	Huff-Daland HA Fighter on ramp	Ibid.
145	Huff-Daland HA Fighter on beach	Ibid.
146	N-1 A4342 aircraft trial report, front of page 17	National Archives RG 86, ID none.
146	N-1 A4342 aircraft trial report, reverse of page 17	Ibid.
147	N-1 seaplane	National Archives, RG 80G.
147	N-1 seaplane on ramp	Ibid.

148	Lewis machine gun	Ibid.
148	R-9 torpedo seaplane	Ibid.
149	R-9 torpedo seaplane loading on tug	Ibid.
150	Aeromarine, Model No. 40, A5086	National Archives, RG 80G, ID 42689.
150	Aeromarine, Model No. 40, A5086	National Archives, RG 80G, ID 427042.
151	Curtiss MF Boat with Hispano Suiza motors and pusher propeller	National Archives, RG 80G, ID 651114-651557.
151	NC-4 Liberty engines	National Archives, RG 80G, ID 65114-651557.
153	Sperry light bomber and triplane seaplane	National Archives, RG 80G.
153	Sperry light bomber and triplane seaplane, Roosevelt Field, New York	Ibid.
154	Curtis 18T seaplane A-3325	Ibid.
154	Loening LS seaplane beached	Ibid.
155	Loening M-81 seaplane aircraft trial comments	National Archives, RG 86.
155	Loening M-81 seaplane	National Archives, RG 80G, ID 459246, 459248.
156	Loening M-80 landplane	National Archives, RG 80G.
156	Curtiss CT seaplane	National Archives, RG 86.
157	Curtiss CT seaplane test report extract	National Archives, RG 80G.
158	Naval Aircraft Factory Type PT seaplane	National Archives, RG 80G, ID 424487.
159	Experimental aircraft Models WE amphibian and WS seaplane	National Archives, RG 80G, ID 46327-463449.
163	Aeromarine, Model No. 40	National Archive, RG 80G, ID 42689, ID 427042.
164	Launching HS-2L at CGAS Morehead City, North Carolina	National Archives, RG 80, Historian files.
165	HS-2L about to come up on the step	National Archives, RG 80, Historian files.
165	Curtiss HS-2L in flight	National Archives, RG 80, Historian files.
165	CGAS Morehead City Station crew at station decommissioning, July 27, 1921	Coast Guard photograph, Historian files.

166	Seventy-five-footer, or "six-bitter"	Coast Guard photograph, Historian files.
168	O2U-2C	RG 80G, Navy Department Photograph No. 80-G-15177.
169	Reserve NAS Squantum shown on Massachusetts Rand-McNally Air Map of the day	Rand-McNally.
170	Chance-Vought O2U-2 specifications sheet	Coast Guard photograph, Historian files.
171	CDR C.C. von Paulsen, commanding officer, Base 7 and CGAS Ten Pound Island, and ENS L. M. Melka, May 20, 1927	Coast Guard photograph, Historian files.
172	CGAS Ten Pound Island with Loening OL-5 in hangar	Coast Guard photograph, Historian files.
172	CGAS Ten Pound Island photographs	*Coast Guard Magazine,* 1941, 44, Historian files.
172	CGAS Ten Pound Island first pilots and hangar crew (commanding officer CDR C. C. von Paulsen, rear row, third from left)	*Coast Guard Magazine*, 1941, Historian files.
173	Loening OL-5 during maintenance at CGAS Ten Pound Island	Coast Guard photograph, Historian files.
173	Loening OL-5 during maintenance at CGAS Ten Pound Island	Ibid.
173	Loening OL-5 landing in Gloucester Harbor	Ibid.
174	Loening OL-5 anchored off CGAS Ten Pound Island ramp	Ibid.
174	Loening OL-5 resting on beaching gear on CGAS Ten Pound Island ramp	Ibid.
175	Loening OL-5 resting on beaching gear on CGAS Ten Pound Island ramp preparing for launch	Ibid.
175	Loening OL-5 machine-gun check on CGAS Ten Pound Island ramp	Ibid.
176	Vought UO-4	Ibid.
176	Vought UO-4	Ibid.

177	Vought UO-4 flown by LT William Foley, USCG, to CGAS Salem, from CGAS Cape May via Ten Pound Island	Ibid.
177	OL-5 on patrol with two six-bitters	Ibid.
178	OL-5 and six-bitters pursuing rumrunners	Ibid.
179	USCGC *Modoc*	Ibid.
180	CGAS Cape May with old Navy dirigible hangar before its destruction	Ibid.
181	Coast Guard destroyer *Monaghan*	Ibid.
182	Coast Guard destroyer *Cummings*	Ibid. Coast Guard Academy Museum, New London, Conn.

Chapter 9, unless indicated otherwise, aircraft photographs were obtained from National National Archives, College Park, Maryland, Reference Group 80. Not all photographs were marked with identification numbers (ID). Document images and photographs associated with same correspondence were obtained from National Archives, Washington, D.C., Reference Groups 72 and 86, "Correspondence of the Secretary's Office relating to aviation 1917–1921."

184	1921, USS *Arizona* (BB-39) turret catapult with Newport 28 aircraft	Cagle, "The Wings Unfold," *Wings of Gold* (Summer 1986), 49.
185	Atlantic Fleet first catapult test August 13, 1920, pilot LCDR V. C. Griffin, USN	Ibid.
185	August 13, 1920, USS *Oklahoma* (BB-37) Vought aircraft on number-two turret	Ibid.
186	Atlantic Fleet catapult test, August 13, 1920, pilot LT A. C. Wagner, USNRF	National Archives, RG 72.
186	Atlantic Fleet catapult test, August 13, 1920. Vought seaplane coming alongside USS *Oklahoma* motor sailer for recovery and hoist to ship's catapult	Ibid.
188	BUORD 2nd endorsement letter to Navy Judge Advocate General acknowledging Stone invented powder catapult	Ibid.

189	Earlier pneumatic turntable catapult tested at Navy Aircraft Factory. Later was converted to Stone's Mark V P- typepowder turntable catapult	National Archives, RG 80G.
191	USS *Jupiter*, Coal Barge 302	U.S. Naval Institute photo archive.
191	USS *Langley* (CV-1)	National Archives, RG 80G.
192	First *Langley* landing	Ibid.
192	Escorts making smoke to hide USS *Langley*	National Archives, RG 80G, ID 3543.
193	Carl Norden's May 22, 1922, letter to LCDR Stone	National Archives, RG 86.
194	LCDR Stone's acceptance letter to Norden, p.1	Ibid.
195	LCDR Stone's acceptance letter, p.2	Ibid.
197	Carl Norden's April 14, 1924, letter to Stone, p. 1	Ibid.
198	Carl Norden's April 14 letter, p. 2	Ibid.
201	Theodore H. Barth's October 26, 1925, letter	Ibid.
201	NAS Hampton Roads	National Archives, RG 80G.
202	Aeronautic, Test No. 1, arresting gear, *Saratoga,* p. 1	National Archives, RG 80.
203	Aeronautics Test No.1, arresting gear, *Saratoga,* p. 2	Ibid.
204	Aeronautic Test No. 1, arresting gear, *Saratoga,* p. 3	Ibid.
205	Aeronautic Test No. 1, arresting gear, *Saratoga,* p. 4	Ibid.
206	USS *Saratoga* hangar deck	Ibid.
206	USS *Saratoga* and O2U aircraft takeoff	Ibid.
207	1926, USS *Saratoga* anchored, with Jenny aircraft on deck	Ibid.
207	1930, USS *Lexington*	National Archives, RG 80G, ID 460921.
210	Sikorsky S-39 off Newport, Rhode Island	Coast Guard photograph, Historian files.
210	Shreck Boat Company O-38, Number OO-1, later V-2, purchased October 1936	Ibid.
211	Viking Boat Company Shreck O-38	Ibid.
211	Viking Boat Company Shreck O-38	Ibid.

212	Viking Boat Company Shreck O-38	Ibid.
213	Douglas OS-38-C	Ibid.
214	PJ-1 on ramp resting on beaching gear	Ibid.
215	PJ-1 water landing	Ibid.
215	PJ-1 embarking medical evacuation patient	Ibid.
216	PJ-2 in flight over harbor	Ibid.
216	PJ-2 water takeoff	Ibid.
217	Consolidated N4Y training planes	Ibid.
217	Consolidated N4Y training plane	Ibid.
218	CGAS Cape May, 1932.	Ibid.
219	RD-4	Ibid.
219	USS *Akron*, J-3, tethered to USS *Patoka* (AO-9)	National Archives, RG 80G.
220	RADM William A. Moffett, USN, and LCDR Ros, USN, on *Akron*'s bridge	National Archives, RG 80G.
221	Douglas RD-4 Dolphin	Coast Guard photograph, Historian files.
222	RD-3	Ibid.
223	RD-1	Ibid.
223	RD series radio rack suite	Ibid.
225	New Standard NT-2	Ibid.
226	New Standard NT-2	Ibid.
227	Chance-Vought O2U-2 received in 1934	Ibid.
227	Chance-Vought O2U-2 received in 1934	Ibid.
228	Chance-Vought O2U-2 received in 1935	Ibid.
229	Coast Guard Grumman JF-2 in the Arctic as part of USN's Byrd polar Expedition	Ibid.
229	Grumman JF-2 makes first flight in Antarctica with USCGC *Northwind* on Operation High Jump	Ibid.
230	Painting of CGC *Northstar* on Greenland Patrol, returning JF-2-5 Duck scout, by Gus Swensen	CAPT Manard F. Young, USCG (Retired, deceased), Greenland Patrol art collection, author's files.
230	Notation on back of Swensen's painting	Ibid.
231	Grumman JF-2 on launching ramp at CGAS Port Angles, Washington	Coast Guard photograph, Historian files.

231	Grumman JF-2 preparing for USN's Byrd Arctic polar expedition	Ibid.
232	JF-2	Ibid.
233	Certificate of record, National Aeronautic Association, World Seaplane Record, December 20, 1934	Ibid.
233	LCDR Elmer F. Stone, December 20, 1934, breaks the world speed record for seaplanes	Ibid.
234	JF-2 lifted on board USCGC Spencer	Ibid.
235	JF-2 preparing for lowering to water for takeoff	Ibid.
235	JF-2 on board USCGC Storis	Ibid.
236	R-Q1	Ibid.
236	R-Q1	Ibid.
237	RT-1 Delta	Ibid.
238	RT-1 Delta at CGAS Arlington, National Airport, Virginia	Ibid.
238	Northrop RT-1 Delta	Ibid.
239	Lockheed R30-1 Electra	Ibid.
239	R30-1	Ibid.
240	J2W	Ibid.
240	J2W on skis at the Waco Aircraft Company hangar in Troy, Ohio	Ibid.
241	Fairchild J2K-1	Ibid.
241	Fairchild J2K-2	Ibid.
242	Hall Aluminum PH-2 on ramp with beaching gear	Ibid.
243	PH-2 removing beaching gear on CGAS Cape May launching ramp	Ibid.
243	PH-2 on CGAS Brooklyn tarmac	Ibid.
244	PH-2 parked, resting on beaching gear	Ibid.
244	PH-2 taking-off, CGAS Brooklyn seadrome	Ibid.
245	CGAS Elizabeth City PH-2 with NAS Norfolk, Virginia, beaching crew offloading litter basket patient	Ibid.

Appendix B

NOTES

Introduction

1. Roger E. Bilstein, Flight in America: From the Wrights to the Astronauts (Baltimore: Johns Hopkins University Press, 2001), 33.

2. U.S. Naval Aviator Number List with date aviator wings earned; CAPT Maury Cagle, "The Wings Unfold," Association of Naval Aviators Wings of Gold (Summer 1986), 46.

3. U.S. Naval Aviator Number List with date aviator wings earned; Robert Erwin Johnson, Guardians of the Sea (Annapolis, Md.: U.S. Naval Institute, 1987).

4. Cagle, "The Wings Unfold," 47.

5. Rear Admiral Taylor, USN, memorandum, August 1917, Reference Group [hereafter RG] 45, Secretary of the Navy [hereafter SECNAV] files, National Archives, Washington, D.C.

Chapter 2: Naval Aviation Conception and Birth: 1898–1912

1. Cagle, "The Wings Unfold," 42. Dr. Robert L. Scheina, Coast Guard Historian, "Coast Guard Aviation: A Proud Record," Association of Naval Aviators Wings of Gold (Summer 1986), 9.

2. Cagle, "The Wings Unfold," 43.

3. Ibid., 44.

4. Ibid., 44, 45; Robert Merkin, 50th Anniversary of Naval Aviation 1910–1961 (El Segundo, Calif.: Douglas Aircraft Company, 1961), 19.

5. Merkin, 50th Anniversary of Naval Aviation 1910–1961, 18.

6. Cagle, "The Wings Unfold," 45.

7. Ibid; Merkin, 50th Anniversary of Naval Aviation 1910–1961, 19.

8. Cagle, "The Wings Unfold," 45.

9. Roy A. Grossnick, United States Naval Aviation, 1910–1995 (Haddonfield, N.J.: Ross & Perry, June 2001).

10. Cagle, "The Wings Unfold," 45.

11. Grossnick, United States Naval Aviation, 1910 1995; Cagle, "The Wings Unfold," 45.

12. Grossnick, *United States Naval Aviation, 1910–1995*; Cagle, "The Wings Unfold," 45.

13. Ibid.

14. Ibid.

15. Merkin, *50th Anniversary of Naval Aviation 1910–1961,* 21.

16. Cagle, "The Wings Unfold," 48.

17. Merkin, *50th Anniversary of Naval Aviation 1910–1961,* 21.

18. Grossnick, *United States Naval Aviation, 1910–1995*.

19. Ibid.

20. Ibid., 19, 20, 47; Merkin, *50th Anniversary of Naval Aviation 1910–1961,* 19.

21. Merkin, *50th Anniversary of Naval Aviation 1910–1961,* 21.

22. Ibid.

23. Grossnick, *United States Naval Aviation, 1910–1995*.

Chapter 3: Development and Growth: 1913–1919

1. Benjamin W. Labaree et al., *America and the Sea: A Maritime History,* American Maritime Library, vol. 15 (Mystic, Conn.: Mystic Seaport Museum, 1998).

2. Robert Browning, PhD., Coast Guard Historian, *Commander Elmer Fowler Stone, USCG, 1887–1936,* Official Coast Guard Aviation History website, Coast Guard Headquarters, Washington, D.C. February 21, 2012.

3. Labaree et al., *America and the Sea*.

4. Grossnick, *United States Naval Aviation, 1910–1995*.

5. Ibid.

6. Ibid.

7. Ibid.

8. Captain Commandant, U.S. Coast Guard letter designating Stone a line officer of *Onandaga,* February 14, 1914.

9. Captain Commandant, U.S. Revenue Cutter Service, Office of the Secretary of the Treasury, letter to Mr. Elmer F. Stone, April 21, 1910, Coast Guard Historian files, Coast Guard Headquarters, Washington, D.C.

10. Secretary of Treasury, letter to Mr. Elmer F. Stone, April 26, 1910.

11. Captain Commandant, U.S. Coast Guard, letter order to Third Lt. E.F. Stone, directing an investigation of aviation matters bearing on the Coast Guard, March.

12. Assistant Secretary of the Treasury, letter to Capt. B. M. Chiswell, Commanding Officer, Cutter *Onondaga,* Subject: Commendation in Connection with Rescue of Crew of Schooner *C. C. Wehrum,* June 24, 1915, Coast Guard Historian files, Coast Guard Headquarters, Washington, D.C.

13. "New Port News, Virginia History" website, www.vahsonline.org/Newport.news-atlanticcoast-aeronautical-station, February 21, 2012.

14. Eklund Don Dean, "The Story of Lighter than Air Development in America: Early Aero Entepreneurs—Lifting Americans into the Air Age. Captain Thomas S. Baldwin: Pioneer American Aeronaut," PhD dissertation, 1970, University of Colorado.

15. Coast Guard Historian, Robert Browning interview by CAPT Robert B. Workman Jr., USCG (Ret), June 2004.

16. Merkin, *50th Anniversary of Naval Aviation 1910–1961,* 22.

17. Captain Commandant, U.S. Coast Guard, letter orders to Third Lt. E. F. Stone, directing an investigation of aviation matters bearing on the Coast Guard, March 21, 1916, Coast Guard Historian files, Coast Guard Headquarters, Washington, D.C.

18. John Bentley, "Yearly Count of New Types of Aircraft Owned or Used by the Coast Guard Since Flying Became an Entragal [*sic*] Part of Its Duties (1915–1970)," Coast Guard Historian files, Coast Guard Headquarters, Washington, D.C., Coast Guard Headquarters (Office of Operations copy), API/83.

19. Grossnick, *United States Naval Aviation, 1910–1995*.

20. Ibid.

21. Ibid.

22. Ibid.

23. Ibid.

24. Ibid.

25. Alex Roland, *Model Research: The National Advisory Committee for Aeronautics, 1915–1958* (Washington, D.C.: National Aeronautics and Space Administration, 1985), 1:6ff.

26. Grossnick, *United States Naval Aviation, 1910–1995*.

27. Ibid.

28. Bentley, "Yearly Count of New Types of Aircraft Owned or Used by the Coast Guard."

29. T. O'Brien and Dr. Robert L. Scheina, "Coast Guard: In at the Beginning," Association of Naval Aviators *Wings of Gold* (Winter 1977), 8–9; Capt. Frank A. Erickson, USCG (Ret.), "The First Trans-Atlantic Flight," *Coast Guard Academy Alumni Bulletin* (May/June 1977). Louis B. Casey, "Curtiss Flying Lifeboat," *American Aviation History Society Journal* 10, no. 2 (Summer 1965), 102–4; Cagle, "The Wings Unfold," 47; Merkin, *50th Anniversary of Naval Aviation 1910–1961,* 19; Lt. Cdr. Holden C. Richardson, USN, undated, typed narrative describing events and personnel participating in development of NC aircraft and First Transatlantic Flight [hereafter Richardson, narrative], 5, RG 45, SECNAV/Chief of Naval Operations [hereafter CNO] files, National Archives, Washington, D.C; Curtiss Aeroplane and Motor Corporation, New York, *The Flight across the Atlantic* (Washington, D.C.: U.S. Department of Education, 1919) [hereafter *Flight across the Atlantic*], 23. This book, limited to two hundred copies, bears in the margin handwritten comments by the pilot, LT E. F. Stone, USCG.

30. Captain Commandant, letter orders to Third Lt. E. F. Stone, Subject: Duties in Connection with Aviation (Assignment to Instruction in Aviation at Naval Aeronautic Station, Pensacola, Fla.), March 29, 1916, Coast Guard Headquarters Historian files, Coast Guard Historian files, Coast Guard Headquarters, Washington, D.C.

31. O'Brien and Scheina, "Coast Guard," 9.

32. Ibid.

33. Ibid.

34. Ashley D. Pace, interview by Coast Guard Liaison Officer, Naval Air Training Command, Naval Air Station [hereafter NAS] Pensacola, Florida, 1986.

35. Ibid.

36. Commandant, U.S. Navy Aeronautic Station, Pensacola, Fla., letter to Third Lt. E. F. Stone, Subject: Orders as Naval Aviator, April 10, 1917, Coast Guard Historian files, Coast Guard Headquarters, Washington, D.C.; Captain Commandant, letter orders to Third Lt. E. F. Stone, Subject: Increase in Pay (Flight Pay), May 8, 1917; Coast Guard Headquarters Historian files.

37. Capt. Frank Erickson, USCG, Coast Guard Aviation narrative, ca. 1940, located in his personnel record, Coast Guard Historian Office, Coast Guard Headquarters, Washington, D.C. [hereafter Coast Guard Historian] files.

38. Grossnick, *United States Naval Aviation, 1910–1995.*

39. Bilstein, *Flight in America,* 33; Dauntless, 15; Cagle, "The Wings Unfold," 47; Johnson, *Guardians of the Sea.*

40. Cagle, "The Wings Unflod," 46, 47.

41. Bilstein, *Flight in America,* 6.

42. Browning, *Commander Elmer Fowler Stone, USCG, 1887–1936.*

43. Individual personnel records, Coast Guard Historian files.

44. Grossnick, *United States Naval Aviation, 1910–1995.*

45. Navy Department, letter, file N-31/GLN, to Third Lt. Elmer F. Stone, NAS Rockaway, L.I., N.Y., Subject: Change of Duty (Report to Chief of the Bureau of Construction and Repair, Navy Yard), May 15, 1918, Coast Guard Historian files, Coast Guard Headquarters, Washington, D.C.

46. Coast Guard Headquarters news release 64-68/EAS, "Vice Admiral S. V. Parker, USCG, Ret., Coast Guard Aviator, Dies," July 17, 1968, 2.

47. Navy Department, Third Naval District, letter to Third Lt. Elmer F. Stone, Subject: Detached *Huntington,* to Temporary Duty in Command NAS Rockaway, L.I., N.Y., October 12, 1917.

48. Coast Guard Headquarters news release 64-68/EAS.

49. Richardson, narrative.

50. Robert Browning, interview by Capt. Robert B. Workman, Jr., USCG (Ret.), June 2004, Coast Guard Historian.

51. *Jersey Journal,* front page, Sunday, July 30, 1916; Richard Pyle, Associated Press release, July 31, 2006.

52. Browning, interview.

53. Ibid.

54. Grossnick, *United States Naval Aviation, 1910–1995.*

55. Roger E. Bilstein, *Orders of Magnitude: A History of the NACA and NASA, 1915–1990* (Washington, D.C.: U.S. Government Printing Office, 1989), 4.

56. Grossnick, *United States Naval Aviation, 1910–1995.*

57. Bilstein, *Orders of Magnitude.*

58. Grossnick, *United States Naval Aviation, 1910–1995.*

59. Capt. John R. Stewart, USNR (Ret.), "Assembly Line Warriors," Association of Naval Aviators *Wings of Gold* (Winter 1986), 49–51. Unless indicated otherwise, sources cited in notes 62–65 were obtained from RG 72, job numbers 0146-949, 0146-778, 0146-788, 0146R-86, National Archives, Washington, D.C.

60. Grossnick, *United States Naval Aviation, 1910–1995;* Browning, *Commander Elmer Fowler Stone, USCG, 1887–1936;* USS *Huntington* log book, RG 24, 33161, December 1, 1916, to December 31, 1917, National Archives, Washington, D.C.

61. Browning, *Commander Elmer Fowler Stone, USCG, 1887–1936.*

62. Grossnick, *United States Naval Aviation, 1910–1995.*

63. USS *Huntington* log book.

64. Browning, *Commander Elmer Fowler Stone, USCG, 1887–1936.*

65. U.S. Army Board of Heraldry.

Chapter 4: First Transatlantic Flight NC Flying Boats—Design and Assembly: 1918

1. Lt. John H. Towers, USN, 1914, memorandum, RG 45, SECNAV files, National Archives, Washington, D.C.

2. Taylor, August 1917 memorandum.

3. "Atlantic Prize Flight," November 21, 1918, and "Flight," February 16, 1919, both *London Daily Mail*.

4. G. C. Westervelt, H. C. Richardson, and A. C. Read, *The Triumph of the NCs* (New York: Doubleday, 1920).

5. Maurice Holland and Thomas M. Smith, *Architects of Aviation* (New York: Ayer, 1951), 7–25.

6. Richardson, narrative.

7. Rear Adm. Norman Hall Military Personnel Record, Coast Guard Historian files; Richardson, narrative.

8. Holland and Smith, *Architects of Aviation;* Westervelt, Richardson, and Read, *Triumph of the NCs,* 6–12; Richardson, narrative; Lt. Cdr. J. C. Hunsaker (CC), USN, memorandum, Subject: Collaborators, [hereafter Hunsaker, memorandum], 2, RG 45, SECNAV/CNO files, National Archives, Washington, D.C.

9. Ibid.

10. *Flight across the Atlantic,* 13–21.

11. Ibid., 21–24.

12. Ibid.; Browning, interview; Erickson, "First Trans-Atlantic Flight"; Casey, "Curtiss Flying Lifeboat"; Cagle, "The Wings Unfold," 47; Merkin, *50th Anniversary of Naval Aviation 1910– 1961,* 19; Richardson, narrative, 5; *Flight across the Atlantic,* chap. 3.

13. Richardson, narrative, 3.

14. Ibid., 6.

15. Hunsaker, memorandum, Subject: Collaborators, 1.

16. Richardson, narrative, 2.

17. Ibid., 6.

18. Ibid.

19. Jesse G. Vincent, "Liberty Engine," Society of Automotive Engineers *Transactions* 14 (1919), Part 1, 385–432.

20. Cdr. John H. Towers, USN, memorandum, to CNO (OPAIR S-63-1), October 31, 1918, file 068-A, RG 72, National Archives, Washington, D.C.

21. *New York Times Press,* July 2, 1918 (5:4); July 3 (9:1); July 5 (20:5); July 7 (8:1).

22. Planning Committee, Navy Department, Office of Operations (Op-35), secret (declassified) undated memorandum to CNO, Subject: Trans-Atlantic Flight, 1, signed Capt. J. T. Tompkins, USN, Cdr. J. H. Towers, USN, and Lt. Cdr. G. DeC. Chevalier, USN [hereafter Planning Committee, memorandum], RG 45, SECNAV/CNO files, National Archives, Washington, D.C.

23. Ibid., 3.

24. Ibid., 5.

25. *Jane's All the World's Aircraft, 1919* (C. G. Grey [1969], Fred T. Jane), 488–99.

26. Planning Committee, memorandum.

27. Ibid.

28. Richard E. Byrd, *Skyward* (New York: Putnam, 1928), chaps, 4, 5.

29. Ibid.

30. Lieutenant Commander Bellinger, letter to CNO (Aviation), file f/068-A-354, April 1, 1919, RG 72, box 73, BUAERO Correspondence 1917–1925, National Archives, Washington, D.C.

31. Ibid.

32. Hunsaker, (CC) USN, Memorandum, Subject: Collaborators, 3.

33. Navy Department, letter, Subject: Three Engine Flying Boat Proposal, December 21, 1917, RG 72, SECNAV Files, National Archives, Washington, D.C.

34. Major W. J. H, memorandum to Lt. Col. A. A. Maybach, USA, U.S. Army War Plans Division, July 17, 1918, copy in CNO OPAIR file, RG 72, BUAERO 1917–1925, U.S. National Archives, Washington, D.C; Evan J. David, *Christening of the First American Made Handley Page: Plans for Transatlantic Flight Taking Concrete Form* (n.p.: July 7, 1918), 534–35.

35. Josephus Daniels, SECNAV, memorandum to Bureaus of Construction and Steam Engineering, Subject: Three Engine Flying Boat Proposed, December 21, 1917, RG 45, SECNAV/CNO files, National Archives, Washington, D.C.

36. Richardson, narrative, 2.

37. Ibid., 6–8.

38. Ibid., 9.

39. Ibid., 12–13, 15.

40. Ibid., 11–12.

41. Smithsonian Institution, "Curtiss NC-4 Engineering Drawing and Description: NC-4 Flying Boat," May 1919, Coast Guard Historian files.

42. Richardson, narrative, 10.

43. Ibid., 9.

44. Hunsaker, memorandum, Subject: Collaborators, 3–4.

45. Ibid., 4; Richardson, narrative, 5, 9a.

46. Bilstein, *Flight in America,* 28–29; Martin Classen, *Material Research and Development in the Army Air Arm, 1914–1945* (November 1946), 15.

47. Navy Department, letter, 1917, Subject: Three Engine Flying Boat Proposal.

48. Richardson, narrative, 3.

49. Ibid., 9a; R. E. Basler, memorandum, January 1, 1919, to Lt. Cdr. Garland Fulton, Chief of Naval Operations files, 1917–1925, U.S. National Archives, Washington, D.C.

50. Hunsaker, memorandum, Subject: Collaborators, 5.

51. Browning, interview.

52. Hunsaker, memorandum, Subject: Collaborators, 6.

53. Richardson, narrative, 32.

54. Ibid., 9.

55. Ibid., 9a–13; F. G. Coburn, "Problems of the Naval Aircraft Factory during the War," Society of Automotive Engineers *Transactions* 14 (1919), part 1, 304–32.

56. Richardson, narrative, 10.

57. Author's visual inspection of NC-4, displayed National Naval Aviation Museum, Pensacola, Fla.; Richardson, narrative, 9a.

58. Ibid., 7.

59. Ibid., 8.

60. Ibid., 6.

61. Hunsaker, memorandum, Subject: Collaborators, 6.

62. Navy News Bureau, release, May 14, 1919, RG 72, SECNAV files, National Archives, Washington, D.C.

Chapter 5: First Transatlantic Flight NC Flying Boats Shakedown: 1918–1919

1. Hunsaker, memorandum, Subject: Collaborators, 6.
2. Richardson, narrative, 13.
3. Hunsaker, memorandum, Subject: Collaborators, 6–7.
4. Ibid., 7; Richardson, narrative, 14–15; *Washington, D.C., Evening Star,* November 9, 1918.
5. Richardson, narrative, 14–15.
6. Ibid., 15; Hunsaker, memorandum, Subject: Collaborators, 7.
7. Richardson, narrative, 15.
8. Ibid., 16.
9. Ibid.
10. Cdr. Towers, confidential (declassified) letter CNO OPAIR file 068-A to Cdr. Hunsaker, Subject: Design Review Minutes, February 16, 1919, RG 72, box 72, OZ 1–OZ 4, vol.1.2, Bureau of Construction and Repair General Correspondence 1917–1925, U.S. National Archives, Washington, D.C.
11. Ibid.
12. Ibid.
13. Ibid.
14. Ibid.
15. Richardson, narrative, 17; secret (declassified) Official Navy Accident Investigation Report, with photographs, RG 45, SECNAV/Chief of Naval Operations files, National Archives, Washington, D.C.
16. Ibid., 17–18; Hunsaker, memorandum, Subject: Collaborators, 8.
17. Cdr. John Towers, USN, memorandum for file O-Z-4(A), C-341411, April 5, 1919, 1, RG 72, BUAERO General Correspondence 1917–1925, Bureau of Construction and Repair, OZ 1–OZ 4, vol. 1.2, National Archives, Washington, D.C.
18. Ibid., 1.
19. Hunsaker, memorandum, Subject: Collaborators, 8; Richardson, narrative, 18.
20. Ibid., 19; Towers, memorandum for file, April 5, 1919, 1–2.
21. Richardson, narrative, 19.
22. Ibid.
23. Navy Department, Bureau of Construction and Repair, to CNO (Aviation), Subject: Trans-Atlantic Flight: Temporary Duty of Lieut. Stone, C.G., in Connection with, March 19, 1919, memorandum file 18694-A, Cdr. E. F. Stone Military Personnel Record, Historian files, Coast Guard Headquarters, Washington, D.C; Franklin D. Roosevelt, Navy Department, letter to First Lt. Elmer F. Stone, Subject: Detached Bureau of Construction & Repair, Navy Department; to Duty in Connection with the Trans-Atlantic Flight, April 21, 1919, Coast Guard Historian files.
24. Ibid.
25. Richardson, narrative, 4; Cdr. Towers orders to Command NC Division 1, RG 72, Correspondence of the Secretary of Navy's Office, Relative to Aviation 1917–1921 (3068-A-1), box E-22, 3062–3068-286, National Archives, Washington, D.C.
26. *Flight across the Atlantic,* 32.
27. Richardson, narrative, 19–20; NC-1 Hangar Fire Board of Investigation, May 5, 1919, OPAIR file 068-A-513; Commanding Officer, NC Division One, letter 068-A-533, Subject: Relative to Fire in No. One Hangar, RG 72, box 73, BUAERO Correspondence 1917–1925, National Archives, Washington, D.C; Assistant Secretary of the Navy, naval communication to Cdr. John H. Towers, OpAir file 069-A, May 6, 1919, RG 72, box 72, BUAERO Correspondence 1917–

1925, National Archives, Washington, D.C; Navy Dept JAG, letter Misc (J) 060-A-533, Subject: Relative to Fire in No. One Hangar, May 9, 1919, RG 72, box 72, BUAERO correspondence 1917–1925, National Archives, Washington, D.C.

28. Towers, memorandum for file, April 5, 1919.

29. Ibid., 24; Navy News Bureau immediate release, morning papers, Monday, May 12, 1919, "Special Celestial Navigation Instruments and Tables for NC Aircraft," May 10, 1919, Navy News Bureau release morning papers, Monday 12, 1919, "Novel Instruments Especially Designed for Overseas Navigation by NC Seaplanes," May 10, 1919, RG 72, SECNAV files 1917–1925, National Archives, Washington, D.C; Commander, NC Seaplane Division 1, National Archives, 1919 year file, letter TA-2-T, Op-Air 068-A-635 to CNO, 6, RG 72, Records of Bureau of Aeronautics, Secretary of the Navy and CNO, entry 13, box 1, Correspondence Relative to Transatlantic Flight; Commanding Officer NC Division One, memorandum 068-A-224, to Capt. Simpson, Hydrographic Office, Subject: Relative to Short Methods of Navigation of Aircraft, March 28, 1919, RG 72, Records of Bureau of Aeronautics, Secretary of the Navy and CNO, entry 13, box 1, Correspondence Relative to Transatlantic Flight, 1919; Hydrographic Office, April 5, 1919, memorandum 068-A-260, to Lt. Cdr. Byrd, stating Supplementary Tables of altitudes and azimuths of stars will soon be sent, RG 72, Records of Bureau of Aeronautics, Secretary of the Navy and CNO, entry 13, box 1, Correspondence Relative to Transatlantic Flight; memorandum 068-A-93, for Cdr. Towers, Subject: Aero Gyro Compass, Proposed Test of Sperry, Co. Experimental Aero Gyro Compass, March 5, 1919, RG 72, Records of Bureau of Aeronautics, Secretary of the Navy and CNO, entry 13, box 1, Correspondence Relative to Transatlantic Flight, 1919; CNO, T. B. Howard, memorandum 069-A-45, Subject: Relative to Letter from Carrie Gyroscopic Corp, March 4, 1919, RG 72, Records of Bureau of Aeronautics, Secretary of the Navy and CNO, entry 13, box 1, Correspondence Relative to Transatlantic Flight; J. Hughes, *History of Air Navigation* (Allen and Unwin, London, 1946); U.S. Naval Institute *Proceedings* 44, no. 181 (March 1918), 567–84.

30. Richardson, narrative, 21.

31. *Flight across the Atlantic,* 32–33; Richardson, narrative, 21.

Chapter 6: First Transatlantic Flight: 1919

1. Planning Committee, memorandum, 1.

2. Ibid., 3.

3. Ibid.

4. Commander, Division 1 Pac. St Johns 5-15-19, naval communication I AIR-1383 to OpNav, "C-5 arrived St. Johns," RG 72, SECNAV files 1917–1925, National Archives, Washington, D.C; "U.S. Navy Class 'C' Dirigible," *Aerial Age Weekly,* August 25, 1919, 1095–98; *Evening Telegram,* St. Johns, Newfoundland, May 13, 1919, 4:1, and May 15, 1919, 6:3; *New York Times,* January 12, 1919, 3:5, January 13, 1919, 4:5, and January 16, 1919, 16:7; *New York Tribune,* May 15, 1919, 2:2.

5. Commander, Division 1 Pac. St Johns, naval communication I AIR - 1383 to OpNav, May 16, 1919, "C-5 broke moorings, drifted to seaward," RG 72, SECNAV files 1917–1925, National Archives, Washington, D.C; Record of Court of Inquiry, 1919, Convened On Board USS *Chicago,* "Loss of U.S. Navy C-5 Dirigible," NAV file 26283-2529, BUAERO file 068-273, May 16–19, 1919, RG 72, BUAERO Correspondence 1917–1925, National Archives, Washington, D.C.

6. Lt. Cdr. P. N. L. Bellinger and Lt. Stone, letter f/068-A-354 to CNO (Aviation), April 1, 1919, RG 72, box 73, BUAERO Correspondence 1917–1925, National Archives, Washington, D.C.

7. Jane's *All The World's Aircraft,* 1919.

8. Mark Kerr, *Land, Sea and Air: Reminiscences of Mark Kerr* (New York: Longmans, Green, 1927); Frida H. Brackley, *Brackles: Memoirs of a Pioneer of Civil Aviation* (Chatham, U.K.: W. & J. Mackay, 1952), 695.

9. Graham Wallace, *The Flight of Alcock and Brown, June 14–15, 1919* (London: Putnam, 1955).

10. Harry G. Hawker and Kenneth MacKenzie Grieve, *Our Atlantic Attempt* (London: Methuen, 1919).

11. Jane's *All The World's Aircraft,* 1919, 488a–499.

12. Richardson, narrative, 19.

13. Ibid., 26; *Flight across the Atlantic,* 34; Erickson, "First Trans-Atlantic Flight."

14. Bess B. Read, "The Private Letters of Putty Read," *Pensacola National Naval Aviation Museum Foundation* (1986), Cdr. Read's crew selection, Major Richardson's narrative, 26.

15. Navy News Bureau, immediate release, "Acting Secretary Roosevelt Authorizes the Following: The Radio on the NC Seaplane Evolves into Two Transmitters . . . ," May 14, 1919, RG 72, SECNAV files 1917–1925, National Archives, Washington, D.C.

16. Richardson, narrative, 27; *Flight across the Atlantic,* 34–36.

17. ENS Herbert C. Rodd, radio officer, NC-4 radio log of first transatlantic flight, RG 72, CNO/ SECNAV file; *Flight across the Atlantic,* 37.

18. Richardson, narrative, 27.

19. Ibid., 27–28; Commander, NC Seaplane Division One letter TA-2-T, Op-Air 068-A-635 to CNO, n.d., Subject: Trans-Atlantic Flight: report of, with reports from Commanding Officers, 1, NC-1, NC-2 and NC-4, RG 72, box 73 (entry 50, OZ 1–OZ 4 [Bellinger and Mitchner Reports]), BUAERO Correspondence 1917–1925, National Archives, Washington, D.C.

20. Richardson, narrative, 28–29; Commander, NC Seaplane Division One letter TA-2-T, 1.

21. *Flight across the Atlantic,* 37.

22. Richardson, narrative, 31; Lt. Cdr. Holden C. Richardson, USN, untitled narrative, 1–2, RG 72, SECNAV files 1917–1925, National Archives, Washington, D.C. [hereafter Richardson, untitled narrative].

23. Commander, NC Seaplane Division One letter TA-2-T, 1–2.

24. Richardson, untitled narrative, 2–3.

25. Ibid., PG 3, 4.

26. Richardson, untitled narrative, 5–6; Commander, NC Seaplane Division One letter TA-2-T, 1–2.

27. *Flight across the Atlantic,* 46.

28. Ibid., 37.

29. Ibid., 37, 39, 41.

30. Ibid., 41, 43; Richardson, untitled narrative, 7–9.

31. Richardson, narrative, 22.

32. Ibid.

33. Commander, NC Seaplane Division One letter TA-2-T, 2; Richardson, untitled narrative, 9–10; *Flight across the Atlantic,* 41, 43, 45.

34. Ibid.

35. Richardson, untitled narrative, 11.

36. Ibid., 12–13.

37. Ibid., 14; Commander, NC Seaplane Division One letter TA-2-T, 2; *Flight across the Atlantic,* 46, 48.

38. *Flight across the Atlantic,* 49; Commander, NC Seaplane Division One letter TA-2-T, 2.

39. Commander, NC Seaplane Division One letter TA-2-T, 2–3; Richardson, untitled narrative, 15.

40. Richardson, untitled narrative, 16–26.

41. *Flight across the Atlantic,* 45; Richardson, narrative, 12–13, 15.

42. *Flight across the Atlantic,* 45.

43. Ibid., 45–46, 55.

44. Ibid.

45. Lt. Breese, Engineer, report to CNO/SECNAV, RG 72, box 73, BUAERO Correspondence 1917–1925, National Archives, Washington, D.C.

46. Wallace, *Flight of Alcock and Brown.*

47. *The Aeroplane* (n.p.: Hutchinson, May 28, 1919), 16:2102–103.

48. Kerr, *Land, Sea and Air.*

49. Richardson, untitled narrative, 31.

50. Rodd, NC-4 radio log.

51. Hawker and Grieve, *Our Atlantic Attempt.*

52. Richardson, untitled narrative, 32–33; Commander, NC Seaplane Division One letter TA-2-T, 3.

53. "NC's Might Just as Well Fly the English Channel Back and Forth," *New York Times,* May 8, 1919, sec. 16, 14; Read, "Private Letters of Putty Read," 8.

54. Browning, *Commander Elmer Fowler Stone, USCG, 1887–1936.*

55. Lt. E. F. Stone, report to CNO/SECNAV, RG 72, box 73, BUAERO Correspondence 1917–1925, National Archives, Washington, D.C.

56. *Flight across the Atlantic,* 85.

57. Richardson, untitled narrative, 32.

58. Rodd, NC-4 radio log.

59. Richardson, untitled narrative, 34.

60. Ibid., 3.

61. Read, "Private Letters of Putty Read," 8.

62. SECNAV, letter to Lt. Elmer F. Stone, The President of the United States takes pleasure in presenting the Navy Cross, November 11, 1920, Cdr. E. F. Stone Military Personnel Record, Coast Guard Headquarters, Washington, D.C.

63. Commander, NC Seaplane Division One letter TA-2-T, 4.

64. Ibid., 3.

65. Ibid., 4; Navy Department, Office of Naval Intelligence, Director of Intelligence, letter to First Lt. E. F. Stone, September 25, 1919, 8-65, RG 72, CNO/SECNAV file, Cdr. E. F. Stone Military Personnel Record, Coast Guard Headquarters, Washington, D.C.

66. Ibid.

67. See chapter 11.

68. Ibid.

69. SECNAV letter to First Lt. Elmer F. Stone, USCG, Subject: Commendation (Pilot, NC-4), August 23, 1919, Cdr. E. F. Stone Military Personnel Record, Coast Guard Headquarters, Washington, D.C. Unless noted otherwise, reference data were found in RG 72, job numbers 0146T-849, 0146-T-53, 0152-248, Board of Inspection and Survey, Reports of Acceptance Trials of Naval Aircraft 1917–1919, National Archives, Washington, D.C.

Chapter 7: Evolving the Naval Aviation Test Organization: 1913–1926

1. Cdr. Robert C. Whitten, USNR (Ret.), "The Father of Naval Aviation: William A. Moffett," Association of Naval Aviators *Wings of Gold* (Summer 1989), 52; Grossnick, *United States Naval Aviation, 1910–1995.*

2. Navy Department, Subject: Detached *Huntington.*

3. Navy Department, Subject: Change of Duty.

4. Navy Department, letter to Third Lt. Elmer F. Stone, USCG, file N-31/LF, Subject: Repeated Travel, June 10, 1918, Coast Guard Historian Files.

5. Browning, *Commander Elmer Fowler Stone, USCG, 1887–1936.*

6. Pace interview.

7. CG Historian, oral interview, April 2004.

8. Ibid.

9. ADM Robert B. Pirie, USN (Ret.), "The Development of Early Flight Testing on Naval Aviation," Association of Naval Aviators *Wings of Gold* (Winter 1983), 36.

10. Ibid., 37.

11. Board of Inspection and Survey, Reports of Acceptance Trials of Naval Aircraft 1917–1919, RG 72, job numbers 0146-949, 0146-778, 0146-788, 0146R-86, 0146T-849, 0146-T-53, 0152-248, National Archives, Washington, D.C.

12. Board of Inspection and Survey, Reports of Acceptance Trials of Naval Aircraft 1919–1932, RG 38, job number 448-30, National Archives, Washington, D.C.

13. Board of Inspection and Survey, Reports of Acceptance Trials, photographs of "contract" airplanes 1918–1940, RG 38, job number 448-30, reference NNSP, National Archives, College Park, Md.

14. Ibid.

15. Ibid.

16. Navy Department, Bureau of Navigation, letter to Lt. Elmer F. Stone, U.S.C.G., Subject: Temporary Additional Duty (Proceed to NAS Hampton Roads for Trials of MF Flying Boat, N-1 Seaplane and Torpedo Trials of R-9 Seaplane), July 14, 1919, Coast Guard Historian Files; Grossnick, *United States Naval Aviation, 1910–1995.*

17. Navy Department, July 18, 1918, Bureau Construction and Repair letter to Stone, Subject: Temporary Additional Duty.

18. Board of Inspection and Survey, photographs of "contract" airplanes 1918–1940.

19. Commander Third Naval District Memorandum to Cdr. John Towers, USN, Request Lt. Stone, USCG test dirigible envelope at NAS Montauk, September 7, 1918, Coast Guard Historian Files.

20. Board of Inspection and Survey, Reports of Acceptance Trials.

21. Ibid.

22. Navy Department, Bureau of Navigation, letter to Stone, July 14, 1919.

23. Ibid.

24. Ibid.

25. Board of Inspection and Survey, Reports of Acceptance Trials, job number 448-30.

26. Navy Department, Bureau of Navigation, letter to Stone, July 14, 1919.

27. Navy Department, Bureau of Navigation, letter, file N311/de, to Lt. Elmer F. Stone, U.S.C.G., Subject: Temporary Additional Duty (To Dayton, Ohio, ... in Connection with Methods of Testing U.S. Army Aircraft w/Liberty Engines at McCook Field), August 8, 1919, Coast Guard Historian Files.

28. Board of Inspection and Survey, Reports of Acceptance Trials.

29. Ibid.

30. Bureau of Construction and Repair, date unknown, letterVCG, snw, 52A, Coast Guard Historian Files.

31. Board of Inspection and Survey, Reports of Acceptance Trials.

32. Ibid.

33. Ibid.

34. Ibid.

35. Ibid.

36. Ibid.

Chapter 8: Marine Corps Aviation and Coast Guard Aviation
Develop to Support Their Service Missions: 1917–1938

1. LtCol Edward C. Johnson, USMC, *Marine Corps Aviation: The Early Years 1912–1940,* PCN 19000316800 (Washington, D.C.: U.S. Marine Corps, History and Museums Division Headquarters, 1977), 11, 12, 82.

2. Ibid., app. C., "Marine Corps Aircraft, 1913–1940."

3. C. Douglas Kroll, *Commodore Ellsworth P. Bertholf: First Commandant of the Coast Guard* (Annapolis, Md.: Naval Institute Press, 2002).

4. Ibid.

5. Ibid; Assistant Secretary of Treasury, letter to Lt. Cdr. E. F Stone, U.S. Coast Guard, May 4, 1920, Cdr. E. F. Stone Military Personnel Record, Coast Guard Headquarters, Historian files, Washington, D.C.

6. Kroll, *Commodore Ellsworth P. Bertholf.*

7. Erickson, narrative.

8. *Annual Report of the United States Coast Guard, Fiscal Years ending 1920–1923* (Washington, D.C.: Coast Guard Headquarters, Legal Library, 1981).

9. CDR Malcolm F. Willoughby, USCGR(T), *Rum War at Sea* (Washington, D.C.: U.S Government Printing Office, 1964), 1–10.

10. Robert Scheina, *Coast Guard Aviation,* 17.

11. Erickson, narrative, 419.

12. Capt. William P. Wishar, USCG (Ret.), "Some Recollections of Early Coast Guard Aviation," *U.S. Coast Guard Academy Alumni Association Bulletin* 32, no. 1 (January–February 1970), 48–51. Captain Wishar was the first commanding officer of the first Coast Guard air station, at Morehead City, N.C.

13. Assistant Secretary of Treasury, letter to Lt. E. F. Stone, USCG, June 1, 1922, Subject: Regulations for Consideration of the President Relative to Pay and Allowances of Personnel Detailed to Duty Involving Flying, Stone Personnel Record, Coast Guard Headquarters, Historian files, Washington, D.C.

14. LCDR E. A. Coffin, USCG, "After Four Years, Interesting History of Section Base Seven of Gloucester Is Record of Achievement," *U.S. Coast Guard Magazine* 2 (June 1929).

15. Scheina, *Coast Guard Aviation,* 51, 52.

16. Ibid., 43.

17. Scheina, *Coast Guard Aviation,* 51; Erickson, narrative, 419; Coffin, "After Four Years, Interesting History of Section Base Seven of Gloucester Is Record of Achievement," 43.

18. Wishar, "Some Recollections of Early Coast Guard Aviation," 51–52.

19. O'Brien and Scheina, "Coast Guard," 9; Paul Freeman, *Abandoned and Little-Known Airfields in Massachusetts, Southeast Boston Area* (n.p.: 2002, revised September 2007).

20. Wishar, "Some Recollections of Early Coast Guard Aviation."

21. Coffin, "After Four Years, Interesting History of Section Base Seven of Gloucester Is Record of Achievement," 11–26; Erickson, narrative, 419.

22. Erickson, narrative; Browning, *Commander Elmer Fowler Stone, USCG, 1887–1936.*

23. Erickson, narrative; Browning, *Commander Elmer Fowler Stone, USCG, 1887–1936.*

24. Coffin, "After Four Years, Interesting History of Section Base Seven of Gloucester Is Record of Achievement," 11–26.

25. Ibid., 43; Scheina, *Coast Guard Aviation,* 18.

26. Erickson, narrative, 419.

27. Wishar, "Some Recollections of Early Coast Guard Aviation," 51–52.

28. Erickson, narrative, 419; Browning, *Commander Elmer Fowler Stone, USCG, 1887–1936.*

29. Commandant, USCG (Admiral Billard), letter to Department of the Navy, Chief, Bureau of Aeronautics (Admiral Moffett, USN), June 6, 1925, Cdr. E. F. Stone Military Personnel Record, Coast Guard Headquarters, Historian files, Washington, D.C; Robert Scheina, "Coast Guard Aviation," *Pterogram* (Spring 2001), 1. This is the periodical of the Coast Guard Aviation Association, also known as the "Pterodactyls." Cdr. Towers, telegram to Capt Irwin, serial no. HT 5193-17, file NRFC, Subject: Capt. Commission for Stone, September 25, 1919, RG 72, SECNAV files 1917–1925, National Archives, Washington, D.C.

30. Navy Department, Subject: Relieved of All Duty with the Navy.

31. Browning, *Commander Elmer Fowler Stone, USCG, 1887–1936.*

32. Erickson, narrative, 419.

33. Ibid.

34. Browning, *Commander Elmer Fowler Stone, USCG, 1887–1936,* 11–13.

35. Ibid.

36. Willoughby, *Rum War at Sea,* 151–52.

37. Scheina, *Coast Guard Aviation,* 18.

38. *Aces of the Air,* with an Introduction by Captain Eddie Rickenbacker, 214–15; CDR Norman Hall, *Air Traffic Control: System Operated by CG* (n.p.: McLoughlin Bros, 1930), 214–15. CAPT Frank Erickson, USCG, pioneer for helicopter operation, knew and conducted oral interviews with many of the early naval aviators, including Stone. Endnotes referencing an "Erickson, narrative"—a draft manuscript for a book telling the story of Coast Guard aviation, located in Capt. Erickson's Military Personnel Record in Coast Guard Headquarters, Historian files—refer to these interviews.

Chapter 9: Catapults and Aircraft Carriers: 1917–1926

1. Browning, *Commander Elmer Fowler Stone, USCG, 1887–1936.*

2. Erickson, narrative.

3. Ship Installation Division (Carrier Branch) Program Records 1922–1929, RG 72 (2705-565, 6852-376, 3646-342, 28027 4/15/19, 28027-279), National Archives, Washington, D.C.

4. Ship Installation Division (Carrier Branch) Program Records 1922–1929.

5. Browning, *Commander Elmer Fowler Stone, USCG, 1887–1936.*

6. Ibid.

7. Ibid.

8. Stone memorandum to BUAERO, April 4, 1923, with endorsements one through eight; Carl F. Jeansen, letter to BUORD, April 14, 1923, para. 3: "On 14 December 1921, Lieutenant E. F. Stone suggested to me the use of powder as motive power for launching airplanes from catapults." Bureau of Ordnance, Confidential (Declassified) 1912–1926, 37716-365, RG 74, 34622-365, National Archives, Washington, D.C.

9. Stone memorandum, April 4, 1923; Jeansen letter, April 14, 1923.

10. Bureau of Ordnance, confidential (declassified) 1912–1926, RG 74, 37716-289, 37716 9/25/20, 37716-296, 37716-309, 37716-343, 37716 3/13/23, 37716-365, 37716-392, 37716-492, 37715-496, 37716-602; Bureau of Aeronautics, General Correspondence Initiated in Bureau of Construction and Repair 1917–1925, RG 72, 51-3, 203-0, 900-1, 202-13 to 203-2, vol. 1.1; all National Archives, Washington, D.C.

11. Bureau of Ordnance, 1912–1926, 37716-365; Jeansen, letter, first endorsement to Commandant, Washington Navy Yard.

12. Bureau of Ordnance, confidential (declassified), 1912–1926, RG 74, 37716-619, 37716-627, National Archives, Washington, D.C.

13. Ibid.

14. Bureau of Ordnance, confidential (declassified) 1912–1926, RG 74, 37716-616, National Archives, Washington, D.C.

15. Ibid., 37716-619, 37716-627.

16. Ibid., 37716-638.

17. Ibid., 37716-706.

18. Cagle, "The Wings Unfold," 48.

19. Ibid.

20. Ibid.

21. Whitten, "'Father of Naval Aviation,'" 53.

22. Cagle, "The Wings Unfold," 48.

23. Whitten, "'Father of Naval Aviation,'" 53.

24. Lt. Stone, BUAERO letter to Carl Norden and to Warren Noble Engineering Corporation of North Carolina, "Requirements for MKI Experimental Arresting Gear for USS *Langley,* and Inviting a Contract Proposal," April 1, 1922, Bureau of Aeronautics, Ship Installation Board, RG 72, General Correspondence Initiated in Bureau of Construction and Repair 1917–1925, National Archives, Washington, D.C.

25. Warren Nobel Engineering Corporation, letter, proposed design and drawings, May 16, 1922, Bureau of Aeronautics, Ship Installation Board, RG 72, General Correspondence Initiated in Bureau of Construction and Repair 1917–1925, National Archives, Washington, D.C; Carl Norden, letter, "Arresting Gear Engineering Design with Formulas and Calculations," May 22, 1922, Bureau of Aeronautics, Ship Installation Board, RG 72, General Correspondence Initiated in Bureau of Construction and Repair 1917–1925, National Archives, Washington, D.C.

26. Bureau of Ordnance, confidential (declassified) letter S7716/367(T3-G5-O, VBJ), to BUENG, via BUAERO, May 7, 1923, RG 74, 1912–1926, 37716, National Archives, Washington, D.C.

27. Stone letters to Norden dated December 24, 1923 and January 15, 1924, Bureau of Aeronautics, Ship Installation Board, RG 72, General Correspondence Initiated in Bureau of Construction and Repair 1917–1925, National Archives, Washington, D.C.

28. Ibid.

29. Ibid.

30. Ibid.

31. Ibid.

32. Ibid.

33. Erickson, narrative.

34. Commandant, USCG letter, June 6, 1925.

35. Department of the Navy, Chief, Bureau of Aeronautics, letter to Commandant, USCG, January 8, 1925, Cdr. E. F. Stone Military Personnel Record, Historian files, Coast Guard Headquarters, Washington, D.C.

36. Bureau of Aeronautics, Ship Installation Board, BUORD S7716/367(T3-G5-O, VBJ) letter, "Reserved Four MK VII, MOD 6 Torpedo Air Compressors Intended for Installation on Battleship No 50 and Battle Cruiser N. 6 to Go to *Lexington* and *Saratoga* for Aircraft Catapults," to BUENG, via BUAIR, May 7, 1923, RG 72, General Correspondence Initiated in Bureau of Construction and Repair 1917–1925, National Archives, Washington, D.C.

37. Ibid.

38. Ibid.

39. Ibid.

40. Navy Department, Subject: Relieved of All Duty with the Navy.

41. Barth letter to Stone dated December 7, 1925, Bureau of Aeronautics, Ship Installation Board, RG 72, General Correspondence Initiated in Bureau of Construction and Repair 1917–1925, 202-13 to 203-2, vol. 1.1, National Archives, Washington, D.C.

42. Erickson, narrative.

Chapter 10: Years of Technical Advancement and Growth: 1930–1935

1. Printing on back of Coast Guard photograph of Sikorsky S-39, Coast Guard Historian files.

2. Coast Guard Headquarters, Washington, D.C., Historian files.

3. Printing on back of Coast Guard photograph, OS-38C, tail no. 394, Coast Guard Historian files.

4. Erickson, narrative, 419; Wishar, "Some Recollections of Early Coast Guard Aviation," 53.

5. Printing on back of Coast Guard photograph, PJ-1 *(Altair),* Historian files.

6. Coast Guard Headquarters, Historian files.

7. Erickson, narrative.

8. Coast Guard Headquarters, Historian files.

9. Erickson book draft, chap 5.

10. Scheina, *Coast Guard Aviation,* 18; Erickson, narrative.

11. Office of Assistant Commandant, U.S. Coast Guard, "Records of Movements of Vessels of the United States Coast Guard; 1790–December 31, 1933," RG 26, Records of the U.S. Coast Guard, National Archives, Washington, D.C; Erickson, narrative.

12. Commandant, USCG, May 29, 1933 letter, file ST-71 651, Subject: Commendation—Assistance Rendered at Time of Casualty to Navy Dirigible *Akron* J-3, Stone Military Personnel Record, Coast Guard Headquarters, Washington, D.C.

13. *Washington Times,* April 4, 1933; Stone Military Personnel Record, Coast Guard Headquarters, Washington, D.C.

14. Printing on back of Coast Guard photograph, Douglas RD-4, Historian files.

15. "Major Events in Coast Guard Aviation History," Coast Guard Headquarters, Historian files.

16. Rear Adm. Frank A. Leamy, USCG Official Personnel Record, Coast Guard Headquarters, Historian files.

17. "Major Events in Coast Guard Aviation History."

Chapter 11: A New Treasury Secretary Expands Aviation Missions: 1934–1938

1. Scheina, *Coast Guard Aviation,* 18.

2. Ibid.

3. Printing on back of Coast Guard photograph, NT-2 New Standard, Historian files.

4. Printing on back of Coast Guard photograph, Chance-Vought O2U-2, Historian files.

5. Coast Guard Headquarters, Historian files.

6. Printing on back of Coast Guard photograph, JF-2, Historian files.

7. Commandant USCG, memorandum to Secretary of Treasury, December 14, 1934, file CO-600, Subject: World Record Tests—Airplane, Coast Guard Historian files.

8. Historian, Stone 1887–1936 Coast Guard history website.

9. Commandant USCG, memorandum to Secretary of Treasury, February 23, 1936, file CO-71 600, Subject: Coast Guard Aviators—Instruction in Instrument Flying, Progress Of, Coast Guard Historian files.

10. Scheina, *Coast Guard Aviation,* 18.

11. Coast Guard Headquarters, Historian files.

12. Ibid.

13. Printing on back of Coast Guard photograph, Northrop RT-1 Golden Goose, Historian files.

14. Historian files.

15. Printing on back of Coast Guard photograph, Lockheed R30-1 Electra, Historian files.

16. Printing on back of Coast Guard photograph, Waco J2W, Historian files.

17. Historian files.

18. Erickson, narrative.

19. Printing on back of Coast Guard photograph, Curtiss SOC-4, Historian files.

20. Promotion orders to commander and permanent change of station orders to Coast Guard Air Detachment, San Diego, California. Military Personnel Record in Coast Guard Headquarters, Historian files.

21. Official City of San Diego history, Official San Diego History website

22. CDR Clarence (Deacon) F. Edge, USCG (Ret.), letter to VADM Donald (Deese) C. Tompson, USCG (Ret.), October 22, 1990, author's files.

23. Historian, Stone 1887–1936, Coast Guard Historian History website.

Appendix B: Technology Inspired by the First Transatlantic Flight: 1919–1938

1. Read, "Private Letters of Putty Read," 10.

2. Commander, NC Seaplane Division One letter TA-2-T, 5.

3. CDR Benjamin Dutton, *Navigation and Nautical Astronomy* (Annapolis, Md.: Naval Institute Press, 1942).

4. Navy News Bureau, May 10, 1919; Commander, NC Seaplane Division One, letter TA-2-T, 6; Commanding Officer NC Division One, Subject: Relative to Short Methods of Navigation of Aircraft; Hydrographic Office, memorandum to Lt. Cdr. Byrd, April 5, 1919, stating that *Supplementary Tables of Altitudes and Azimuths of Stars* would soon be sent, 068-A-260, RG 72

Records of Bureau of Aeronautics, Secretary of Navy and CNO, entry 13, box 1, Correspondence Relative to Transatlantic Flight, 1919; memorandum for Towers, Subject Aero Gyro Compass; T. B. Howard, Subject: Relative to Letter from Carrie Gyroscopic Corp.; Arthur J. Hughes, *History of Air Navigation* (London: Allen and Unwin, 1946).

5. Navy News Bureau, May 10, 1919.

6. Historical information on back of H-10 photo, USCG Historian files, Washington, D.C.

7. Navy News Bureau, May 10, 1919.

8. *HU16E Pilot Handbook,* NAVWEPS 01-85-AC-1 (Washington, D.C.: Bureau of Naval Weapons, July 15, 1961).

9. Navy News Bureau, May 14, 1919.

10. Ibid., 5.

11. Grossnick, *United States Naval Aviation, 1910–1995;* Merkin, *50th Anniversary of Naval Aviation 1910–1961.*

12. Ibid.

13. Ibid.

14. Browning, interview.

15. Grossnick, *United States Naval Aviation, 1910–1995;* Merkin, *50th Anniversary of Naval Aviation 1910–1961.*

16. Ibid.

INDEX

of, 59; transatlantic flight, 105; transatlantic flight leadership team, 64; transatlantic flight route, survey of, 63–64, 88; Trepassey Harbor, flight to, 94

Breese, James L.: aircraft trials and testing, 136–37, 142, 144; NC team and crew, 83, 91; NC-4 transatlantic flight, 101, 111, 114, 144; Plymouth, flight to, 116; transatlantic flight leadership team, 64; Trepassey Harbor, flight to, 96

British Air Force Medal, 119, 120

Burgess Company, 17, 18, 34

Burgess D-1 flying Boat, 25

Byrd, Richard Evelyn, Jr.: contributions of and hall of honor plaque, 3, 4; Navy air arm, expansion of, 2; NC-1 team, 83; polar expedition, 228, 229, 231; sextant, development of, 271–72; transatlantic flight leadership team, 64; transatlantic flight route, survey of, 63

C-5 dirigible, 61, 62, 87–88, 89

Carolina F Boat, 139, 152

catapults: A-1 launch, 18, 19; AB-2 launch, 32; barge, launch from, 21, 32; C-1 launch, 20, 21; development and installation of, vii, 20, 41, 178–79, 183–90, 197, 198–99, 252–53; gunpowder catapult, 187, 188, 189–90, 202; on *Huntington*, 46–47, 49–52; hydraulic catapults, 200, 208; pneumatic catapults, 21, 184–86, 187, 189, 191, 193, 194, 200; problems related to, 46, 184; requirement for, 20, 191; ship underway, launch from, 21, 32, 33, 46; steam catapults, 208; testing of, 196; torpedo launchers and development of, 17, 184; Wright brothers use of for flight off ship, 9, 159

Chambers, Washington Irving: A-1 flights, 16; A-2 flights, 16; as Aide for Matériel, 8, 20; aircraft construction materials, 18; aircraft demonstrations, arrangements for, 9; aircraft requisition, 15; catapult, development of, 17; contributions of and hall of honor plaque, 3, 7; jet turbine engines, opinion about, 16; Naval Academy assignment, 15; naval air arm, organization of, 21; Naval Flying Corps, plan for organization of, 21; responsibilities of, 8

Chance-Vought O2U-2 aircraft, 167, 168, 169, 170, 206, 226–28

Chevalier, Godfrey DeC., 2, 3, 4, 16–17, 33, 46, 63–64

Chiswell, Benjamin M., 30, 34, 35, 36, 37, 218

Coast Guard, U.S.: air arm, attitudes toward, 251–52; air arm, birth of, 26–30, 218; air arm, expansion of, 224–25; air arm, legislation to establish, 37; air arm and naval aviation, xi, 24–25, 163–78, 179–80, 181–82; air stations, transfer to, 127, 163; aviation, Stone role in development of, 27, 30, 58, 166, 208, 251–53; collaboration among services and joint mission areas, xiii–xiv, xv, xx, 3, 24; establishment of, 25, 161, 162; first aviation group, 38; force reductions, 161, 162; funding for, 30, 33, 161–62; mission areas, 181–82, 224–25, 234; Navy, interservice transfers to, 161–62; Navy, transfer to, 40, 161; officers, training of, 39–40; rank and rate structure, 126, 276–77; rank and rates, reductions in, 127–28; Treasury Department, return to, 161–62, 183; World War I, air operations, patrols, and missions during, 18; World War I, naval aviation capabilities for, xix–xx, 1–2, 3, 40

Coast Guard Academy, U.S., 2

Coast Guard Air Detachment (CGAD), 225, 226

Coast Guard Air Stations (CGAS): Biloxi, 242; Brooklyn, 242; Cape May, 127, 163, 179, 180, 209, 217, 218; Charleston, 241; Dinner Key, 179, 209–10, 275; Elizabeth City, 242, 245; Gloucester, 168, 217; Miami, 218, 242, 275; Morehead City, 127, 163, 164, 165; Salem, 168; St. Petersburg, 241; San Diego, 242, 245, 249–50; San Francisco, 242; Ten Pound Island, 167–69, 172–75, 217

Coffin, Eugene A., 2, 3, 58, 74, 83

commerce and trade: merchant ships during the war, 24; safety of maritime commerce, 2; schooners and coastal trade, 23–25; technological changes and changes in, 1–2; transport of and U-boat attacks, 41–43

communications: Coffin expertise in, 74; Coffin role in development of, 58; instruments and equipment for, 85; between land, ships, and

CAPT Robert B. Workman Jr., USCG (Ret.), born in Long Beach, California, is married to the former Gail P. Young of New London, Connecticut. Bob and Gail have two children, Robert and Rosemary, seven grandchildren, and one great-granddaughter. Bob is a graduate of the U.S. Coast Guard Academy, class of 1959. He flew both helicopters and fixed-wing aircraft, including the last of the flying boats.